Favorite Recipes® of
HOME ECONOMICS TEACHERS

"LIFE-SAVER"
COOKBOOK

©Favorite Recipes Press MCMLXXVI
Post Office Box 3396, Montgomery, Alabama 36109

Library of Congress Cataloging in Publication Data
Main entry under title:

"Life-saver" cookbook.

Includes index.
1. Cookery. 2. Handicraft. I. Title: Favorite
recipes of home economics teachers.
TX652.L48   641.5   76-22705
ISBN 0-87197-107-0

Recipe on page 174.

Recipe on page 166.

DEAR HOMEMAKER:

This newest edition in the Home Economics Teachers' Cookbook series is dedicated to you — the economy-conscious homemaker on a budget. Truly, it is exactly what you have been asking for — a reasonably-priced book full of nutritional as well as economical recipes and thrifty craft ideas that can actually "save your life" in these inflationary times. This is why we call it the Home Economics Teachers' "Life-Saver" Cookbook.

Home Economics Teachers have long been experts in all areas of home management. And, because they delight in sharing their time, energy and money-saving recipes as well as their ingenious ideas for inexpensive arts and crafts projects, you can become an expert, too! Besides the many "Life-Saver" Crafts and Recipes, you'll find a number of excellent household hints which can help make your housework faster and easier. Yes, this "Life-Saver" Cookbook is *the* answer to every homemaker's dream.

As we say "Hats Off" to the Home Economics Teachers across the country who made this dream a reality, we also want to say "Thank You" to each and every homemaker — for your contributions to HET fund raising will benefit many worthwhile school and community projects that might never have been possible without your interest and support.

The Home Economics Teachers' "Life-Saver" Cookbook was conceived with you in mind and you have helped to make it a real success. It is our hope that you and your family will enjoy this unique cookbook for years to come.

Sincerely,

Nicky Beaulieu

Nicky Beaulieu

BOARD OF ADVISORS

RUTH STOVALL, Chairman
Branch Director, Program Services Branch
Division of Vocational-Technical
  and Higher Education
Alabama Department of Education

CATHERINE A. CARTER
Consultant, Consumer Homemaking
  Education
Illinois Division of Vocational
  and Technical Education

ANNE G. EIFLER
Senior Program Specialist
Home Economics Education
Pennsylvania Department of Education

BARBARA GAYLOR
Supervisor, Consumer and Homemaking
  Education
Michigan Department of Education

JANET LATHAM
Supervisor, Home Economics Education
Idaho State Board of Vocational Education

CHRISTINE E. NICKEL
Consultant, Home Economics Education
Wisconsin Board of Vocational Technical
  and Adult Education

BETTY ROMANS
State Advisor, Texas Association
  Future Homemakers of America
Consultant, Homemaking Education
Texas Education Agency

FRANCES RUDD
Supervisor, Home Economics Education
Arkansas Department of Education

ODESSA N. SMITH
State Supervisor, Home Economics Education
Louisiana Department of Education

4

Table of Contents

Today's "Life-Savers"

Creativity and imagination are two of today's greatest "Life-Savers" for the economy-minded homemaker. While the household budget, with its rising food, clothing and energy costs, is becoming more and more strained, homemakers are becoming more and more inventive. They are spending their money more carefully, and are using food, time and household materials more wisely. They look continually for shortcuts, and when one is found that works, breathe a sigh of relief and say, "Whew, what a 'Life-Saver'!"

Microwave oven cooking, which is featured in this edition, is certainly one of the newer time and energy saving methods! This is what the Home Economics Teachers' "Life-Saver" Cook and Crafts Book is all about – ways to save, creatively and imaginatively, in order to get the most from your money, meals, materials and time. The book is divided into two parts, "Life-Saver" Crafts and "Life-Saver" Recipes. But, the Home Economics Teachers are glad to say that it is more than a crafts book or a recipe book. They believe it is a "Life-Saver" because it emphasizes turning what seems useless into something useful, while saving time, money and calories, stretching the budget and conserving energy.

Each of the two "Life-Saver" sections is divided into several chapters in order to fully cover all of the individual food and craft categories. The 5 craft chapters include those which can be made from yarn and string, fabric, paper and wood, plastic, and a potpourri of materials. The 4 recipe chapters include those for quick and easy, low-calorie, microwave oven, and all-purpose cooking. Each of the craft or recipe ideas was contributed by a home economics teacher who has tried it often, knows its dependability and is glad to share it with you.

The "Life-Saver" Crafts section deals with an astounding number of apparently worthless things which you can use to save time and money. Just think of all the things you throw in the trash almost everyday: milk cartons, fabric and yarn scraps, stockings, used greeting cards and tin cans. All of these things have a *saving* potential. From them you can create handmade holiday decorations, thus avoiding long and expensive shopping trips. Also you can make uniquely personal party gifts and shower favors. Plus you can create all kinds of handy home articles that you might otherwise do without.

You will find that each craft is well organized with clear, concise instructions. Moreover, much of the equipment needed to complete the various projects you already have around the house: scissors, glue, staples, needle and thread, sandpaper, paint and brush.

To make the most from each "Life-Saver" Craft, it is important to remember that the emphasis is on "Save." First of all, get in the habit of thinking before you throw away something very useful. Then, most important of all, use what you save! Once all of this becomes second nature to you, a whole new world of thriftiness, creativity and satisfaction will be yours!

The "Life-Saver" Recipe section includes ideas for a new approach to kitchen economy. Food management has been important

for so long that homemakers everywhere know systematically about using to the fullest extent the foods they grow and buy. But, they are still working to "de-calorize" their meals, and to spend less time and conserve more energy in the kitchen. The Home Economics Teachers have contributed their own favorite recipes and household hints to help you achieve these goals.

The recipes are also complete, practical and easy to follow. The ingredients that go into each one are generally easy to find, easy to use, and economical. As an imaginative and concerned homemaker, you will be confident and proud to serve these dishes offered to you by Home Economics Teachers. And, when you find that you are spending less time in the kitchen, serving fewer calories and cutting down on energy costs, you will know why home economist call these "Life-Saver" recipes!

The Home Economics Teachers offer these crafts and recipes to you as "Life-Savers" and ways to express yourself without exhausting the budget. Many hours of their time in research has been spent to develop them . . . each is unique and ingenious in its own way. But don't hesitate to add plenty of your own imagination and creativity. Then, each recipe that you include in your menu and each craft that you create will reflect your unique personality. Even the most knowledgeable home economics teacher can think of no greater "Life-Saver" than that!

Homemakers everywhere know just how necessary a needle and thread can be. From simple mending to more complicated stitchery, there's no limit to the projects that can be done with these two homemaker's friends — especially when you know *how* to work with yarn and string. And, the Home Economics Teachers want to help you learn how to do just that! Whether you are decorating your home or looking for a special gift, they have some marvelous, money-saving craft ideas that could be the *"life-savers"* you've been hoping for.

Decorating with plants is both an inexpensive and beautiful way to bring life and color to a room. And, when you add your personal touch with hanging planters made of string, you'll find you've achieved just the right effect without putting a strain on your budget. Handmade yarn flowers and yarn flower pictures are also lovely decorator items — items that can be made cheaply from leftover yarn yet appear to be the same expensive accessories you've admired in stores.

Making gifts of yarn and string is rewarding as well as fun. Just think how proud you would be to give your family and friends a gift made especially for them. A *Knitted Pin Cushion* for mother and a *Colorful Afghan* for baby are just two of the darling gift ideas that can be made from inexpensive remnants of yarn and string.

Yes, the emphasis is on saving — saving time, saving money and saving leftover household articles. Thanks to the many wonderful yarn and string craft ideas from Home Economics Teachers, you are now on your way to a life full of saving enjoyment!

YARN AND STRING

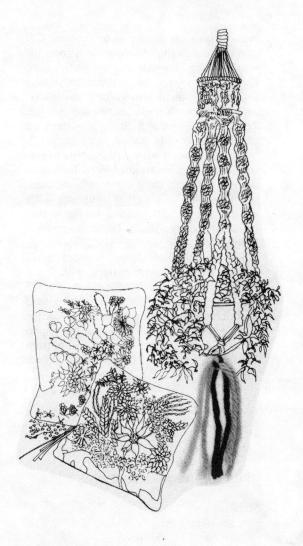

9

CORNICE DRESS-UP IN NEEDLEPOINT AND BARGELLO

Materials:

> *Measuring tape*
> *Monowave canvas*
> *Shears*
> *Fabric to match draperies*
> *Continental stitch needlepoint and*
> *   straight stitch Bargello pattern*
> *Graph paper*
> *Masking tape*
> *4-ply worsted yarn in desired colors*
> *Yarn needle*
> *Stapler*

Measure area on cornice to be covered. Cut canvas accordingly, allowing for 6 rows for overlap along long edges for a smooth finish. Canvas strips may be stitched in double thickness for about 4 rows for a continuous strip if more than 36 inches are needed. Trace needlepoint and Bargello pattern on graph paper for easy reading and color placement. Tape canvas with masking tape to prevent snags and unraveling. Work individual pattern in length to fit cornices being used, selecting colors of yarn that complement the existing decor. Stitch canvas to fabric that matches drapery; staple fabric to cornice. Helpful hints for cornice: Stitch canvas on fabric by machine. Cover bottom 5 1/2 inches of cornices with pattern, with fabric covering rest, if depth of pattern is 5 1/2 inches finished. Rows of pattern being used must be counted when marking canvas for cutting. Allow 35 rows for each cut if pattern is 23 rows, 6 rows on top and bottom for folding under, of 36-inch width original canvas.

Mrs. Jane E. Healy
Ellenville Central High School
Ellenville, New York

CROCHETED HANGER COVERS

Materials:

> *1 skein rug yarn*
> *Size J or K crochet hook*
> *Wooden dress hangers*

Ch 8, using yarn and crochet hook; work 7 sc. Ch 1; turn. Work as many rows of sc as needed for length of hanger; leave end of yarn long enough to sew together on hanger. Push dress hanger hook through center of cover. Sew end and across bottom; sew across other end. Wrap hook with yarn; tie a bow. One skein rug yarn will cover several hangers.

Mrs. Donna Rasmussen
Central Middle School
Montevideo, Minnesota

CROCHETED KNITTING BAG

Materials:

> *2 4-oz. skeins sayelle yarn in*
> *   contrasting colors*
> *1 size H crochet hook*
> *1 pair plastic handles*
> *1/2 yd. printed calico, combining*
> *   2 colors of yarn*

Crochet in dc 2 rectangular pieces 14 x 10 inches, using 1 color yarn. There will be approximately 40 dc and 20 rows. Sl st 9 dc and ch 2 on 20th row. Make 26 dc for 4 rows; this will make edge to which handle will be attached. Make gusset of 10 dc and long enough to go on 3 sides of rectangle, using contrasting yarn; sc gusset to front and back rectangle. Crochet motif for one side of bag, using same color yarn as gusset; attach motif by sewing with yarn. Sew on handles. Cut and sew lining from calico; sl st to top edge of bag.

Mrs. Lucille S. Pantel
Ellenville Central School
Ellenville, New York

CHILD'S CROCHETED BASSINET PURSE

Materials:

> *Scissors*
> *1 22-oz. or 32-oz. detergent bottle*
> *Paper punch*
> *00 crochet hook*
> *1 oz. sport weight yarn*
> *Additional contrasting color yarn (opt.)*

Flannel scraps
Nylon stocking
Doll

Cut top from plastic bottle to leave 3-inch base; punch holes evenly around top edge.
Rnd 1: dc in each hole.
Rnd 2: dc 2 stitches in each dc of rnd 1. Repeat rnd 2 until piece measures 3 inches or covers base when folded down.
Beading:
Rnd 1: dc 1 stitch every 3rd dc with 2 chain stitches between.
Rnd 2: 2 dc, ch 2, 2 dc in each space for shell design. Break off yarn.
Rnd 3: sc in contrasting color.
Fold down over base. Crochet canopy and fasten to edge of bassinet, if desired. Chain stitch drawstrings of desired length; thread through beading. Make 1-inch pompons for sides of canopy and ends of drawstrings, if desired. Make mattress of flannel; stuff with nylon stocking. Make blanket of flannel. Place doll in bassinet.

Mrs. Gladys Olson
Monmouth High School
Monmouth, Illinois

CROCHETED SNOWFLAKES

Materials:
  Size 11 crochet hook
  Medium weight white crochet thread
  Liquid starch
  Waxed paper
  Corrugated cardboard

Chain 8; sl st into 1st ch to make circle.
Rnd 1: ch 4, * dc into center, ch 2, repeat from * 10 times, sl st into 2nd ch from first ch 4.
Rnd 2: sl st into center of next spoke holes, ch 6, * tr into next spoke hole, ch 3, repeat from * 10 times. Sl st into 3rd ch of first ch 6 of rnd 2.
Rnd 3: ch 10, join in top of next tr, repeat from * 11 times, sl st in top of first tr.
Final Rnd: * ch 15, sc in 5th ch from hook, ch 10, sc in top of tr of rnd 3, ch 13, sc in 3rd ch from hook, ch 8, sc in 3rd ch from hook, ch 8, sc in 3rd ch from hook, ch 10, join in top of next tr of rnd 3, repeat from * 5 times, pull thread through to end. Break off. Starch with full strength liquid starch. Stretch on waxed-paper covered cardboard, using pins to stretch into shape. Loop a white thread or plastic thread in tip of star point for hanger. Hang on Christmas tree, in windows, on mantel or stairway.

Doris W. Larke
Woodruff High School
Peoria, Illinois

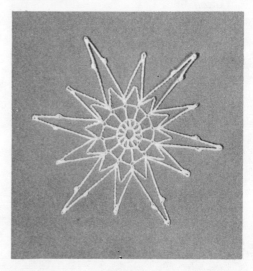

CROCHETED EASTER BUNNY

Materials:
> Crochet hook G
> Yarn
> Small rubber band
> 2 pipe cleaners
> 3 beads
> Cotton
> Plastic egg

Rnd 1: sc 30 stitches onto small rubber band.
Rnd 2: sc 30 stitches.
Rnd 3: dc 30 stitches; tie in 2nd color of yarn at end of 3rd rnd, if desired.
Rnd 4: dc 30 stitches.
Rnd 5: dc into every other stitch or 15 times.
Rnd 6: tr c into every dc of previous rnd, 15 times. Tie off, leaving an 8-inch piece of yarn. Weave this string through top of tr c. Bend 2 pipe cleaners in half for ears. Clove hitch an 11-inch piece of yarn to top of the pipe cleaners. Pull yarn tight and wrap around end of pipe cleaner. Place ears in top

of tr c and pull piece of yarn woven in top tight. Thread end of yarn into darning needle and secure ears. Cut an 18-inch piece of yarn and weave through bottom of tr c. Stuff head with small amount of cotton. Pull yarn tight and tie into bow. Insert plastic egg through rubber band at bottom. Glue on beads for eyes and nose.

Juanita S. Holtmeier
Clark-Vitt Jr. High School
Union, Missouri

YARN FORK FLOWERS

Materials:
> Large fork
> Assorted colors of yarn
> Wire for stems

Hold large fork; weave yarn in and out between prongs 7 or 8 times. Place long piece of green yarn between center prongs; tie tight knot around center of weaving. Remove pompon from fork. Wind and glue green yarn around wire for stem. Green yarn may be clipped for short stem. Repeat for additional flowers.

Le Nora Hudson
Oklahoma School for Deaf
Sulphur, Oklahoma

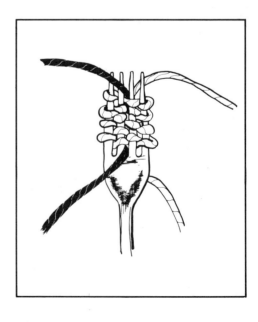

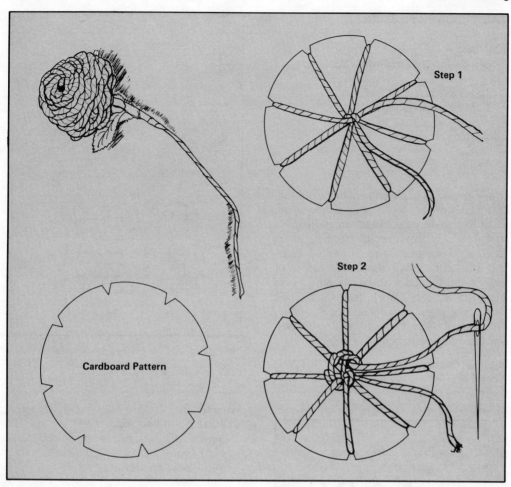

Step 1

Step 2

Cardboard Pattern

POMPON YARN FLOWERS

Materials:

Lightweight cardboard
Orlon or sayelle yarn
Yarn needle
Wire for flower stems
Floral tape
Artificial floral leaves

Cut a circle 4 inches in diameter from cardboard. Cut 8 notches at regular intervals in cardboard. Cut piece of yarn 2 1/2 yards long. Wrap yarn around spokes in circle, from top to bottom, holding 3-inch end securely. Tie 3-inch end to the last yarn spoke. Thread long end of yarn into needle. Go under 2 strands of yarn with needle, then backstitch over 2nd strand to form a loop. Continue backstitching over each spoke, leaving slightly loose, until all yarn is used except for about 4 inches. Run needle along side of 1 spoke back to center and hold loosely. Turn card over and clip yarn in center. Hold yarn ends together and attach to wire with loop in end. Cover with floral tape and attach artificial leaves. These may be made with 2 or 3-inch stems and used in a greenery-covered Styrofoam ring for wreath, if desired.

Mary M. Yevin
Granite City Sr. High School South
Granite City, Illinois
Mrs. Bette M. Cox
South High School
Denver, Colorado

Yarn and String

YARN FLOWER PICTURE

Materials:
> *12 x 14-inch piece of white decorator*
>   *fabric*
> *3 sizes looms*
> *4-ply yarn in assorted colors*
> *Glue*
> *Needle*
> *Thread*
> *Picture frame*

Draw outline of arrangement on white fabric. Make flowers on looms in desired colors according to loom package directions. Prepare vase by working interlocking chain stitch in 2-ply green yarn in desired shape and size. Glue small flowers in center of large flowers; tack with needle and thread for extra security. Work leaves on fabric with 2-ply green yarn in satin stitch wherever needed. Glue flowers and vase on outline of arrangement; frame picture.

Mrs. Jesse Clausel
Kossuth High School
Kossuth, Mississippi

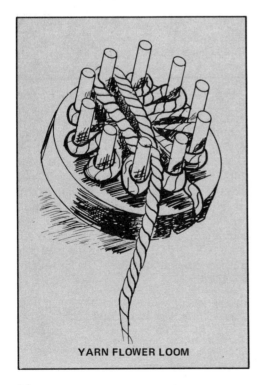

YARN FLOWER LOOM

HAVE A BALL, BABY

Materials:
> *1 pair No. 6 knitting needles*
> *Needle with large eye to sew up ball*
> *Yarn scraps, 1 color or various colors*
> *Nylon hose for stuffing*

Cast on 18 stitches.
Row 1: Knit.
Row 2: Slip 2 stitches as to purl, put yarn to back, knit 15 stitches, slip 1 stitch, work rows 1 and 2 twice.
Rows 3 through 6: Repeat rows 1 and 2 twice.
Row 7: Change color, purl 18 stitches.
Row 8: Purl.
Repeat rows 1 through 8, making 10 stripes. Change yarn to starting color, repeat rows 7 and 8. Bind off. Sew bound off edges to cast-on edge. Draw up one end. Stuff with hose. Draw up other end and fasten. This is washable and dries fast.

Emely Sundbeck
Manor High School
Manor, Texas

KNITTED SLIPPERS

Materials:
1 4-oz. skein worsted yarn
No. 8 American or No. 6 Canadian
 knitting needles
Tapestry needle

Cast on 29 stitches, using doubled yarn.
Row 1: k 9, p 1, k 9, p 1, k 9.
Row 2: Knit.
Repeat rows 1 and 2 until piece measures
5 1/2 inches. Work in ribbing of p 1, k 1 for
3 inches.
Finishing:
Knit 2 together across next 2 rows. Cut off
yarn, leaving 5-inch end on work. Thread
end into tapestry needle; pass needle
through remaining stitches. Sew sides together to end of ribbing. Sew heel seam.
Make pompon; sew on top of slipper.

Marjorie Harris
Greeley Public School
Greeley, Nebraska

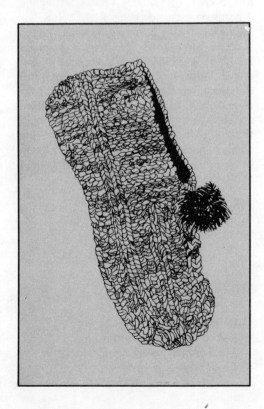

BABY AFGHAN

Materials:
 No. 9 needles
 Yarn

Cast on 140 stitches.
Rows 1 and 2: K 1, P 1 entire rows.
Row 3: Knit.
Row 4: Purl.
Rows 5 and 6: P 1, K 1 entire rows.
Row 7: Knit.
Row 8: Purl.
Repeat rows 1 through 8 until piece mea-
sures about 30 inches. Bind off.
Edging:
Chain 3, 1 dc in next stitch, skip about 2
stitches and sc in next stitch. Completed
afghan should measure 30 x 38 inches.

Louisa M. Krebs
Central High School
Rapid City, South Dakota

KNITTED CHRISTMAS BELLS

Materials:
 1 pair No. 3 knitting needles
 1 tapestry needle
 1 4-oz. skein red yarn
 1 small bell
 1 ft. red checked ribbon, 1 in. wide,
 for each bell

Cast on 12 stitches.
Row 1: Knit 5, purl 7, turn.
Row 2: Purl 12, turn, this will be inside of
bell.
Repeat these 2 rows for 36 rows. Bind off,
leaving 6 inches of yarn. Thread yarn through
tapestry needle; run needle through end of
each purl row. Knitted edge forms bottom
of bell. Draw top of bell up tightly; fasten.
Weave sides of bell together with remaining
thread. Attach ribbon on top for bow; attach bell on inside with yarn, having bell
hang down just to inside of bottom edge of
bell. One 4-ounce skein of yarn will make
about 12 bells.

Elizabeth Green
Loretto High School
Loretto, Tennessee

Yarn and String

KNITTED PINCUSHION

Materials:
1 pair No. 7 or 8 knitting needles
Small balls of leftover yarn of two
  or three harmonizing colors
1 thimble

Cast on 20 stitches for each of the 3 strips. Knit 1 strip 7 inches long. Knit 2nd strip 5 inches long and 3rd strip 3 1/2 inches long, casting off ends of each strip. Fold lengthwise. Stitch edges together, then stitch ends together, making circles. Place smallest circle in medium-sized circle; baste together on underside. Place this in largest circle; baste together. Place thimble in center.

Lorene L. Arent
Wausa Public Schools
Wausa, Nebraska

COLORFUL AFGHAN

Materials:
1 pair No. 9 knitting needles
Leftover yarn

Cast on 50 stitches of colored yarn for each strip. Knit each strip as long as needed for afghan, adding different colors of yarn as desired. Knit as many strips as needed for width of afghan. Cast on 12 to 15 stitches of neutral colored yarn for strips to join multicolored strips together. Join strips together. Makes a colorful afghan for family room or car, using leftover yarn.

Sue Volkmer
Hemingford High School
Hemingford, Nebraska

LARGE-EYED MACRAME OWL

Materials:
48 yd. jute or yarn
2 wooden branches
2 2-inch metal rings
2 lg. wooden beads

MACRAME OWL

Cut 6 cords 8 feet in length. Use 6 cords doubled; attach to 1 branch with lark's heads. Make 2 rows of 3 square knots. Make 3 square knots with middle 4 cords, letting the 4 cords on each side hang. Right below last square knot make 2 alternating square knots. Make 6 more rows of alternating square knots, 3, 2, 3, 2, 3, 2. Attach ends to 2nd branch with horizontal half hitches. Pull ends together; tie with a small piece of cord to make tail, trim and fuzz. Make eyes from metal rings. Cut 4-inch pieces of jute; attach to rings with lark's head until rings are covered. Trim and fuzz ends. Attach rings to body by a large bead, tying ends behind body.

Jill Kralicek
Oak Park High School
Kansas City, Missouri

STRING BALLOON

Materials:
1 small to medium bowl
1 ball of multicolored crochet thread
1 oval-shaped balloon
1 bottle of liquid starch

16

working in 2-inch bands, until can is covered. Clip final end of rope at top to lie flat; let can dry. Wrap contrasting twine around rope in pattern; glue onto rope. Coat can with varnish spray to waterproof planter.

Mary E. Harrington
Doherty High School
Worcester, Massachusetts

GIFT CARD HOLDER

Materials:
  Can opener
  Hammer
  Empty juice can
  Yarn
  Scraps of braid (opt.)
  Glue

Cut both ends from can; hammer edges until smooth. Wrap yarn around can from top to bottom, going inside can and up around outside. Cover closely and fairly tight. Fasten ends with thread or glue. Fasten braid around top and bottom for decoration. Braided yarn may also be used. Cards are slipped under yarn and extend out.

Mrs. Rosemary K. Harwood
North Stanly High School
New London, North Carolina

Place ball of thread in bowl; pour starch over thread. Blow up balloon to desired size and tie. Wind twine around balloon, leaving an oval opening in front. Wind the balloon with as much thread as desired, the more thread used the prettier the balloon will be. Hang by the top to dry for 24 hours. Break balloon and remove from shell. May be used as an Easter basket or filled with flowers for a centerpiece.

Patricia G. Green
Virgie High School
Pikeville, Kentucky

ROPE-COVERED PLANT CONTAINER

Materials:
  1 16-oz. empty can
  White glue
  1 ball natural-colored rope
  Scissors
  Small amount of contrasting twine
  Clear coating varnish spray

Work from base of can up; spread thick coat of glue in 2-inch band around container. Let glue dry until tacky; start winding natural-colored rope around can. Continue process,

Yarn and String

YARN HANGING PLANTER

Materials:
Rug yarn
Scissors
Flowerpot, glass jar or other
container for plants

Measure 12 yards rug yarn. Fold yarn over 4 times. Leave fold at 1 end; cut other end to make 8 strands 54 inches long. Loop folded end over an inverted chair leg; this will be the beginning loop. Tie 4 knots at 2-inch, 4-inch and 6-inch intervals. Divide yarn into 4 double strands; knot again at 4-inch interval on each double strand. Divide yarns again. Make double strands with alternate yarns. Measure 4 inches; tie in knots. Bring all yarns together; tie 15 inches below knot or to desired length. Cut 6 inches below knot for fringe. Remove from chair leg; hang. Place flower container in hanger.

Sister Marionita Gergen, OSF
Ryan High School
Omaha, Nebraska

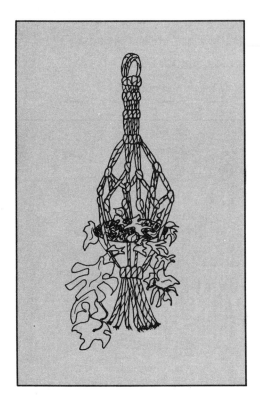

TIED PLANT HANGER

Materials:
1 3-oz. skein of yarn plus 2 colors
of leftover yarn
1 plastic ring

Cut 30 strands of the 3-ounce skein of yarn, each strand 48 inches long. Loop strands through ring to middle of length of strands. Bring together tightly just below ring and tie securely with second color of yarn. Wrap to form 1/2-inch band of color. Separate into 3 equal sections, 20 strands to each section. Tie and wrap each of these sections, about 3 inches down from top, in same manner as above. Divide each of these sections so that you now have 6 sections; take one section and place with one from another group. Tie together securely about 6 inches above ends of strands. Repeat with remaining sections. Tie the 3 groups together at bottom, leaving about a 3-inch tassel. Pull strands apart and place pot in between. You may pull strands together several inches above pot and tie if desired.

Mrs. Mary E. Cantwell
Mt. Markham C School
West Winfield, New York

YARN-COVERED WIRE HANGER

Materials:
1-in. wide transparent tape
2 identical wire coat hangers
Scissors
2 balls rug yarn in matching or
contrasting colors

Tape the 2 wire hangers together at tip of hook, at base of hook, at curves and in middle. Cover all straight portions of wire hangers by putting tape lengthwise down wires and wrapping around to seal in wires. Tape ends of both balls of yarn to tip of hanger hook, with yarn balls hanging off hook. Take 1 ball of yarn and make a blanket stitch by carrying ball under the wire, over the wire and through the loop that is formed.

Move the ball through loop of yarn; pull so twist lies on right side. Repeat, as desired, up to 4 times. Move remaining ball of yarn over wire, then under wire; pull twists to left side. Repeat. All of 1 color twists are on right and all other color are on left. Repeat all around hanger until entire hanger is covered. Tie bow with remaining yarns at base of hook.

Mary Ellen Trowbridge
North Thurston High School
Lacey, Washington

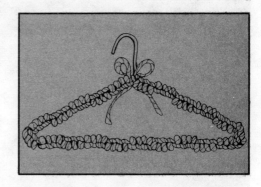

Quick Trim Idea

This simple idea is a real quickie to add a bit of trim to a blouse, child's dress or place mats. Make a row of machine stitching about 1/4 inch from edge of neckline or sleeve, using a fairly long stitch length. Weave in and out of each machine stitch with 2 strands of embroidery floss. Do not pull too tight. One can use harmonizing or contrasting floss or sometimes black adds just the right touch.

Mrs. Margaret Onerheim
Evans Jr. High School
Ottumwa, Iowa

Saving Money On Hooked Rug Yarn

Skeins of rug yarn
Yardstick or T square
Masking tape
Sharp utility knife

Wrap yarn closely around yardstick without overlapping, leaving an inch of yardstick exposed at each end. Cut a piece of masking tape the length of yardstick; apply to one side of wrapped yarn. Be sure to secure masking tape to open ends of yardstick to aid in cutting. Cut full length of yarn with util-ity knife; remove from yardstick. Yarn will adhere to masking tape for easy removal. Cut along both edges of T square, if used. This simple process will save 50% or more of the cost of precut yarn.

Margaret K. Shollenberger
Girard High School
Girard, Pennsylvania

Stitchery Hint

Stitch your name or initials and date into your handmade creation of stitchery and needlepoint. This makes it personalized and in years to come of antique and sentimental value to relatives.

Betty J. Brandt
Gibbon Public School
Gibbon, Minnesota

Stringing Beads Hint

Smooth a little nail polish on the end of thread when stringing beads. This stiffens the thread so a needle isn't needed.

Elsie Klassen
Georges P. Vanier School
Tohigo, Alberta, Canada

Fabric

Fabric is all around us everyday, adding warmth, color, texture and design to our lives. Whether it creates the clothes we wear, or the curtains, sheets, towels and tablecloths that decorate our homes, fabric is always versatile and durable. Because of these qualities, most fabrics can be used again and again in limitless ways.

By saving and reusing fabric scraps imaginatively, there are many things that you can make — and hardly spend a cent. The American quilt is probably the earliest example of this creative frugality. With the material scraps saved from dresses, flour sacks and curtains, women created breathtaking quilts, so durable that they are still in use today.

Think how your child, or even your grandchild, might love a patchwork pillow that you made by hand — and from seemingly useless scraps of fabric! Handmade cloth flowers can do so much to brighten a friends kitchen, or your own family room. Inexpensive, or even frayed, washcloths and towels are perfect for making attractive throw pillows and washable baby bibs. Cloth afghans, pot holders and personalized Christmas decorations are other items you and your family can enjoy making.

Even though you may not have saved fabric scraps, a good selection of inexpensive remnants is always available at fabric stores. And, from now on, think before you throw away denim, double knit, burlap, or most any other fabric, because you may be throwing away a gift! Home Economics Teachers know the value of saving and using, "Make something old into something new" is their advice. You will have fun doing it, and save money, too!

Fabric

FLOWER GARDEN AFGHAN

Materials:
  Scraps of polyester double-knit fabric
  Sewing thread
  Embroidery thread
  Cardboard or sandpaper for 2-inch
    square pattern

Cut squares from double-knit fabric, using pattern. Use a variety of colors and patterns. Sew squares together to form attractive color combinations. Press seams open. Embroider with featherstitch to cover seams. Cut bias strips of polyester material of desired width for edges. Sew the strips together; sew around edges. Turn and stitch to other side.

Mrs. Ruth L. DeFriese
Young High School
Knoxville, Tennessee

WOOL AFGHAN

Materials:
  Postcard-sized sandpaper pattern
  Unbonded woolen fabric from old coats
    or similar items

Size O metal crochet hook
28 ounces 4-ply yarn
Large crewel needle

Cut 160 pieces of fabric, using pattern. Mark corners with dots, then mark 9 equally spaced dots between corner dots of long sides and 5 equally spaced dots between corner dots on short sides. Crochet, beginning at corner, 4 sc in each corner dot and 2 sc in each of the other dots, leaving an 18-inch piece of yarn on last corner to weave pieces together. Weave 20 pieces together along long edges into long strip. Continue weaving pieces together until all pieces are used. This will be 20 pieces long and 8 pieces wide. Crochet or make fringe for the edges. Pieces may be crocheted together instead of woven, if desired.

Clara Oneil
North Junior High School
Rapid City, South Dakota

APPLE SACHET

Materials:
  Scissors
  Needle

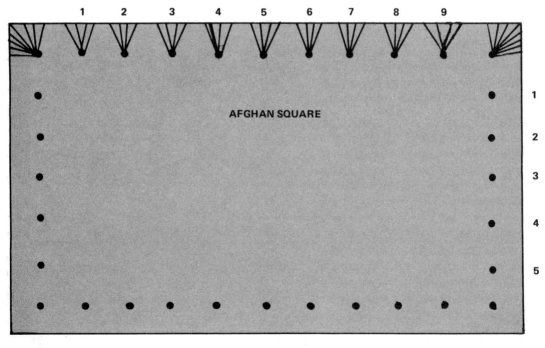

Thread
Red, black and green felt
Tissue
Powder

Cut 2 identical apple shapes from red felt; cut a 1-inch stem from black felt. Cut 2 leaves from green felt. Sew apple-shaped pieces together 3/4 of the way around with needle and thread, using overcast stitch; stuff with tissue and powder. Sew opening together; sew on leaves and stem.

Nadia Hamilton
Harbor Creek Jr. High School
Harbor Creek, Pennsylvania

APPLYING FABRIC APPLIQUES TO GARMENTS

Materials:
Scissors
Lightweight plastic bag from cleaners
Fabric applique

Cut a piece of plastic slightly larger than applique. Place plastic on garment; place applique on plastic. Place brown paper over plastic and applique, being sure plastic is covered with brown paper. Iron with hot iron, pressing hard. Let cool for several minutes; remove brown paper. Applique will be attached to garment and excess plastic to brown paper. Garment may be washed gently several times; plastic holds applique in place until sewn with zigzag stitch on sewing machine.

Mrs. Mary D. Brown
Crowell High School
Crowell, Texas

BABY BIB FOR GIFT

Materials:
Small hand towel fringed at each end
Pins
2 yd. folded bias tape

Fold down 4 to 5 inches of towel to make a yoke with fringe across front; sew across towel just above yoke fringe. Fold towel in half lengthwise; cut out semicircle for neck.

Pin both sides of bias tape to neck edge, having center of tape at center of neck edge. Sew through tape and neck thicknesses. Use extended tape to tie bib around baby's neck. May sew bias tape around circle cut for neck opening and attach to bib with ribbon; use as wiper.

Mrs. Juanita Pitts
Linden-Kildare High School
Linden, Texas

WASHCLOTH BABY BIB

Materials:
Washcloth
Folded bias tape

Cut out semicircle measuring about 4 inches across and 2 inches deep on one side of washcloth. Bind semicircle with bias tape, leaving about 12 inches tape on each side to use as ties. Stitch edge of bias tape extensions together.

Elaine Hillyer
Chinook Jr. High School
Bellevue, Washington

BREAD CLOTH

Materials:
Scissors
1 15-in. square linen or similar fabric
Pins
Bias tape

Cut half circle from center of each edge of linen. Pin bias tape around edge of fabric; stitch. Turn tape under; overlap ends. Stitch. Fold corners of linen to center to cover bread.

Mable Whisnant
East Lincoln Sr. High School
Denver, North Carolina

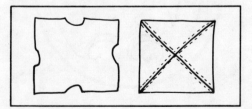

Fabric

BEDROOM CURTAINS FROM PILLOW CASES

Create beautiful bedroom curtains for short 3-foot windows to match room decor from pillow cases. Simply rip out seam of each pillow case. Leave hems sewn; hem sides evenly. Sew in top heading; curtains are finished. Curtains are also interchangeable, right to left, as hems are even. May be reconverted to pillow cases if room decor is changed. One pair pillow cases makes 2 curtains.

Ruth H. Methvin
Fall River High School
McArthur, California

CARPET REMNANT OWL NOTE PAD

Materials:
    Heavy scissors
    Rubber-backed carpet remnant
        or sample
    Felt scraps
    Rug yarn
    Glue
    Note pad
    Pencil

Cut design from remnant for owl, about 15 inches long and 11 inches across at largest point. Cut wings and mortarboard from felt of blending color. Cut 2 large circles from white felt, 2 smaller circles from yellow felt and 2 smallest circles from black felt for eyes; cut beak and feet from felt. Glue all pieces in place. Make eye glasses from yarn; glue in place. Outline owl with yarn; glue in place. Glue on strip of felt for pencil holder; glue on note pad. Make tassel from black yarn; glue in place. Let dry. Place pencil in pencil holder.

Irma Haley
Castleford High School
Castleford, Idaho

CASSEROLE CARRIER

Materials:
    Scissors
    Cotton fabric
    Paper pattern for circles
    Pins
    Bias tape

Cut out 2 circles 14 inches in diameter from fabric. Cut out a 7-inch circle from center of 1 circle. Cut two 16 x 2-inch strips of fabric. Sew bias tape around opening of 7-inch circle. Sew bias tape to small fold on wrong side of circle. Turn bias tape to right side of fabric; topstitch along edge, leaving ends open for drawstring. Cut a 36-inch strip of bias tape; fold over. Stitch together. Pull through casing of 7-inch center opening. Place circles, wrong sides together. Sew each 16-inch strip together for straps; turn. Place ends of straps on opposite sides of circle, leaving about 4 inches between straps. Pin in place. Stitch one side of bias tape around edge of circle on bottom side. Bring other side of tape over top side; stitch along edge. This sews circle edges and straps together. Place casserole in center opening; pull up bias string to secure dish. Carry with straps.

Mrs. Cora Carroll
White Deer High School
White Deer, Texas

CHRISTMAS CANDLE

Materials:

    Red fluffy washcloth
    Pins
    White bar of soap
    Tape
    1 2-in. strip of bright yellow
      fluffy yarn
    2 14-in. squares red net
    1 yd. Christmas ribbon
    Plastic sprig of holly or poinsettia

Fold washcloth from corner to corner in diagonal fold. Roll tightly from one side of fold to form candle; pin. Pin flat bottom to center of soap, using at least 8 to 12 pins. Tape yarn in center of cloth for wick. Wrap net around bottom of soap; tie around candle with ribbon. Decorate with holly.

Jerrie L. Evans
Vallivue High School
Caldwell, Idaho

TREE ORNAMENTS

Materials:

    Scissors
    Scraps of fabric
    3-in. Styrofoam balls
    White glue
    Straight pins
    Rickrack or other trim

Cut pointed oval bias strips 1/4 to 1/2 inch shorter than measurement of Styrofoam ball from top to bottom, cutting enough to cover ball. Place small band of glue around edge of 1 strip; pin to top of ball. Stretch to fit curve of ball; pin to bottom of ball. Repeat with remaining strips until ball is covered; let dry. Remove pins. Cut strips of rickrack the diameter of the ball. Apply glue to back of rickrack; place around ball between strips. Pin in place; let dry. Cut strip of rickrack 12 inches long; tie into bow. Cut strip of rickrack 3 inches long; tie in knot around bow. Pin to top of ball. May use contrasting colors or prints to cover Styrofoam balls.

Mrs. Marian S. Holcombe
Enfield Jr. High School
Oreland, Pennsylvania

UNUSUAL CHRISTMAS DECORATION

Materials:

    1 potato chip can
    Glue
    1 9 1/2 x 10-in. piece of velvet
      fabric
    1 yd. metallic braid
    Gold or silver glitter
    Styrofoam
    Felt
    Small scene for inside of can
    1 sm. candle
    1 sm. glass to fit top of can

Cut an oval-shaped hole in one side of can towards bottom. Glue velvet to can, turning under edges. Cut hole in velvet for hole in can; glue edge to inside of can. Glue braid around top and bottom of velvet; glue around hole. Glue glitter behind cut hole to make background for scene. Cut Styrofoam to fit inside bottom of can; glue in place. Cut felt circle to cover outside bottom of can; glue in place. Place scene inside can on Styrofoam. Place candle in glass; anchor with melted wax. Place glass in top of can.

Mrs. J. M. Allen
Wall ISD
Wall, Texas

EASY CARE AND DUAL USE TABLECLOTH

Materials:

    Quilted fabric
    Bias binding

Cut quilted fabric large enough to fit table plus a 12-inch overhang. Sew bias binding around edges. Bias binding may be made from nonquilted matching fabric, if desired. This is an easy to wash no-iron tablecloth that may be used, backing side up, as silencer cloth under lightweight tablecloths.

Elaine Hillyer
Chinook Jr. High School
Bellevue, Washington

Fabric

EASY PLACE MATS

Materials:
- Quilted fabric
- Pins
- Bias tape
- Sewing machine

Cut fabric in 17 x 12-inch rectangles or ovals. Pin bias tape to edges; stitch to give a neat finish. May make a ruffled or pleated edge for variety, if desired.

Elaine Schramm
Plateau Valley School
Collbran, Colorado

FABRIC BALL

Materials:
- Shears
- Colorful fabric scraps
- Shredded foam

Cut out 8 pieces of fabric scraps into 3 x 10 1/2-inch shapes according to illustration. Stretch and sew a 1/4-inch seam on one side of 2 pieces; repeat for all 4 pairs. Sew 2 pairs together, making half the ball. Sew 2 halves together on one side; sew remaining seam, leaving a 2 to 3-inch opening. Turn right side out; stuff with shredded foam. Hand stitch opening. Ball is machine washable and dryable. Six shapes make a football; 8 shapes make a round ball.

Mrs. Millie Griswold
Lincoln Jr. High School
Wyandotte, Michigan

FABRIC FRUIT

Materials:
- Scissors
- Gingham and calico fabric
- Thread
- Stuffing
- Scraps of green felt

Pear

Trace pear pattern; cut 4 patterns from gingham fabric. Stitch pieces together on wrong side beginning and ending at dots. Top of pear is almost closed; bottom is open. Clip seams at curves; turn to right side. Stuff pear. Make row of running stitches around bottom opening. Pull thread tight; fasten off. Circle of felt may be sewn over opening, if desired. Cut 4 leaf patterns from green fabric; stitch 2 together on wrong side, leaving opening at bottoms. Turn; add small amount of stuffing. Stitch bottoms closed. Sew row of stitches down center of each leaf; stitch leaves into top of pear. Two patterns of green felt, sewn down center, may be used for leaves, if desired.

Peach

Trace peach pattern; cut 4 patterns from gingham fabric, using grain line. Stitch pieces together on wrong side, leaving opening at top of one seam. Clip seams at curves; turn to right side. Stuff peach; slip stitch opening. Cut peach leaf patterns from green fabric or felt; follow instructions for making pear leaves. Attach leaves to peach.

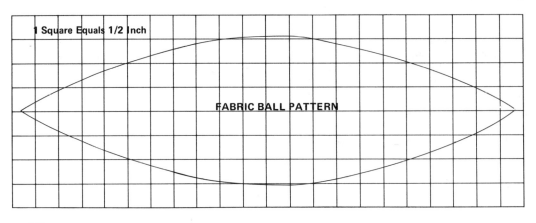

1 Square Equals 1/2 Inch

FABRIC BALL PATTERN

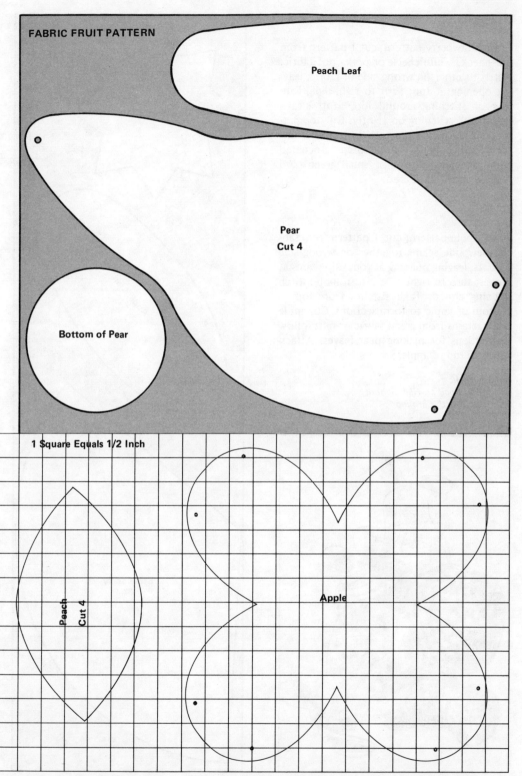

FABRIC FRUIT PATTERN

Peach Leaf

Pear
Cut 4

Bottom of Pear

1 Square Equals 1/2 Inch

Peach
Cut 4

Apple

Fabric

Strawberry

Trace strawberry pattern; cut 1 pattern from red check, white check or polka dot fabric. Stitch together on wrong side of fabric, leaving opening at top; turn to right side. Run row of stitching around top. Stuff strawberry; pull stitching up tightly. Cut top pattern from green felt; attach to top of strawberry, using green thread. Stem crocheted from matching thread or small green cord may be added, if desired.

Apple

Trace apple pattern; cut 1 pattern from fabric. Sew side seams together on wrong side to dots, leaving opening at top. Clip seams at curves; turn to right side. Stuff apple; stitch opening closed. Take stitches from top to bottom of apple to form sections. Cut apple leaf patterns from green fabric or felt; follow instructions for making pear leaves. Attach leaves to top of apple.

Billie J. Puckett
Albemarle Road Jr. High School
Charlotte, North Carolina

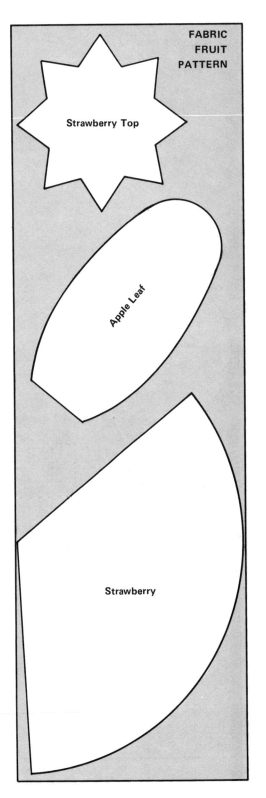

FABRIC FRUIT PATTERN

Strawberry Top

Apple Leaf

Strawberry

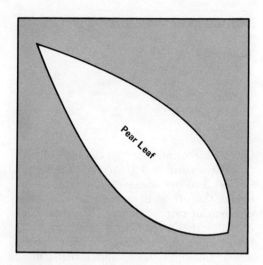

Pear Leaf

FABRIC POTHOLDER

Materials:
> Worn-out mattress cover
> Printed fabric scraps
> Seam binding

Cut two 6 x 7-inch pieces from outside edge of mattress cover. Cut a printed design from scrap for applique. Applique onto one mattress cover piece. Place 2 pieces together. Stitch seam binding around edges. Form loop for top of seam binding; sew onto corner. Printed fabrics with fruit designs make excellent appliques.

Carmaleta Walker
Edmond Memorial High School
Edmond, Oklahoma

CALICO FLOWERS

Materials:
> Scissors
> Scraps of small-printed fabric or
>   checked gingham
> Glue
> Pipe cleaners
> Floral wire
> Balls from ball fringe
> Floral tape

Cut 10 identical heart shapes of fabric for each flower. Use 2 heart shapes for each petal. Coat wrong side of fabric of 1 heart with glue. Place pipe cleaner down center of heart from indention extending through point. Place another heart evenly over first, enclosing top part of pipe cleaner between the 2 hearts. Repeat for 4 more petals. Place floral wire in middle of the 5 pipe cleaners; force ball of fringe over end of wire for center of flower. Wrap pipe cleaners tightly with floral tape to form stem. Repeat for as many flowers as desired. Folded chenille rods may be used instead ball fringe. A red clay pot trimmed with rickrack makes an attractive container.

Mrs. Ruth Wilson
MacArthur Jr. High School
Beaumont, Texas

ORGANDY ROSES

Materials:
> Scissors
> Organdy
> White glue
> Small paintbrush
> Florist wire
> Florist tape

Cut 7 petals of organdy for each rose. Petals should measure 1 1/2 to 2 inches in length and about 1 inch in width. Petals should have 1 rounded end and 1 tapered, almost oval, end. Mix equal parts of glue and water; apply to petals with paintbrush. Let dry until tacky. Roll rounded ends between thumb and forefinger across top and on either side of top. The first few will be difficult; keep practicing until petals are easy to roll. Let petals dry; bend into petal shapes. Cut a strip of organdy about 2 inches wide and 5 inches long for center of rose. Fold strip in half lengthwise; slip end of 6-inch piece of florist wire in fold. Twist and fold organdy around wire to form bud; hold in place. Place petals around bud, making sure rolled edges of petals turn outward. Secure with florist tape; wrap until petal ends and stems are enclosed. Repeat for number of roses desired. Organdy may be dyed before cutting petals if colored roses are desired.

Mrs. Ann Hughes
Pea Ridge High School
Pea Ridge, Arkansas

Fabric

NYLON HOSE FLOWERS

Materials:

Scissors
Old nylon hose
Color remover
Dye
Copper wire
Flower stamens
Floral wire
Floral tape

Cut off toes and tops of hose; remove color from hose. Dye nylon desired colors; cut nylon into 3-inch squares. Make loops of wire according to desired size petals or leaves required. Place 1 wire loop diagonally on 1 square; fold over nylon, gathering edges at base. Wrap with wire. Arrange petals as flower around stamen; wrap with floral wire and floral tape to form stem. Bend into flower shape. Repeat for desired number of flowers.

Carol Sullivan
Woodsboro High School
Woodsboro, Texas

BURLAP FLOWERS

Materials:

Burlap
Heavy gauge stem wire
Pliers
Floral tape
Glue

Cut burlap into 4-inch squares. Pull center string of 1 square to remove from square. Continue pulling and removing strings from same direction from either side of center until a 3/4-inch band of burlap is left on 2 opposite sides of squares. Fold burlap square in half, matching the 3/4-inch bands. Cut wire into stem lengths. Make a loop on one end of a stem with pliers. Loop hook over the bands at one end. Begin rolling the double band into cylinder shape; continue until roll is completed. Secure roll with floral tape; continue down stem with tape until covered, using glue to help steady tape. Repeat for number of flowers desired.

Mrs. Margaret W. Lyles
Westminster High School
Westminster, South Carolina

PADDED TREASURE BOX

Materials:

1   2-qt. milk carton
Fabric
Fiber fill padding
Trimming (opt.)
Button (opt.)

Cut off top of milk carton; cut each corner carefully to within 3 3/4 inches of bottom. Cut off 3 of the sides evenly, leaving 1 side for lid. Cut off lid to measure same as sides of box. Cut strip of fabric 4 1/2 inches wide and 21 inches long. Fold back 4 inches of fabric with right sides together; sew 2 side seams 3/8 inches wide. Clip corners; turn and press. Slide finished lid over lid of box; slide fiber fill padding on both sides of lid. Wrap fabric around box padding; leave bottom free of padding. Paper clip end of fabric to front of box. Cut fabric 4 1/2 inches wide and 14 inches long for sides of box. Paper clip 1 end of fabric to 1 of the remaining uncovered sides of box. Wrap fabric around sides of box again, padding sides and leaving bottom free of padding. Paper clip last end to edge of box. Fold under all edges of fabric on corners of box; slip stitch. Remove paper clips. Box may be lined, if desired. Attach trimming; add button and loop to front of box. Velvet, satin and fur fabrics make an elegant box.

Marjorie M. Heaston
Foothill Intermediate School
Walnut Creek, California

CALICO CLAY POT

Materials:

Scissors
Calico scraps
Dec-O-Llage or Elmer's glue
Clay pot with saucer
Felt

Cut calico into about 1 1/2 x 2-inch pieces or desired sizes to cover clay pot in old-fashioned crazy quilt design. Shake Dec-O-Llage thoroughly before using. Glue pieces of calico onto pot and saucer with Dec-O-Llage; glue piece same depth within pot. Press each piece firmly with fingers in rolling motion from center of calico outward; wipe away excess glue. Let dry for 1 hour. Brush 3 or 4 light coats of Dec-O-Llage over pot and saucer, letting dry between coats for 30 minutes or until milky film disappears. Cover bottom of saucer base with felt.

Mrs. Mary Ada Parks
Anna-Jonesboro High School
Anna, Illinois

GREETING CARDS

Materials:
Nonwoven interfacing
Standard-sized envelopes
Iron-on transfers
Tube paints, magic markers or crayons
Paper towels

Cut folded piece of interfacing to fit envelope; press transfer on outside of interfacing with warm iron. Color design with paints; write an appropriate message on outside and inside. Cover with paper towel; press with warm iron to set color.

Clara May Charlesworth
Northeast High School
Pasadena, Maryland

PATCHWORK CURTAINS

Materials:
Cardboard
Scissors
Scraps of material
Sheet of lining material

Cut 6-inch square pattern from cardboard. Cut 200 squares for a 4 x 4-foot window from material, using cardboard pattern as guide. Sew squares together in solid-print sequence or in any desired pattern. Line finished curtains with sheet.

Carol Ransom
East Jordan Middle School
East Jordan, Michigan

TACKLE BOX SEWING BASKET

Materials:
Metal tackle box
Vinegar
Steel wool
Gesso
Sandpaper
Acrylic spray paint in desired color
Mod-Podge or Dec-O-Llage
Leftover fabric scraps
Waxed paper or sheets of plastic
Scissors
Brayer
Rickrack, braid or ribbon in 2 colors
Velverette Craft Glue
Acrylic spray

Wash tackle box with vinegar and water; remove any rust with steel wool. Apply 1 coat of Gesso over inside and outside of box; let dry. Apply second coat, if needed, sanding between coats. Spray inside of box with 2 coats of acrylic paint; let dry between coats. Apply coat of Mod-Podge over inside of box; let dry. Apply coat to outside of box; let dry. Place fabric scraps on waxed paper. Brush Mod-Podge over fabric; let dry, lifting fabric before dry to prevent sticking to waxed paper. Turn fabric; repeat procedure on other side. Fabric may now be cut without raveling. Cut fabric scraps into enough patchwork squares to cover outside of box. Apply coat of Mod-Podge to small section of box and to back of fabric that will cover that section. Glue fabric to box, overlapping fabric, if desired. Roll out excess glue and air bubbles with brayer. Continue procedure until entire outside of box is covered with fabric in patchwork pattern. Wash brayer with soap and water when finished. Glue 1 trim around edge of each patchwork square and contrasting trim to long edges of box with Velverette Craft Glue. Apply coat of Mod-Podge over trim. Apply coat of acrylic spray over outside of box; let dry.

Mrs. Vera S. Smith
Strong High School
Strong, Arkansas

Fabric

TENNIS RACQUET COVERS

Materials:
Brown paper
Fabric
Zipper
Pellon
Cording

Two types patchwork are used for 2 covers pictured, seamed squares and crazy patch. Both may be made on the machine, though the seamed squares shown here are quilted by hand. Draw a pattern on brown paper around a tennis racquet, leaving at least 1 1/2-inch allowance for thickness of frame of racquet and seam allowance. Fold pattern in half for back pieces, allowing 5/8 inch for zipper. Back should be made from sturdy material such as denim or canvas but may be made of patchwork too, if desired. Stitch zipper in back pieces. Sew pieces of fabric together in patchwork design to make an area of fabric large enough to accommodate pattern for front. The squares may be seamed together by machine, then placed on Pellon and quilted by hand or machine. The crazy patches are worked directly onto Pellon with zigzag machine stitch. Join front and back together with corded piping. Stitch seam binding around lower edge; turn up and hem in place.

Photograph for this project on page 36.

ECONOMICAL AND FAST PATCH QUILT

Materials:
Scrap fabrics
One bed sheet or about 5 yards
    material
Crochet thread

Cut scrap fabrics into desired number of squares of equal size. Sew together, using 5/8-inch seams. The back of quilt is made from bed sheet, material or another patchwork piece. Place right sides of back and front together. Stitch around edges, leaving an opening for turning. Turn inside out; slip stitch opening together. Tack each square in 4 places, depending on size of square, using crochet thread; tie each tack in a knot.

Sandra Owen
St. Charles Jr. High School
Lebanon, Kentucky

WASHCLOTH PILLOW

Materials:
Rug yarn or acrylic washable yarn
2 washcloths identical in size
Size 4 metal crochet hook
Washable pillow stuffing

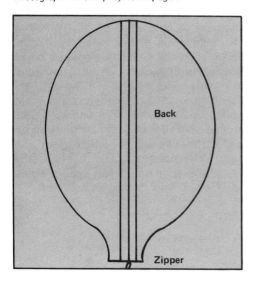

Cut about 200 pieces of yarn, 5 inches long. Pin corners of washcloths together, right sides out. Push crochet hook through 2 washcloths, close to edge at corner. Fold 1 piece of yarn in half; pick up yarn at fold and pull through washcloths, then pull ends through loop. Secure all corners in this fashion, then complete all sides with the loops, leaving and opening for stuffing. Stuff with desired amount of stuffing. Close opening with yarn loops as above. Design may be varied by using identical washcloths for front and back or printed for front and solid color for back or 1 or 2 colors of yarn for fringe.

June D. Allan
Mark Twain Jr. High School
Los Angeles, California

TOTE BAG

Materials:
3/8 yd. burlap or other heavy fabric
3/8 yd. lightweight lining fabric,
   preshrunk
Thread to match fabrics

Make pattern from Fig. 1 measurements out of brown paper bag. Cut bag from heavy material and lining from lightweight fabric, using pattern and placing narrow edge on fold of fabric along lengthwise grain of fabric. Stitch lining to bag along curved edges with 1/2-inch seams with right sides together (Fig. 2); trim seams to 1/4 inch. Turn bag right side out by passing fabric through narrow handle; bring right sides of bag together and right sides of lining together to form rectangle. Stitch around rectangles with 1/2-inch seam, leaving a 5-inch opening in bottom seam lining. Reinforce corners; trim seam to 1/4 inch. Reach into 5-inch opening; pull tote handle through opening. Turn bag, lining side out. Turn raw edge of 5-inch seam allowances under; stitch folds very close together. Turn lining to inside of bag. Press curved edges.

Mrs. Linda Anderson
Somonauk High School
Somonauk, Illinois

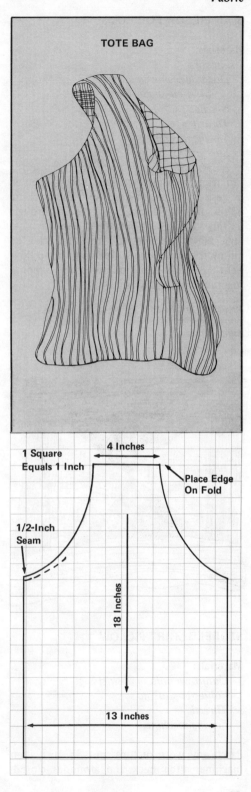

TOTE BAG

1 Square Equals 1 Inch

4 Inches

Place Edge On Fold

1/2-Inch Seam

18 Inches

13 Inches

Fabric

JEAN PILLOW FOR BOYS

Materials:
Scissors
Discarded jeans in at least 2
*   different shades*
Needle
Thread
Sewing machine
Stuffing for pillow

Cut jeans into pieces; baste pieces together in desired design, having front and back of pillow of equal shape. Stitch pieces through bastings on sewing machine; remove bastings. Sew right sides of front and back of pillow together, leaving opening; turn pillow right sides out. Stuff pillow; stitch opening together with needle and thread.

Mrs. Mary Ada Parks
Anna-Jonesboro High School
Anna, Illinois

STUFFED SHIRT PILLOW

Materials:
Outgrown polo or T-shirt
Polyester stuffing
Thread
Sewing machine

Patch any worn or torn spots in shirt, then machine stitch neck and armholes closed.

Stuff shirt with filling to desired shape. Sew bottom of shirt together. Kids will love their new stuffed shirt pillows.

Mrs. Elizabeth B. Lengle
Warrior Run High School
Turbotville, Pennsylvania

BUTTON-ON PURSE

Materials:
Scissors
Felt, plastic or leather
Needle
Thread
Yarn

Cut 2 circles 3 inches in diameter from felt; shape edges of circles as desired. Cut 2 leaves from felt; tack in place to inside of 1 circle. Make small pompon with yarn; sew to outside center of 1 circle. Place circles together, pompon side out; stitch 1/8 inch from edge, leaving top open to insert coins. Cut slit through both circles for buttonhole. Button onto child's dress for safe keeping of coins.

Le Nora Hudson
Oklahoma School for Deaf
Sulphur, Oklahoma

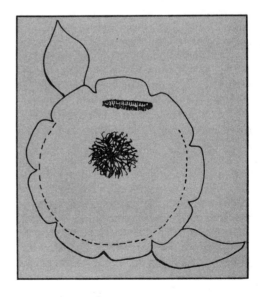

Project on page 72.

COSMETIC CASE

Materials:
   Pins
   2 12 x 7-inch pieces of matching
      fabric
   Scissors
   1 button or gripper

Pin the 2 pieces of fabric with right sides together; round off one end evenly. Sew around edges in 1/2-inch seam, leaving a 2-inch opening on straight end. Trim corners; clip curved end. Turn fabric right sides out; press. Slip stitch opening. Fold straight end up 4 1/2 inches from edge; stitch edges together. Fold down curved end. Complete closure with button and buttonhole.

Mrs. Ruby R. Cannon
Royal Palm School
West Palm Beach, Florida

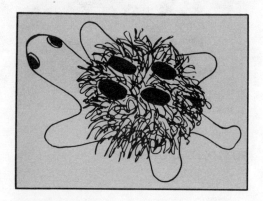

REFRIGERATOR ANIMALS

Materials:
   Scissors
   Felt scraps
   Glue
   Ball fringe
   Small plastic eyes
   Magnet strips
   Thin wire

Cut turtle shape from felt 1 1/2 inches long; glue on 1 ball fringe of contrasting color.

Project on page 32.

Glue on 2 plastic eyes. Glue 1/4 x 1/2-inch strip of magnet to underside of turtle. Cut small spots from felt; glue to ball fringe. Cut caterpillar shape from felt. Cut 3 balls from fringe; glue onto felt. Glue 2 plastic eyes to ball fringe at 1 end of caterpillar. Cut 2 antenna from wire; bend into shape. Glue next to eyes. Cut small spots from felt; glue to remaining ball fringe. Glue strip of magnets to underside of caterpillar.

Joy Pool
Northlawn Jr. High School
Streator, Illinois

QUILTED POTHOLDER

Materials:
   Scraps of plain and print cotton
      fabric
   Flannel

Cut two 9-inch squares of fabric. These may be of same fabric or 1 print and 1 solid color or any combination desired. Cut one 9-inch square of flannel. Pin flannel square between 2 fabric squares. Quilt square on right side with small running stitches. Bind edges with bias strip of fabric.

Elizabeth M. Coccia
East Greenwich Jr. High School
East Greenwich, Rhode Island

PUFF QUILT

Materials:
   Scraps of fabric
   Clean used nylon hose
   Pearl cotton

Cut 4-inch squares of fabric. Sew 2 squares together on 3 sides, allowing 1/4-inch seam. Turn right sides out. Roll hose from top to bottom. Slip hose carefully into pocket. Slip stitch 4th side together. Make a tie in center of each square to secure hose, using pearl cotton. Make as many puffs as needed for desired size of quilt. Attach the puffs together with herringbone stitch of pearl cotton.

Mrs. Lucille S. Pantel
Ellenville Central School
Ellenville, New York

Fabric

SENSIBLE CRAZY QUILT

Materials:
Fabric scraps
1/2-yard pieces of new materials
Material for backing
Bias binding

Collect fabric scraps from your sewing basket and supplement with a 1/2 yard each of several new fabrics to complete a color and or fabric plan. Pieces will overlap, so allow more than enough material to cover the total surface. Spread backing flat; place cut pieces in an overlapping arrangement, varying pieces in size and shape. Pin in place. A single machine line will hold down 2 pieces. Set machine for full width of satin stitch, then stitch raw edges. Finish outer edge with bias binding. The stitching will produce a gay pattern on the underside if the quilt backing and the thread are of contrasting colors. Attractive enough, in fact, to make the quilt entirely reversible.

Louisa M. Krebs
Central High School
Rapid City, South Dakota

TIE-AROUND CRAYON APRON

Materials:
Scissors
Solid color cotton fabric

Cut fabric in rectangular shape to fit child, allowing for gathers, if desired, and allowing 2 1/2 inches for hem. Sew narrow hem on sides and bottom of apron. Turn bottom of apron up 2 1/4 inches to right side of apron; machine stitch 15 lines through turned hem and apron to form pockets for crayons. Cut and attach a waistband long enough to allow for ties.

Marguerite S. Darnall
Corona Sr. High School
Corona, California

ROUND DISHCLOTH

Materials:
Pins
20 inches terry cloth
Scissors
1 pkg. wide bias tape

Make circular pattern from newspaper or brown paper 18 inches in diameter. Pin pattern on terry cloth; cut out fabric. Pin bias tape around edge of terry cloth circle; baste. Sew tape on with sewing machine; remove basting. Rickrack may be sewed on for decoration; bias tape may be added to outside to hang dishcloth.

Sondra Keener
Solon High School
Solon, Ohio

BUTTON WALL HANGING

Materials:
Scissors
1 large piece of felt
Sewing machine
Thread
Needle
Felt scraps
Fabric scraps
Stuffing
Buttons
Dowel

Cut felt to desired size for wall hanging. Sew casing in top for dowel. Cut double thicknesses of felt and fabric scraps in shapes such as tree, stars, moon, car, people and animals. Sew shapes together, leaving small openings. Insert small amount of stuffing; stitch closed. Sew buttonhole at top edge of each shape. Sew buttons on felt to achieve desired picture. Insert dowel; hang up.

Mrs. Karen Oliver
University Hills Jr. High School
San Antonio, Texas

ANGEL WALL HANGING

Materials:
> Gold spray paint
> 3 4-in. square plastic picture
>   frames
> 1 5-in. x 5-ft. black or dark green
>   felt strip
> Elmer's glue
> 3 miniature angels, butterflies
>   or other items
> 1 1 x 4-in. board
> 1 ornamental hook

Spray picture frames with gold paint; wipe down carefully to give antique look. Space frames on felt strip; glue down. Glue miniatures to felt inside frames. Wrap top of felt around board; glue to hold together securely. Screw hook into board.

Mrs. Marie Purvis
Odessa Public Schools
Odessa, Texas

BELL HANGING FOR CHILD'S BEDROOM DOOR

Materials:
> 1 soup can lid
> Shears
> Nail
> Colored yarn
> Wide ribbon or decorative fabric
> Stapler

Draw 2 lines through lid at right angles, dividing lid into 4 equal parts. Cut lid with shears to 1/2 inch from center on all 4 lines. Pound nail hole for center hole. Bend cut quarters of lid down; curve ends in slightly. String bell on yarn; knot yarn. Pull yarn through hole; knot on top of bell. Leave about 4 inches yarn on top. Cut ribbon into desired length; cut V shape in lower end. Staple yarn to ribbon; staple bow at top of yarn, if desired. Hang decoration on door. May place 2 or 3 bells on 1 hanging.

Margaret Morgan
Austin High School
Austin, Minnesota

PICTURE PERFECT PROTECTOR

Materials:
> Scissors
> Gingham or knit material
> Cardboard to fit picture
> Glue
> Favorite card or poem
> Lace trim, flower appliques or
>   rickrack
> Picture frame or shadow box

Cut material to fit cardboard; glue onto cardboard. Place card and trim on background material in desired pattern; glue down. Slide gently into picture frame, being careful not to wrinkle background.

Elaine Pugh
Hugoton High School
Hugoton, Kansas

have a nice day!

Fabric

EASY WALL HANGINGS

Materials:

    *Discarded upholstery material
      or drapery samples
    Embroidery thread or yarn
    Needles
    Scissors*

Select material with bird, floral or scenic designs. Embroider around birds to outline in color harmonies, as desired. Hem and hang. Embroidered piece may be framed and hung as sampler or used as pillow top.

*Elnor Alkio
Pendleton Sr. High School
Pendleton, Oregon*

GREETING CARD FRAME-UPS

Materials:

    *1 plain frame, with or without glass
    Glue
    Rickrack trim
    Thick corrugated cardboard
    Ruler
    Pencil
    Greeting card or other small picture
    Utility knife or single-edged razor
      blade
    1/4 yd. fabric
    Stitch Witchery or rubber cement*

Remove cardboard backing and glass from frame; glue rickrack to inner edges of frame (Fig. 1). Cut cardboard to fit inner edges of frame (Fig. 1). Cardboard backing that came with frame may be used for pattern. Measure area of card or picture to be framed allowing at least 1/2 inch over edges. Center on cardboard; mark area. Cut out space for picture. Cut fabric 4 inches wider and 4 inches longer than cardboard; center cardboard on wrong side of fabric with Stitch Witchery, following package directions. Cut fabric at center of cardboard as shown (Fig. 2). Pull through hole; attach with Stitch Witchery. Repeat to fold down extra fabric around edges, clipping corners as shown (Fig. 2). Place the card behind opening in matting; center. Glue

in place. Replace glass in frame; place mounted card in frame.

*Glenda Muller
Ballard High School
Huxley, Iowa*

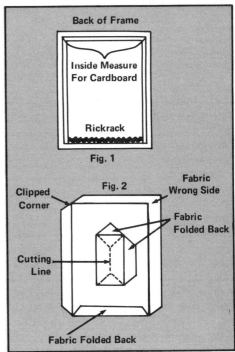

Back of Frame

Inside Measure
For Cardboard

Rickrack

Fig. 1

Fig. 2

Clipped
Corner

Cutting
Line

Fabric
Wrong Side

Fabric
Folded Back

Fabric Folded Back

SPICE ROPE

Materials:
    Cloves or other spices
    4 6-in. squares calico or early
        American print
    String
    1 18-in. piece of rope, hemp or yarn

Place cloves in center of each square of calico. Bring 4 corners of fabric together; secure tightly with string to enclose cloves. Make loop in top of rope. Attach spice sacks to rope by knotting string from sack to rope in several places. Attach card to bottom or top of rope with poem.

The Spice Rope

Hang me in a special place
Where steam or wind blows in my face.
My spicy fragrance fills the room
And brightens up kitchen gloom.

Lynn Lankford
Taylor High School
Taylor, Texas

VELVET WALL HANGING

Materials:
    Velvet
    Bleach

Cut velvet to desired size. Tie for tye dyeing; bleach to desired color. Hem and hang.

Sherry Fay
Sycamore High School
Sycamore, Illinois

Recycling Worn-Out Nylon Hose

Hose make a soft washable stuffing for stuffed toys or a good filler for the quilt-as-you-go quilts.

Marie Heltzel
Union County High School
Lake Butler, Florida

PATCH CANS

Materials:
    Coffee can
    Gesso or white latex paint
    Paintbrush
    Scraps of cotton fabric
    Pinking shears
    Craft glue
    Varnish or Mod-Podge

Paint can with Gesso, if needed; let dry. Cut fabric with pinking shears into various shapes. Mix 3/4 parts glue with 1/4 part water. Glue fabric shapes onto can, overlapping edges; smooth with fingers to release air bubbles. Let dry overnight. Varnish with 2 or 3 coats to seal. Use different sized cans to make canisters, cookie jars, wastebaskets, pencil holders and gift boxes.

Mrs. Rhonda Ward
Old Glory Rural High School
Old Glory, Texas

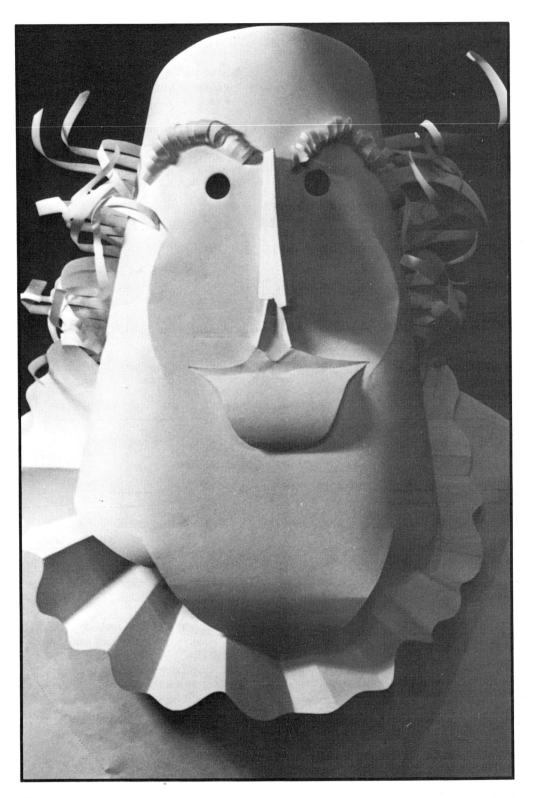

A stack of paper bags, a box of old greeting cards and a drawer of empty spools can be found in practically everyone's home. Yes, saving things "Just in case" we need them is a common habit. But, how many of us ever make use of what we've saved?

Paper and wood are two extremely versatile materials that can be used, then reused to make everything from wastebaskets to toys. Because wood and paper products make ideal craft supplies, they are real "life-savers" for the homemaker who utilizes them.

While old newspapers can be reused in a variety of ways, one of the most money-saving ideas is to make logs for the fireplace from them. Or, why not solve all your gift-giving problems with darling *Foot Notes* that can be made with construction paper? Since paper of all kinds is easily obtainable and easy to work with, there's no end to the projects you can do. Tissue paper, crepe paper or cardboard — all can be transformed into practical and decorative items.

Working with wood is both fun and artistically rewarding. Wall plaques and planters made from scraps and interesting shapes of wood are lovely additions to any home. And, as a family project, both you and the children will enjoy making wooden toys and games to give their friends on birthdays and Christmas. To be sure, there's nothing more satisfying than changing ordinary wood objects found in the home or natural wood pieces into unique, handcrafted articles.

Now, instead of wondering what to do with the many paper and wood products left around, you know what to do! The Home Economics Teachers' "life-saver" crafts have come to help.

Paper and Wood

Paper and Wood

CHRISTMAS CARD PLACE MATS

Materials:
>   Tagboard
>   Christmas cards
>   Scotch tape
>   Transparent contact paper

Cut tagboard into 14 x 18-inch rectangle. Cut picture side from Christmas cards; place on tagboard in desired combination. Tape backs of cards to front of tagboard. Cut contact paper size of tagboard; place over cards carefully. Apply contact paper to back of tagboard. Place mats may be wiped off when soiled. Cards for other occasions may also be used.

Ruth Larson
Hickman High School
Columbia, Missouri

CHRISTMAS TREE ORNAMENTS

Materials:
>   Scissors
>   Old greeting cards
>   Colored felt

>   Glue
>   Silver and gold rickrack or other trims
>   Sequins
>   Bright colored string

Cut out animals, dolls or other objects from old greeting cards. Cut felt of desired color to match ornaments; glue together. Decorate with pieces of rickrack or felt. Glue on sequins for eyes or other accent. Attach string to ornaments for hanging.

Mrs. Ruby R. Cannon
Royal Palm School
West Palm Beach, Florida

COMIC BOOK COLORING

Materials:
>   Comic book
>   Waxed paper
>   Clear tape
>   Metal spoon

Place open comic book on flat surface. Cover page with piece of waxed paper; tape edges to hold in place. Scratch waxed paper with spoon until picture from comic book adheres to waxed paper. This is a safe and easy way to keep children busy.

Neldalea Dotray
LaGrove School
Farina, Illinois

FIREPLACE LOGS

Materials:
>   Old newspapers
>   Heavy twine
>   4 lb. bluestone
>   3 lb. rock salt

Roll old newspapers until about 4 inches in diameter; cut lengths to fit fireplace. Tie with heavy twine securely but not too tightly. Place bluestone and rock salt in a crock or wooden or plastic pail; do not use metal container. Add 1 gallon warm, not hot, water; mix thoroughly. Do not heat solution on stove. Place rolls loosely in solution, using rubber or heavy cotton household gloves to protect hands. Don't pack the container tightly because newspaper rolls swell. Let soak for 2 to 3 weeks, turning logs occasionally. Remove logs from solution; dry thoroughly outdoors or over basement beams. Drying takes about 2 weeks, but the longer the better. Bluestone may be purchased at hardware store.

Mrs. Barbara Goedicke
Lindsay Thurber Comprehensive High School
Red Deer, Alberta, Canada

INEXPENSIVE PLANTERS FOR SEEDLINGS

Materials:

Plastic-coated milk cartons
Gravel or small chips of stone
Sand
Potting soil
Seeds
Plant food

Use milk cartons to start growing plants in the house. Cut cartons down to 4 inches; half fill with gravel for drainage. Mix sand and potting soil; fill cartons with sand mixture. Plant seeds; add plant food mixed with water. Let plants grow until ready to transplant. Plant cartons containing plants in ground when weather is warm enough.

Mrs. Sue Slusser
Agra High School
Agra, Oklahoma

NEWBORN BABY'S BIRTHDATE COLLAGUE

Materials:

Scissors
Daily newspaper
Paintbrush
Paint or varnish
12 x 18-inch piece of plywood
Glue
Mod-Podge or Decoupage
Picture hanger

Cut from newspapers and magazines interesting types of information pertaining to a baby's birthdate, such as the day's weather report, headlines for day, hospital birth announcement, and national and international news headlines. Collect other interesting items such as small calendar page of month with date circled, picture of the hospital, a letter with stamp cancelled with date and picture of the newborn baby. Paint or varnish the plywood. Arrange the items on the board in an interesting way, then glue on the board. Mod-Podge or decoupage over top; let dry. Attach hanger to back. This makes a very personal and meaningful gift to a new mom and dad.

Mrs. Dee Ryan
Edina-West Secondary School
Edina, Minnesota

POSTAGE STAMP LETTER HOLDER

Materials:

Envelopes with canceled stamps
Elmer's glue
Round ice cream cartons
Paintbrush
Varathane clear plastic

Soak envelopes in warm water until stamps slip off easily. Place stamps on paper towels to dry. Apply glue to carton in sections; place stamps on carton in desired design. Let dry thoroughly. Apply coat of plastic for finish; let dry.

Mrs. Elsie Clements
Corbett High School
Corbett, Oregon

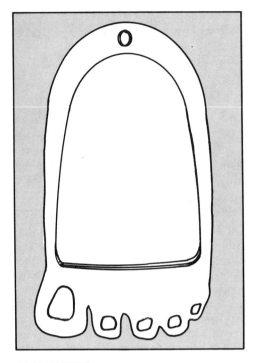

FOOT NOTES

Materials:

2 pieces of colored poster board
2 pieces of construction paper
Paper for inside note sheets
Hole punch
1 brad fastener

Cut poster board into 2 foot-shaped pieces of desired size. Cut 2 construction paper feet, 1/4 inch smaller than poster board feet, rounding off at beginning of toes. Cut graduated sizes of toenails. Glue construction paper feet and toenails to poster board feet. Cut notepaper to fit inside feet. Place paper between 2 feet; punch hole at top. Fasten with paper brad. Slide apart to open.

Audrey W. Craig
Divide High School
Nolan, Texas

TISSUE NOTEPAPER

Materials:

Elmer's glue
Waxed paper
Napkins or any other tissue with design
  or color
Small paintbrush
2 white cloths
Scissors
Envelopes
Sheets of writing paper

Prepare mixture of Elmer's glue in small container, using 1 part glue to 2 parts water. Tear off sheet of waxed paper larger than size of napkin or napkin design. Separate napkin into 1 single sheet or ply; place sheet, right side up, on waxed paper. Wet paintbrush well with glue solution. Brush glue on napkin all the way to end with slow, even strokes, starting from center of napkin. The more wrinkles there are, the better; be sure edges are moistened and there are no air bubbles. Glitter may be sprinkled over napkin, if desired. Let stand until completely dry. Place white cloth on ironing board; place dried napkin with waxed paper on cloth, wax side of paper toward iron. Place another cloth over waxed paper. Press gently with warm iron until napkin is smooth and peels off freely from cloths. Cut napkin the size of envelope. Insert sheet of paper of same size for writing; glue insert to the napkin.

Kay Luckow
Valders High School
Valders, Wisconsin

PAPER CITIES

Materials:

Scissors
Colored construction paper
Glue
Crayons, magic markers or poster paint

Cut regular and irregular shapes from different colors of construction paper; glue onto large sheet of construction paper. Draw store decorations and any other details with crayons. This project will amuse a child for a long time and is inexpensive. This is also a good project for baby-sitting amusement.

Eileen Silva
Escalon High School
Escalon, California

PAPER CITIES

PRESSED FLOWERS

Materials:
Poster paper
1 sm. picture frame
Sm. pressed flowers
Clear contact paper

Cut poster paper to fit frame; arrange pressed flowers on poster paper. Cut contact paper same size as poster paper; place over poster paper to hold flowers. Place in frame.

Marjane Telck
East Jr. High School
Rock Springs, Wyoming

RECIPE FILE

Materials:
Shoe box
Contact paper
4 x 6-in. cards
Card dividers or index tabs
Egg carton

Cover shoe box with contact paper; may decorate white shoe box with felt markers. Write recipes on 4 x 6-inch cards; place in shoe box. Place card dividers between recipe sections. Place whole egg carton behind cards in shoe box to hold cards upright. Cut sections off of egg carton as file increases.

Ann J. Hilliard
Plant City High School
Plant City, Florida

CLOSET ACCESSORIES

Materials:
Cardboard boxes
Shoe boxes
Contact paper

Cover outsides of boxes with contact paper; insides of boxes may also be covered. Place boxes on closet shelf for storage of shoes, blankets, sweaters and other items. Boxes may be covered with leftover wallpaper or scraps of materials, if desired.

Mrs. Rodger Ransom
East Jordan High School
East Jordan, Michigan

CORD KEEPERS

Materials:
Empty rolls from bathroom tissue, waxed
paper or foil
Contact paper
Decals
Pictures
Yarn
Glue

Cover rolls with contact paper or decorate with decals, pictures or yarn, glueing in place. Use for storing extension cords or appliance cords.

Sandra Gilliland
Gustine High School
Gustine, Texas

HOW TO STORE APPLIANCE CORDS

Materials:
Empty toilet tissue rolls
Adhesive contact paper

Cover cardboard rolls with contact paper; label. Fold electrical appliance cords into fourths; place in rolls.

Kay Caksey
Manogue High School
Reno, Nevada

Paper and Wood

ANYTHING CAN

Materials:

Magazines
Any size can
Scissors
White glue
3/4-in. colored vinyl or cloth tape
Shellac or varnish

Use magazine pages the same size as can. Cut full-color pages from magazines; cut off white edges of pages. Roll magazine pages from corner to corner tightly, color side down; glue ends. Continue rolling until enough pages are rolled to go around can. Different cans require different amounts. Glue rolls to can all the way around; let dry. May use masking or scotch tape to hold temporarily, about 1/3 of the way from top and 1/3 of the way from bottom. Cut tops and bottoms of rolls even with edges of cans. Apply colored tape over masking tape, if used, or 1/3 of the way from top and 1/3 of the way from bottom of can. Apply shellac, being careful not to go over rolls too many times to prevent streaking; let dry.

Catherine C. DiNapoli
Madison-Mayodan High School
Madison, North Carolina

ICE CREAM CARTON WASTEBASKET

Materials:

Gold or silver spray paint
Ice cream carton, washed and dried
Lg. magazines
Scissors
Large knitting needle, 3/8-in. wooden
*   dowel, sm. round curtain rod or lg.*
*   long drinking straws*
White glue
1/2-in. wide elastic
Razor blade
Plastic clothesline
Spray varnish

Spray inside of carton with gold spray; let dry thoroughly. Tear out and trim colored magazine pages with no small print. Pages with white borders may be used for spiraled

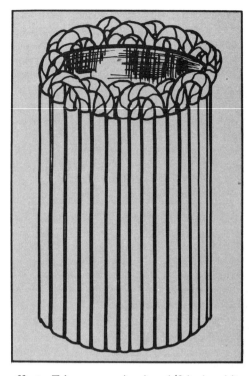

effect. Trim pages, leaving 1/8-inch white border on all edges. Roll each page diagonally on knitting needle, letting knob extend over edge of table to keep roll smooth. Finish roll with corner of page near middle of roll, if possible. Glue corner down; pull out needle carefully. Make about 100 rolls. Spread glue on metal rims at ends of carton and in center, where needed. Glue rolls to carton; keep rolls straight by following occasional lines on carton. Check number of rolls at halfway point; the number must be even. Push rolls closer together while glue is still wet to add 1 roll more if number is uneven. Make bands of elastic; place carefully over rolls. Let stand overnight. Cut off roll edges even with metal rims, using razor blade. Open any holes that may have been closed during cutting process. Cut clothesline into 3-inch lengths; insert ends of each piece in every fourth hole to make loops. Repeat process, making loops in back of first row, until all holes are filled. Spray finished wastebasket with varnish.

Mrs. Mildred Sanders
Clint High School
Clint, Texas

EGGSHELL INLAY BOX PURSE

Materials:
  Fine sandpaper
  Wooden box with lid
  Two 1-inch paintbrushes
  Gesso
  Elmer's glue
  About 2 doz. washed eggshells with
    membrane removed
  Acrylic paint
  Cote and Tote finish
  Hinges, handles and closure

Sand box until smooth. Apply 1 coat Gesso; let dry thoroughly. Apply small amount of glue to box; place 1 piece of eggshell on glue. Push down hard with toothpicks or nails until eggshell cracks and lies fairly flat. Cover the entire surface of box with eggshells, placing the curved side of eggshell on box; do not overlap. Patch any gaps with small pieces of shells. Let glue dry overnight. Sand until fairly smooth. Seal eggshells with 1 thin coat of Gesso. Paint with at least 2 coats of acrylic paint. Let dry overnight. Sand lightly for a solid color or sand until eggshells show through to give an oriental look. This will resemble lizard or snakeskin when sanded enough. Clean off box; let dry thoroughly. Apply 3 to 5 coats Cote and Tote, letting dry thoroughly between coats. Cote and Tote is the only finishing material that will not change the color. Attach hinges, handle and closure. May apply lining of velour material with peel-off backing or felt. Purse can be cleaned with a soapy cloth.

Mrs. Joe Wayne Carter
Hamlin High School
Hamlin, Texas

FAMILY HISTORY TREE

Materials:
  Scissors
  Favorite family snapshots
  Wooden drapery rings
  Paintbrush
  Walnut stain
  Glue
  Pen
  Velvet ribbon
  Christmas tree
  Tree branch
  Vase or stand for branch

Cut snapshots into circles slightly larger than center of wooden drapery ring hole. Stain drapery rings with walnut stain; let dry. Spread glue on outer edge of snapshots; glue snapshots to back of wooden rings. Let dry. Write names and dates on back of snapshots with pen. Cut ribbon into desired lengths; tie into bows on metal loops of wooden rings. Insert ornament hooks onto metal loops. Place tree branch in vase; hang picture on branch.

Mrs. Dee Ryan
Edina-West Secondary School
Edina, Minnesota

Paper and Wood

4 inches

2-½ inches

KEY CHAINS AND TREE TRIMS

Materials:
Assorted patterns
Soft 1/4-inch thick wood
Jigsaw or pocket knife
Sandpaper
No. 3 artist brush
Red, white, green and brown acrylic paints
Small-tipped permanent black ink pen
Acrylic sealer spray

Trace apple design on wood; cut out with jigsaw. Sand until edges and surfaces are smooth. Paint design in desired colors. Let dry. Outline worm, apple, stem and leaf with pen. Spray with acrylic sealer. Drill hole in top for key chain or ornament holder.

Carline Cuttrell
West Lamar School
Petty, Texas

NUT CENTERPIECE

Materials:
Small and large pinecones
Glue

Wooden base in form of ring or solid circle
Various dried pits from fruit such as peaches, apricots and dates
Nuts, such as acorns, chestnuts, hazelnuts and walnuts

Remove individual leaves from large pinecones. Glue leaves around outside and inside edge of ring or outside edge of circle, covering edge completely. Fill in with fruit pits, nuts and small pinecones, leaving an opening for a candle in circle. Ring will be filled in completely. Glue each piece individually. Use as centerpiece or ring makes a lovely wall hanging.

Cathy Lobe
North Central School
Spokane, Washington

COCONUT SHELL PLANTERS

Materials:
Saw
Whole coconuts
Drill
Scissors
Strong twine

Saw off 1/3 of the top of the coconut; remove coconut meat. Saw the small piece of shell in half; discard rounded top. Set large coconut shell in small portion of cut ring.

Hanging Planter

Saw off 1/3 of the top of the coconut; remove coconut meat. Drill 3 equally spaced 1/4-inch holes about 1/2 inch below edge of large shell. Cut 3 pieces of twine 3 yards long. Insert twine in drilled holes; even ends. Tie each piece of twine in single knot over shell. Repeat tying single knots to end of twine, tying same number of knots in each length of twine. Knot 3 pieces together, leaving 3-inch tassel.

Waunice A. Aldridge
Milton High School
Alpharetta, Georgia

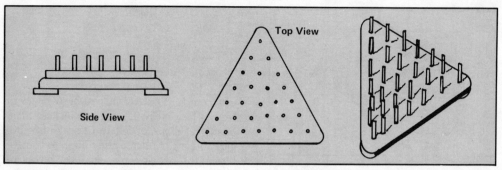

Side View

Top View

APPALACHIAN MOUNTAIN FOLK TOY

Materials:
Saw
Piece of wood
Drill
Wooden dowel
Sandpaper
Steel wool

Saw piece of wood into a triangle, all sides being the same length. Mark off the number of desired holes; drill deep enough to support pegs. Cut pegs from wooden dowel. Sand wood until smooth. The game board can be any size but number of pegs should be odd numbers such as 5, 7 or 9. The diameter and height of peg should be proportional to the size and thickness of the board. An edge or feet may be added.

To Play:

Remove one of the corner pegs and proceed to jump one peg at a time and remove the jumped peg as in checkers. The object is to end the game with only 1 peg left, preferably in the center hole.

Mrs. Mary Ada Parks
Anna-Jonesboro High School
Anna, Illinois

CHRISTMAS TREE SPOOL ORNAMENT

Materials:
Glue
Empty thread spools
Yarn
Scissors
Print fabric scraps
Hair roller picks or plastic needles

Spread glue around center part of spools; wind with yarn. Cut circles of fabric to cover spool ends; glue in place. Remove ball tips from roller picks; stick through yarn. Attach loop of yarn for hanger.

Nancy Stearley
Bloomfield High School
Bloomfield, Indiana

CREATIVE CLAY WALL PLAQUE

Materials:
1 c. cornstarch
2 c. soda
1 1/4 c. cold water
Watercolors, poster paints or felt-tip
pens
Wooden board
Decoupage spray or varnish
Decorative hanger

Combine cornstarch and soda in saucepan; mix thoroughly. Stir in water. Cook, stirring constantly, until mixture reaches slightly moist, mashed potato consistency. Turn out on plate; cover with damp towel. Let stand until cool enough to handle. Knead like dough. Roll out 1/4 inch thick. Cut into fruit shapes such as a watermelon quarter, apple, pear or peach. Let dry. Paint fruit with appropriate colors. Glue onto board. May use 1 fruit on board such as watermelon quarter or may group a selection of fruits. Apply decoupage or varnish. Attach hanger.

Jean Mason
Hi-Plains School
Seibert, Colorado

Paper and Wood

TOY TRACTOR

Materials:

Sharp knife
1 2-in. wooden spool
Wax
4 tacks with small heads
Hammer
1 dowel shorter than diameter of spool
1 strong rubber band length of spool
1/2-in. piece of wax crayon
1 dowel about 6 inches long and 1/4
*   inch in diameter*

Cut notches around edge in each end of spool for traction; wax right end of spool heavily. Drive tacks in left end of spool to hold short dowel; place dowel between tacks so dowel will not turn. Hook rubber band over short dowel. Push rubber band through spool; hook over wax crayon and long dowel at right end. Wind rubber band tightly by turning long dowel round and round. Place tractor on smooth surface; as rubber band unwinds, tractor moves slowly across surface.

Mrs. Claire Hill Shaw
Neal School
Durham, North Carolina

HERB AND SPICE WALL PLAQUE

Materials:
1 board
Desired wood stain
Scissors
Felt
Elmer's glue
Picture hook

Long Italian spaghetti
Choice of spices and herbs
Alphabet macaroni
Tweezers
Lacquer spray finish

Cut board 18 x 5 1/2 inches; bevel edges so top surface is 16 1/2 x 4 1/2 inches. Stain board; let dry. Cut felt to fit back of board; glue to back. Attach picture hook to back of board for hanging plaque. Glue pieces of long spaghetti around outside of board for border. Sketch desired partitions on board with thin ribbons of glue. Break long spaghetti to fit partitions. Place on glue; let dry. Plan spacing and design of spices, herbs and macaroni to place in partitions. Pick up macaroni with tweezers. Dip in glue; attach where desired. Arrange spices and herbs in partitions by placing glue on board, then attaching spices and herbs over glue. May tie small bouquet of clover, wheat and dried poppy head with narrow velvet bow and attach to top corner of board. Spray completed plaque with several coats of lacquer, drying after each coat.

Genevieve Kramer
East Chain High School
Blue Earth, Minnesota

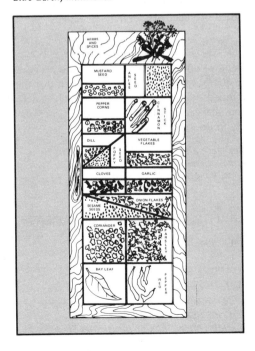

KITCHEN DECORATION

Materials:

 Saw
 1 piece of scrap lumber
 Sandpaper
 Small nails
 Hammer
 1 pop top ring from drink can
 Scissors
 1 piece of burlap or other scrap
  material
 Glue
 1 set measuring spoons
 Spray paint
 Floral clay or bubble gum
 Miniature plastic or dried flowers

Saw lumber into desired size board; sand until smooth. Nail ring on back of board for hanger. Cut burlap to fit board; fringe 1/2 inch of burlap on all edges. Glue to board. Spray spoons with spray paint; let dry. Bend bowls of spoons up; nail spoons into place on burlap. Place floral clay in bowls of spoons; secure flowers to clay.

Audrey V. Craig
Divide High School
Nolan, Texas

THREAD RACK

Materials:

 Sandpaper
 Paintbrush
 Paint
 1 1/2-inch thick square, oblong or
  round board
 Ruler
 Pencil
 Hammer
 Small-headed nails
 Chain, leather or hook for wall hanger

Sand and paint board as desired. A picture may be decoupaged in center. Space and mark nail holes at least 2 inches apart. Hammer in nails at a slight upward angle. Attach chain or leather at top for hanger. Slip spools of thread on nails.

Mrs. Rhonda Ward
Old Glory Rural High School
Old Glory, Texas

WOODEN FLOWERPOT

Materials:

 1 8-ounce tin can
 Glue
 2 doz. forked wooden clothespins
 Varnish
 12 in. gingham ribbon

Wash label off can; clean and dry well. Apply glue to outside of can. Insert clothespins close together over side of can. Cover with varnish; let dry. Tie with ribbon.

Angela Johansen
Sioux Falls Ind. Sch. Dist. No. 1
Sioux Falls, South Dakota

Inexpensive Paint Remover

 1 qt. liquid starch
 2 to 3 tbsp. lye

Mix starch and lye. Spread on furniture; let stand for several minutes. Scrape off.

Shirley Johnson
East High School
Aurora, Illinois

Have you ever looked around your house and made a mental note of all the plastic articles that you can find? Egg cartons, margarine tubs, plastic wrap, or bleach and detergent bottles are only a few of the ordinary things you might come across. And, many of these same items will sooner or later end up in the trash.

What a waste! So many products are marketed in plastic because it is pliable, yet almost indestructible, and can be made into so many shapes and colors. It is these same qualities that make plastic packaging materials so perfect for making inexpensive crafts.

The egg-shaped pantyhose containers are a great example of things you might throw away without realizing their usefulness. With some glitter, rick-rack and old jewelry as trim, you suddenly have a beautifully decorated Christmas or Easter ornament.

Plastic foam egg cartons are extremely versatile "trash". They can be shaped and cut into colorful flowers, or sturdy candy and nut cups. And, they are just right for starting flowers and growing small herb gardens because they hold the dirt well, and drain easily when punched with a few small holes.

Plastic bags can be transformed into a beautiful Christmas wreath to decorate your door. Try "shrink art" in your oven with plastic foam meat trays and transparent plastic medicine bottles, and make really unique jewelry or a key chain!

Home Economics Teachers have saved much of their plastic "trash" and they love the new world of creativity they have found. They want you to start saving, using and enjoying, too — right away!

PLASTIC

Plastic

BIRDHOUSE KLEENEX COVER

Materials:
Sharp knife
1   12 x 12-inch piece of 1/2-in.
*   Styrofoam*
Glue
White lace or lightweight fabric pieces
1   2-in. piece of Tinker Toy or twig
Artificial bird
1 Kleenex boutique box of tissues
4 hat pins

Cut Styrofoam in half; cut 1 piece in half again, forming two 6-inch square pieces. Cut 1 edge of each piece at an angle to let pieces fit together for a roof. Cut 2 triangles, 4 1/2 inches wide and 4 3/4 inches high from remaining piece of Styrofoam. Glue pieces together to form roof; let dry overnight. Cover roof with lace; let dry. Cut a 1-inch hole in one of the triangle pieces. Insert Tinker Toy just below hole for bird perch; glue into place. Fasten bird to perch. Turn Kleenex box on side; place roof on Kleenex box with the bird above the tissue opening. Secure each corner with hat pin.

Mrs. Cecelia Sanchez
Salina High School Central
Salina, Kansas

DECORATIVE SOAP DISH

Materials:
2 plastic detergent bottles of
*   different sizes*
Ice pick or awl
Decal

Cut larger bottle off 2 3/4 inches from bottom; scallop top edge. Cut smaller bottle off 2 inches from bottom in straight line. Punch 6 holes in bottom of container with ice pick for drainage; place smaller container in larger container. Add decal for trim on outside of large container.

Mrs. Martha Kniese
Arickaree School
Anton, Colorado

CHRISTMAS DECORATIONS

Materials:
Plastic wrap
Gold fabric trim
Elmer's glue
Food coloring
Glitter

Spread a piece of plastic wrap on flat surface. Form fabric trim into shapes such as stars, bells or other Christmas shapes, on plastic wrap; glue ends of trim together. Mix several drops of food coloring with glue; spread 1/8 to 1/4 inch thick on center of trim. Sprinkle with glitter; let dry. Remove plastic wrap. Hang decorations as desired.

Cheryl Fisher
Thomas Stone School
Waldorf, Maryland

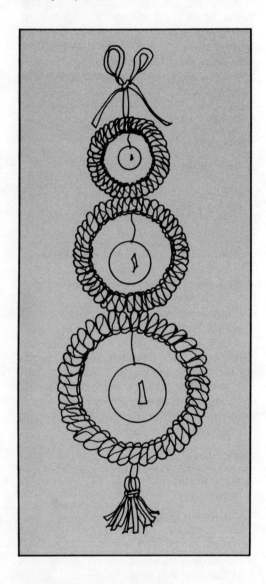

CHRISTMAS WALL HANGING

Materials:
   Plastic lids of 3 different sizes
   Leftover red or green yarn
   Small Christmas balls or other
      decorations

Cut out center of plastic lids, leaving about 1/2 to 3/4-inch rim. Wrap each ring with yarn, using blanket stitch. Attach medium ring to small ring by tying 5 yarns of 1 ring to 5 yarns of other ring with yarn. Attach large ring to medium ring in same manner on opposite side of medium ring. Attach a small Christmas ball to top of each ring with yarn to hang in center of ring. Attach a small bow loop to small ring for hanging. May attach a ball fringe tassel to bottom of large ring, if desired.

Mrs. Marjorie Petefish
Holbrook Public School
Holbrook, Nebraska

CANDY AND NUT CUPS

Materials:
   Scissors
   Styrofoam egg carton
   Glue
   Awl

Cut 3 egg cups of 2 colors; scallop edges. Insert one colored cup into different colored cup. Invert remaining cup and glue together. Decorate as desired with heated awl. Fill with nuts and candy.

Judith Brown
Rawlins School
Rawlins, Wyoming

EASY EASTER EGG

Materials:
   Fabric scraps
   1 egg-shaped hosiery container
   Elmer's glue
   Clear varnish spray (opt.)

Cut fabric in 2 x 3-inch pieces. Cover egg with glue; press pieces of fabric onto egg. Cover fabric with glue; let dry thoroughly. Spray with clear varnish. Bows may be attached, if desired.

Ellin Weaver
Winola High School
Viola, Illinois

Plastic

EGG CARTON DAISIES

Materials:

    Yellow or white Styrofoam egg cartons
    Ball fringe
    18 gauge stem wire
    Daisy leaves
    Green floral tape

Remove lid and lip of carton. Place carton bottom side up; cut into 12 separate cups. Fringe each section by cutting down to the edge of the bottom of the cup. Drop each cup into boiling water; push down with wooden spoon until section spreads for a flat Shasta daisy appearance. Place 2 fringed sections together, rotating corners. Fasten 1 ball of fringe to end of wire stem; push wire through ball, bending end of wire to secure. Push through center of flower. Add leaves as stem is wrapped with floral tape.

Mrs. Bob Farris
Altus-Denning High School
Altus, Arkansas

HOLIDAY EGGS

Materials:

    Woodburning tool
    1 egg-shaped hosiery container
    Glue
    Miniatures
    Lace
    Plastic ring

Cut an oval circle from side of hosiery egg, using woodburning tool. Decorate inside for any holiday occasion, using appropriate scenery and miniatures. Glue egg together carefully at center. Glue lace around the opening. Glue large plastic ring to bottom for a stand.

Mrs. Margaret W. Lyles
Westminster High School
Westminster, South Carolina

EGG CARTON ROSES

Materials:

    Styrofoam egg cartons
    Small 1/4-in. beads

    Stiff wires for flower stems
    Cellophane tape
    Artificial rose leaves
    Florist tape

Separate cups of egg carton. Cut a slit at center of each side of cups. Place a bead at end of wire stem; bend wire over to secure bead in place. Arrange 4 egg cups together, alternating corner points. Press wire through center of cups with the bead end at center of flower. Secure with a piece of cellophane tape. Twist leaf around stem; cover wire with florist tape.

Beverly R. Perry
Cumberland Middle School
Cumberland, Rhode Island

EASTER BASKET PATCHWORK EGGS

Materials:

    Fabric scraps
    Elmer's glue
    Styrofoam eggs or plastic egg-shaped
      hosiery containers
    Clear acrylic spray
    Easter basket

Cut fabrics into desired patchwork shapes for each egg. Apply glue to a small section of egg; glue on patchwork shapes, overlapping in crazy quilt design. Repeat until egg is covered; let dry. Spray with acrylic spray; let dry. Arrange eggs in Easter basket.

Mrs. Hal J. Puett
North Cobb High School
Acworth, Georgia

PANORAMIC EGG

Materials:

    Egg-shaped hosiery container
    Metal cutting shears
    Elmer's glue
    Decorator's icing
    Small figurines

Take container apart. Cut oval opening in both sides of container with metal cutting shears. Glue both pieces of container together at center seam with Elmer's glue, having ovals together. Place 1 teaspoon icing inside egg, such as green for grass or white for snow. Place figurine inside, such as bunny or chicken with jelly beans to look like small eggs on green icing for Easter or Santa figure on white icing for Christmas. Decorate cut edges and glued seam with icing; hang or place on base.

Mrs. Ray R. Robertson
Madison High School
Madison, Nebraska

PANORAMIC EGG

LIPSTICK HOLDER

Materials:
Velvet finish contact paper
Styrofoam disc, 6 to 9 inches in diameter

Secure strip of contact paper to edge of disc. Press tubes of lipstick into Styrofoam with color name on top.

Vicki Rains
North Platte R-I School
Dearborn, Missouri

PLASTIC SEWING BASKET

Materials:
2 1-gal. plastic containers
Ice pick
1 12-in. piece of felt
Cotton or other stuffing
1 5-in. strip small wire
Glue
1 yd. rickrack
Black Magic Marker

Cut 1 plastic container 4 inches from bottom; cut other container 1 1/2 inches from bottom. Punch 2 holes in center of container with 1 1/2-inch side with ice pick. Cut 2 circles of felt 4 inches wide; cut 1 strip of felt 3 inches long and 1/2 inch wide. Place 2 felt circles together for pincushion; sew around edge, leaving opening for stuffing. Stuff pincushion with cotton; punch 2 holes about 1/2 inch apart through unfinished part of pincushion. Sew 3-inch strip of felt together; insert wire through circle. Insert ends of wire through outside of container with holes to anchor handle to top. Insert wire through pincushion holes; twist ends of wire together to hold handle and pincushion in place. Cut off excess wire. Glue rickrack in 2 rows around container with 4-inch side. Print or write A Stitch In Time Saves Nine with Magic Marker around deeper container; place lid over bottom container for sewing basket.

Evangelena L. Barber
Saluda Jr. High School
Saluda, North Carolina

PORCELAIN FINISH FLOWERS

Materials:
1 pt. turpentine
1 pt. clear varnish
1/4 pt. high gloss white enamel
Plastic flowers

Mix turpentine, varnish and enamel together carefully. Dip flowers in varnish mixture; hang by stem to dry. Varnish mixture can be stored for later use.

Mrs. Thelma Maxey
Lorenzo High School
Lorenzo, Texas

Plastic

PLASTIC BAG WREATH

Materials:

*1 1/2 boxes small plastic bags
1 wire coat hanger
2 1/2 yd. velvet ribbon in desired
     color
Fine wire*

Cut plastic bags crosswise into 4 strips; shape coat hanger into a ring. Pick up 1 plastic strip; tie into single tie on ring. Do not knot. Continue tying strips around ring, pushing together tightly and fluffing until ring is full. Make bow with ribbon with long and short streamers; wire to wreath. Other decorations may be added, if desired.

*Gladys H. Dabbs
Oak Grove High School
Bessemer, Alabama*

PLASTIC PICTURE

Materials:

*Scissors
Heavy cardboard
Picture frame
Pebbly plastic curtain with scene
Elmer's glue
Small paintbrush
Shellac
Wide tape*

Cut cardboard to fit into picture frame. Cut scene from plastic curtain, allowing 1 inch on each side to fold under cardboard. Pull plastic tight over cardboard; glue edges on underside. Brush shellac over plastic; let dry. Place in frame; seal back edge with tape. Plastic picture resembles an oil painting.

*Mrs. Julius W. Williams
Independence School
Coldwater, Mississippi*

POTS AND PLANTS

Materials:

*Plastic glue
Frozen dessert topping container and
     lid*

*Plant
Macrame cord, yarn or string*

Glue lid to bottom of dessert topping container; let dry. Transfer plant to topping container. Make hanger of macrame knots; place container in hanger.

*Mrs. Elizabeth B. Lengle
Warrior Run High School
Turbotville, Pennsylvania*

PLASTIC PENDANTS

Materials:

*Transparent plastic pill bottle
Aluminum foil
Aluminum pie plate
Penny or small seashell
Heavy gloves
Darning needle or heavy straight pin*

Turn on oven to broil. Remove cap of pill bottle; place pill bottle on foil-lined pie plate. Place penny inside pill bottle, on bottom or sideways. Place under broiler for 2 to 3 minutes or until bottle is melted. Window in oven door comes in handy to check melting. Bottle is very hot, but may be molded to desired shape, using heavy gloves. Punch hole in top part with needle to make pendant. May be used as paperweight if hole is not punched in plastic.

*Rosalie Wentzell
Stettler Jr. High School
Stettler, Alberta, Canada*

SOAP SAVER

Materials:

*Lightweight plastic foam from old
     ironing board padding*

Cut foam into 9 x 4-inch piece or desired size. Fold bottom up 3 1/2 inches, working lengthwise; fold 2-inch piece back, keeping even with top. Stitch through all thickness on 3 1/2-inch sides. Fill with scraps of soap;

fold 2-inch top over to form envelope. Add decoration, if desired.

Rosalie Wentzell
Stettler Jr. High School
Stettler, Alberta, Canada

SHRINKING MAGIC

Materials:
  Clear plastic meat trays from
    supermarket
  Permanent marking pens
  Aluminum foil
  Metal skewer or thin nail

Wash meat trays thoroughly; dry. Draw design on trays with marking pens. Cover baking sheets with foil; place trays on covered baking sheet. Place in preheated 350-degree oven for 3 to 5 minutes or until shrunk. Remove from oven; let cool on baking sheet. Heat skewer over a flame; punch hole through plastic. Use for key chains or mobiles.

Jane Koerner
South Fork High School
Miranda, California

TISSUE HOLDER

Materials:
  1 roll toilet tissue
  2 round plastic lace mats, 6 inches in
    diameter
  4 to 6 yd. ribbon, same color as toilet
    tissue

Place toilet tissue between mats. Lace ribbon through holes in mats to form sides of holder. Ribbon can be unlaced far enough to add each new roll of tissue; lace again to close opening. Tissue is pulled through opening in ribbon lacing as needed.

Mrs. Claire Hill Shaw
Neal School
Durham, North Carolina

TISSUE HOLDER

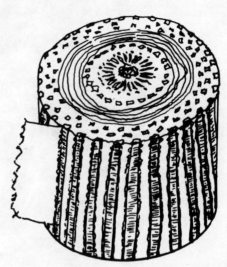

Reusing Plastics

Plastic egg cartons make great containers for starting seeds. Plastic meat trays prevent flowerpots from water staining furniture. Plastic bleach bottles can be turned into dolls' furniture, drums or containers for mixing paint. The top of the bottle may be cut off and used for a candleholder. Hoops can be cut from the remaining bottle and wrapped with ribbon for tree or door decorations with addition of mistletoe, holly or small bells.

Mrs. Barbara Goedicke
Lindsay Thurber Comprehensive H.S.
Red Deer, Alberta, Canada

Stuffings For Toys

Try stuffing toys with plastic dry cleaners bags. Bags are soft, washable and safe inside toy.

Marie Heltzel
Union County High School
Lake Butler, Florida

The touch of Fibber McGehee that lives inside almost everyone loves to save things. Pieces of wire, an occasional interesting jar or metal can, a few unused nails — we put them away in a closet or drawer "just in case", and then forget about them. When the clutter suddenly becomes too much, most of the things get thrown away.

But, the next time you are cleaning out your "Fibber McGehee Closet," think before you throw away some of the things! You might be throwing away something that could be a "life-saver" in creating a gift for a friend, or an item for yourself, your family or your home.

An unusual glass bottle can be covered with masking tape and "painted" with shoe polish for an unusual leather-look vase or lamp base. Metal cans trimmed in various ways become pin cushions and attractive storage containers. Dough art is another fun and economical "life-saver" craft, because you are able to create exactly what you want from the prepared dough.

It is also easy to find things outside your home to inspire your creativity. Cornhusks transform beautifully into a doll any girl will love, or into a lovely seasonal wreath. Dried flowers can be arranged in a vase or mounted in a frame for a striking home decorator accessory.

You never know where you might find just the right "life-saver" to create an inexpensive handmade craft — in the workshop, the attic, in a junk drawer or in your back yard. The Home Economics Teachers offer this array of their own original potpourri crafts for you to try. They also hope their ideas will inspire you to create your own sensational crafts. Have fun!

POTPOURRI CRAFTS

CHRISTMAS PLAQUE

Materials:
> Glue
> 2 plastic flirty eyes
> 1 mold for making plastic grapes
> 1 sm. piece of red yarn for mouth
> 1 red ball fringe
> 1 3 to 4-in. slice of a tree limb
>   with bark
> Red pipe cleaners
> 1 bow of green burlap ribbon
> Hanger

Glue eyes to glass mold; glue on yarn for mouth and ball fringe for nose. Glue mold to board. Make antlers from pipe cleaners; attach to top of mold. Attach bow to mold between antlers. Attach picture hanger to back to hang finished plaque.

Mrs. J. M. Allen
Wall ISD
Wall, Texas

ANTIQUED CLAY PIGEON CANDLEHOLDER

Materials:
> Epoxy glue
> 8 clay pigeons
> Antiquing paintbrush

Glue 3 pairs clay pigeons together with wide edges together to have 3 separate pairs. Glue 3 pairs together on small edges. Glue 1 pigeon, open side up, on top. Glue 1 pigeon, open side down, for base. Antique or paint for desired finish. Add candle and candle ring.

Vivian Reagan
Shaler High School
Pittsburgh, Pennsylvania

DECORATED CLAY PIGEON CANDLEHOLDER

Materials:
> Clay pigeons used in skeet shooting
> Elmer's glue

> Quick-drying spray paint
> Braid or gold leaf

Wipe off unbroken clay pigeons. Place glue along wide edges of 2 pigeons. Allow glue to partially dry. Place pieces together. Make as many pairs as needed for desired height. Stack and glue pairs together. Allow to dry overnight. Spray with quick-drying paint; let dry. Decorate with colorful braid or rub with gold leaf.

Margaret Ingram
Darrington High School
Darrington, Washington

CORNSTARCH MOLDING CLAY

Materials:
> 2 c. salt
> 1 c. cornstarch
> Food coloring
> Waxed paper

Pour 1 cup water into saucepan; bring to a boil. Stir in salt. Mix cornstarch with just enough cold water to dissolve. Stir into salt mixture; cook, stirring constantly, until thick and transparent. Tint with food coloring. Place on waxed paper; cool. Use for modeling.

Suzzun Nuttlng
Salome High School
Salome, Arizona

MODELING GOOP

Materials:
> 2 c. salt
> 1 c. cornstarch

Mix salt and 2/3 cup water in saucepan; heat, stirring with wooden spoon, for 3 to 4 minutes or until mixture is well heated. Remove from heat. Mix cornstarch with 1/2 cup water; stir into salt mixture quickly. Mixture should be consistency of soft dough. Mixture may be left white or divided and mixed with food coloring. Mixture may be kept in plastic wrap in refrigerator. Modeled objects will dry and harden at room temperature in 36 hours; dried objects may be painted.

Shirley Johnson
East High School
Aurora, Illinois

SALT DOUGH

Materials:

    2 c. flour
    1 c. salt
    1 c. water

Combine flour and salt in bowl; mix well. Add water, small amount at a time, mixing until ball is formed. Knead for 7 to 10 minutes or until smooth and firm. Form into desired shapes; moisten connecting surfaces to bond. Bake a completed project in preheated 325-degree oven for 10 to 15 minutes or until hard; cool. Projects may be painted with paint, food dye or varnish.

Suzzan Nutting
Salome High School
Salome, Arizona

CORNCOB PEOPLE MAGNETS

Materials:

    Clean corncobs similar in size
    Small patterned fabric scraps
    Glue
    Iron-on adhesive
    Bits of trim and lace
    Navy beans
    Yarn
    Felt tip pen
    Magnetic strip

Saw each corncob crosswise into 1-inch lengths. Enlarge pattern. Place on fabric scraps; cut out pieces. Gather around edge of lady's bonnet. Place glue around edge and back of corncob piece. Place bonnet around cob; draw up gathers. Reinforce bonnet brim by pressing iron-on adhesive between 2 pieces of fabric. Glue brim to bonnet; glue on trim. Glue navy bean in center of cob for nose. Add yarn bow; use felt tip pen to draw facial features on cob. Attach piece of magnet to back. Make men in similar fashion, using pattern pieces for men. Use magnets to hold notes and grocery lists on refrigerator.

Carolyn Van Amberg
Maurice-Orange City Community School
Orange City, Iowa

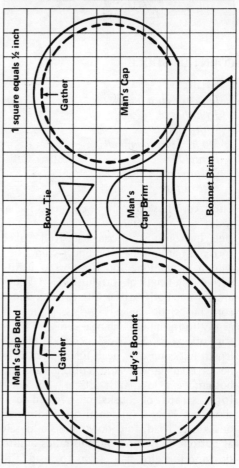

CORN HUSK DOLL

Materials:

Bleached corn husks
18 inches of 18 gauge wire
White glue
3/4-in. Styrofoam balls
Dental floss
Cotton balls
Jute or flax

Cut a corn husk 5 inches long and 3 inches wide; soak in water. Stick 3-inch wire in glue, then into Styrofoam ball. Roll soaked corn husk around ball; tie under chin. Cut a wire 3 inches long for arms; wrap tightly with 4-inch length of corn husk. Tie 1/2 inch away from both wrists. Cut two 3 x 3-inch corn husks; tie up over wrists. Turn back gently to form puff. Tie near center of arms; trim off excess. Tie two 3-inch wide and full length husks up over head for bodice; tie at neck. Fold down. Add cotton balls for bosom; tie a low waist. Place 1/2 x 5-inch long straps of husks crisscrossed over shoulders. Place 7 full length and width corn husks over head; fold down and tie loosely at bottom. Fray three 5-inch strands of jute; tie in center for hair. Glue to head. Cut

3 x 3-inch square of corn husk; glue on head for hat.

Mrs. Penelope J. Byrd
Elk Grove High School
Elk Grove, Illinois

CORN HUSK WREATH

Materials:

*2 lg. packages corn husks used for
    tamales*
Fine wire
Styrofoam wreath
Straight pins or florist pins
Decorations and bow

Soak corn husks in water until pliable. Cut in 2 x 5-inch strips. Fold strips into loops; wrap end with a 2-inch long fine wire. Attach to wreath with pins. Attach a wire hook at top for hanging wreath. Add small sprigs of greens, red berries and attractive bow.

Dana Ray Owens
Schleicher County Independent School
Eldorado, Texas

MACRAME BEADS

Materials:

4 c. flour
2 c. salt
7/8 c. water
Tinker Toys or nails
Paint
Clear varnish

Combine flour, salt and water in bowl; knead the dough for at least 15 minutes. Shape into any size, shape or design of beads. Use Tinker Toy sticks for large beads and nails for small beads to make holes, leaving stick or nail in bead until bead is dry. Dry overnight or longer, turning frequently. May also be dried in 200-degree oven. Cool and paint. Give beads a coat of clear varnish for shine and protection. Use in macrame hangers and other macrame projects.

Sister Joanne Moeller
Kuemper High School
Carroll, Iowa

DECORATOR MOLD HANG-UPS

Materials:

> Plaster of Paris
> Plastic mold, any small plastic
>   container or muffin tin greased with
>   vegetable oil
> Paper clip
> Acrylic paints
> White glue
> Magazine pictures or wrapping paper

Mix plaster according to box directions. Place mold on flat surface; pour in plaster. Bend paper clip at 45-degree angle; place paper clip in middle of back side of mold. Let dry for 1 hour or until hard. Remove from mold. Paint background. Glue picture on mold; let dry. Brush on 2 parts water to 1 part white glue. Gives clear finish and seals paint. Outside of mold may be trimmed with rickrack.

Susan Smith
Fall Mountain Regional High School
Alstead, New Hampshire

DECORATING SOAP

Materials:

> Lightweight prints
> Bar of soap
> Clear candle wax

Cut out prints. Dip fingers into water; wet side of soap to be decorated. Place print on wet soap; rub, removing air bubbles. Let dry for about 10 minutes. Melt wax in double boiler. Hold soap by sides; dip decorated surface 1/4 inch deep into wax. Place on waxed paper until cool; redip, if necessary.

Mrs. Esther Wonderlich
Mt. Pleasant Jr. High School
Mt. Pleasant, Iowa

DECORATIVE CHRISTMAS TREES

Materials:

> Construction paper
> Compass
> Scissors
> Glue

> Absorbent cotton
> Ivory flakes
> Glitter or sequins (opt.)

Draw circles on paper with compass; circles may be as small as 1 1/2-inch radius or as large as 10-inch radius. Cut out circles; cut each circle into 4 equal pieces. Roll each quarter circle into cone shape, overlapping edges and gluing. Cover each cone lightly with glue; stick absorbent cotton in thin layer over cone. Place cones, one over another, until tree is formed. Combine equal parts of warm water and Ivory flakes in bowl; beat with eggbeater until soapsuds hold shape. Spread soapsuds over tree with spatula; swirl into shape. Trim with glitter; let dry. Make as many trees as desired.

Ruth M. Allard
Lyndon Institute
Lyndon Center, Vermont

MARSHMALLOW SNOWMAN

Materials:

> Large marshmallows
> Toothpicks
> Whole cloves

Fasten 2 marshmallows, 1 over the other, with toothpicks; this makes head and midriff. Attach 2 marshmallows to midriff to make legs. Use whole cloves for eyes, nose and buttons; use toothpicks for arms.

Mrs. Paul Drazer
Kouts High School
Kouts, Indiana

Potpourri Crafts

DRYING FLOWERS THE EASY WAY

Materials:
Cornmeal
Borax
Fresh well-shaped flowers
Shoebox or plastic bowl with cover

Mix equal parts of cornmeal and borax. A cup of the mixture will be enough for 1 corsage or flower. Place layer of mixture about 1/4 inch deep in the bottom of box. Place flower on top; work more of the mixture carefully around each petal until flower is completely covered. Cover; let dry for 2 to 3 weeks. Dry flowers with stems removed for a winter bouquet. Add wire stems when dry. Wrap wire with green floral tape; arrange as desired.

Sue Farris
Altus-Denning High School
Altus, Arkansas

HEDGE APPLE FLOWERS

Materials:
Knife
Hedge apples
Aluminum foil
Cookie sheet
Flower wire
Yarn pompons
Florists tape
Artificial leaves

Slice hedge apple 1/8 to 1/4 inch thick; place slices on aluminum foil-covered cookie sheet. Bake in 150-degree oven for 3 to 4 hours or until dry and brown. Make loop at one end of wire; place pompon on wire. Pull wire through center of hedge apple flowers. Wrap florists tape around the base of wire loop, spiraling down wire, adding leaves at intervals.

Neldalea Dotray
LaGrove High School
Farina, Illinois

FLOWERS FOR THE HOSPITAL

Materials:
Plastic or metal convex lens craft
*   frame*
Scrap of velvet fabric size of frame
Glue
Pressed or dried flowers

Remove back from frame. Cover cardboard from frame with velvet fabric, selecting color to complement flowers. Glue fabric to back edge of cardboard. Place flowers on velvet in an artistic arrangement; cover with convex lens. Turn entire frame over carefully. Add back to frame; secure in place. Bouquet may be sent to a patient who is allergic to cut flowers.

Helen B. Boots
Lakeland Village School
Medical Lake, Washington

MICROWAVE-DRIED FLOWERS

Materials:
Flowers
Scissors

Silica gel
Glass jars, cups or bowls
Toothpick, ice pick or knitting needle
Microwave oven
Florist wire
Green floral tape

Choose flowers bright in color, half open and firm. Avoid flowers with thick centers. Cut flowers with about 1/2-inch stem. Dry one flower at a time. Pour layer of silica gel grains into glass container; place flower, stem down, in grains. Sprinkle more silica gel slowly and gently over flower until completely covered, spreading petals evenly with toothpick. Place 1 cup water in corner of oven. Place flower in oven; heat for 1 minute and 30 seconds to 2 minutes. Remove from oven; let stand for 10 to 15 minutes. Remove carefully from grains of silica gel. Use wire as stem; wrap with floral tape. Silica gel can be used over and over; let cool before reusing.

Ruth M. Robare
North Albany Jr. High School
Albany, Oregon

HORSE APPLE FLOWERS

Materials:
   Utility knife
   Horse apples
   Muffin pan
   Florist wire
   Cloth mum leaves
   Hair wire
   Floral tape
   Ball fringe
   White glue

Slice horse apples crosswise about 1/4 inch thick; place each slice over a cup in muffin pan. Bake in preheated 200 to 250-degree oven for about 3 hours or until slices have browned slightly and are dried. Hook florist wire through centers of slices and twist securely, leaving enough wire for stem. Twist leaf onto stem with hair wire; wrap exposed wire with floral tape. Centers may be made by attaching balls from fringe to wire when hooked through flower. A more natural center may be made by covering wire in flower center with white glue; press small seeds into glue. Horse apples are known by a variety of names, such as hedge apples, mock oranges or Osage oranges.

Edith A. Bullock
Theodore Roosevelt High School
San Antonio, Texas

HORSE APPLE FLOWERS

WEED BOUQUETS

Materials:
   Assorted grasses and weeds
   Spray paints
   Chicken wire
   Vases, jars or bottles
   Driftwood

Gather weeds of contrasting shapes and forms. Spray paint with desired colors; let dry. Place piece of chicken wire in vase; arrange weeds attractively. These may be used in driftwood arrangement.

Jean Mason
Hi Plains School
Seifert, Colorado

NONEDIBLE CHRISTMAS BREAD CENTERPIECE

Materials:

>*1 loaf baked twisted bread with sesame seed*
>*1 can spray shellac*
>*1 yd. gingham ribbon about 1 1/2 inches wide*
>*Corsage-type Christmas decoration*

Place bread on baking sheet. Bake in preheated 200-degree oven for 7 hours; cool. Spray thoroughly with shellac. Tie ribbon around loaf in a bow; attach decoration to center of bow.

Mrs. Juanita Pitts
Linden-Kildare High School
Linden, Texas

BREAD DOUGH BASKET

Materials:

>*4 c. flour*
>*1 c. salt*
>*1 1/2 c. hot water*
>*Paintbrush*
>*1 egg, beaten (opt.)*
>*Glossy varnish*

Mix first 3 ingredients in bowl; knead until smooth and pliable. Shape 2 rolls 1/2 inch thick from part of the dough; twist together. Place on greased baking sheet around edge of greased inverted loaf pan. Moisten ends; join carefully. Roll out remaining dough on floured surface to 1/4-inch thickness; cut into strips about 1 inch wide. Place 3 long strips over loaf pan lengthwise, allowing for extra 1 inch at each end. Cut 5 strips; place over width of pan, weaving as placed. One long strip may be woven around sides of pan halfway between top and bottom. Seal with a drop of water between strips when weaving. Cut ends off; attach with drop of water to underside of braid. Fork marks may be made on each end. Bake in preheated 350-degree oven for 30 minutes or until dough is firm enough to be loosened from pan. Reduce oven temperature to 300

degrees. Remove basket from pan; paint all sides with egg for color. Place basket upright on baking sheet; bake for 2 hours to 2 hours and 30 minutes or until hard. Cool. Paint with 2 or 3 coats of varnish.

Mrs. Adeline Brill
Jefferson Jr. High School
Jamestown, New York

WOVEN BREADBASKET

Materials:

>*4 c. flour*
>*1 c. salt*
>*1 c. water*
>*Rolling pin*
>*Knife*
>*Pan*
>*Cookie sheet*
>*Brush*
>*1 beaten egg*
>*Varnish*

Combine flour and salt; add water until mixture forms firm ball. Knead for 5 minutes. Roll out 1/4 inch thick; cut into strips. Interlace strips over inverted greased pan or casserole of desired shape. Moisten ends of strips and press lightly to join. Place on cookie sheet. Bake at 350 degrees for 1 hour. Remove the pan. Place basket, right side up, on baking sheet. Bake for 15 minutes longer. Brush with egg until well coated; bake for 15 minutes. Cool. Coat with varnish. Christmas tree ornaments may be made from dough. Roll out; cut with cookie cutters. Make a hole in top for string. Place on greased cookie sheet; bake for 20 minutes. Cool. Varnish or paint. Tie in string for hanger.

Janice Schaffer
Hudson Sr. High School
New Port Richey, Florida

BREAD DOUGH ROSES

Materials:

>*1 long loaf bread*
>*6 oz. glue*
>*2 tbsp. white shoe polish*
>*1 tbsp. glycerine*

Remove all crust from bread; break bread up into bowl. Pour glue, shoe polish and glycerine over bread. Spread additional glycerine on hands; work bread mixture until combined. Knead until mixture is consistency of bread dough; mixture will be very sticky at first, but keep working. May be stored in plastic bag in refrigerator for long time. Form into roses of desired shapes; let dry. May be painted.

Suzzan Nutting
Salome High School
Salome, Arizona

ROLL BASKET

Materials:
   3 to 4-in. Styrofoam ball
   Roll basket
   Posie clay
   Assortment of dinner rolls and
      breadsticks, some with sesame
      seed
   Florist sticks 6 inches long
   Artificial boxwood
   1 1/2-in. wide florist gingham ribbon
   Flat and glossy decoupage spray (opt.)

Cut piece off Styrofoam ball so ball rests flat on roll basket; secure to basket with posie clay. Place rolls and bread sticks on baking sheet. Bake in preheated 150-degree oven for 10 to 12 hours; cool. Stick florist sticks in bottom of rolls and breadsticks with glue; stick into Styrofoam ball, leaving spaces between. Fill in spaces with boxwood. Wrap ribbon around basket and arrangement; top with bow. May spray breadsticks and rolls with flat decoupage spray; use glossy finish for rolls that are browner for contrast.

Mrs. Connie Phillips
4 District Industrial Training Center
Fenton, Michigan

CATHEDRAL CANDLES

Materials:
   Tempered glass
   Heavy plastic bag
   Hammer

Brandy snifter, glasses or jars
Elmer's glue
Small paintbrushes
Variety of colors of glass stain
Nail polish remover
Votive candle

Clean glass; wrap in plastic bag. Hit with hammer to break. Try to keep glass in fairly large pieces to paint. Can be easily broken after painting. Cover snifter with light coat of glue; let dry. Paint stem of snifter with glass stain; let dry. Place broken glass pieces on flat metal trays; paint tops of pieces in different colors. Do not paint sides. Let dry thoroughly. Do not stack pieces. Clean brushes for future use. Invert snifter. Spread glue on painted side of glass pieces, starting with larger pieces; press firmly onto side of snifter. Fill in holes with small bits of glass, covering entire surface. Let dry thoroughly. Place candle in finished holder. Tempered glass from cars may be obtained from wrecking companies or auto repair companies.

Emely Sundbeck
Manor High School
Manor, Texas

PIGGY BANKS

Materials:
   10 baby food jars
   Screwdriver
   Cloth tape
   Sticker numerals from 1 to 10
   55 pennies
   Sm. coin purse
   Container for jars

Punch slots in jar covers large enough for pennies to slip through, using srewdriver. Cover jagged edges of slots with tape. Paste one numeral on each jar. Place pennies in coin purse. A 4 to 5-year old child can use banks to learn how to form sets, count, make comparisons, learn about money, combine groups, develop respect for property.

Mrs. Gloria J. Smith
Valders High School
Valders, Wisconsin

Potpourri Crafts

CANDLEHOLDER CENTERPIECE

Materials:
> Glue
> 2 baby food jars
> 2 sm. fruit bowls
> Black spray paint

Glue baby food jar to bottom of 1 bowl. Glue second baby food jar to first jar; glue second fruit bowl bottom to second baby food jar. Let dry thoroughly. Spray with paint. Apply second coat of paint; let dry thoroughly. Place ring of artificial flowers and thick candle in one bowl.

Fran Banks
Freedom Jr. High School
Freedom, Pennsylvania

ODD BUTTON SHOW

Materials:
> Odd buttons
> Narrow jar with screw top lid

Place buttons in jar; screw on lid. Place in sewing room for decoration. It is surprising how many times an odd button saves the day when one is lost.

Mrs. Elsie Clements
Corbett High School
Corbett, Oregon

BEADED BOAT

Materials:
> 1 cotton T-shirt
> Large embroidery hoops, slightly larger
>   than boat design
> Piece of muslin material
> Needle
> Thread
> Tiny glass beads

Stretch the front of T-shirt over embroidery hoops where design is to be centered. Baste piece of muslin with design drawn on it to backside of T-shirt to give extra body to beaded design. Baste boat design through T-shirt for guide to sew on beads. Sew beads

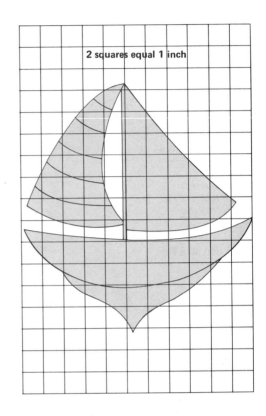

2 squares equal 1 inch

in rows inside boat design. Trim off excess muslin on backside.

Photograph for this project on page 35.

LEATHER BOTTLE WITH PICTURE

Materials:

Interesting looking bottle
Masking tape
Picture from greeting card
Glue
Paste shoe polish
Clear spray shellac or varnish

Cover bottle with torn pieces of masking tape, overlapping edges. Cut picture from greeting card; glue to one side of bottle. Rub bottle evenly with shoe polish to stain. Spray with shellac.

Wanda Ruth Beard
University High School
Warrensburg, Missouri

BARK-COVERED FLOWER VASES

Materials:

Scissors
3/4 to 1-in. masking tape
Pretty-shaped jars
Brown shoe polish

Cut masking tape into 1-inch and 1 1/2-inch pieces. Layer pieces on jar, overlapping slightly and varying size. Rub shoe polish over tape, applying sparingly to achieve a bark-like effect.

Mrs. Gladys Olson
Monmouth High School
Monmouth, Illinois

BOTTLE LAMP

Materials:

Masking tape
1 green bottle
Brown shoe polish or clear varnish
Lamp socket and extension for bottle
Shade

Tear masking tape into small pieces; press onto bottle, starting at bottom. Overlap edges until entire surface is covered. Cover carefully with shoe polish. May leave natural

color, if desired. Insert lamp socket in neck of bottle; attach shade.

Beverly Rieck
Bridgewater High School
Bridgewater, South Dakota

LEATHER-LIKE BOTTLE VASE

Materials:

1 wine bottle
1 roll masking tape
1 can brown paste or shoe polish
1 can clear coating spray
Dried flowers

Cover bottle with small pieces of masking tape, overlapping tape. Repeat process twice, covering bottle completely each time. Apply shoe polish to color shade of leather. Spray with clear spray to seal. Fill with dried flowers.

Mary E. Harrington
Doherty High School
Worcester, Massachusetts

DANCING MOTHBALLS CENTERPIECE

Materials:

2/3 c. water
Food coloring (opt.)
2 tsp. soda
6 mothballs
Glass bowl, goblet, terrarium or fish
  bowl
Vinegar

Combine water, food coloring, soda and mothballs in bowl. Add vinegar until mothballs dance. Add more vinegar when mothballs stop dancing.

Mrs. Marian Baker
Sycamore High School
Sycamore, Illinois

CHEMICAL GARDEN

Materials:

Small pieces of coal or coke
1 6-in. glass dish
4 tbsp. plain salt
4 tbsp. bluing
4 tbsp. water
1 tbsp. ammonia
Food coloring

Place coal in center of dish. Combine salt, bluing, water and ammonia; pour mixture over coal. Drizzle food coloring over coal. Little crystals will begin to form in a short time. Within a few hours the chemical garden will have odd and interesting shapes.

Mrs. Marian Baker
Sycamore High School
Sycamore, Illinois

SANDSCAPES

Materials:

Jars
White sand
Tempera paints
1 sm. funnel
Drinking straws

Fill jar half full with sand; add several drops of water and several drops of liquid tempera paint. Cover jar tightly; shake well. May add more paint for desired color. Remove lid; let sand dry. May use powdered tempera paint instead of liquid paint; sand is dry immediately. Color as many jars of sand as desired. Attach funnel to drinking straw. Pour sand into funnel to place sand in container in design, using as many colors of sand as desired. Sand may be bought at lumberyard.

Sister Margaret Mary Clarke
O'Gorman High School
Sioux Falls, South Dakota

DIPPER WALL DECORATION

Materials:

Spray paint
1 metal dipper
Florist clay or art plaster
Dried or plastic flowers

Paint dipper; let dry. Bend bowl part up; drill hole in handle end of dipper. Place clay in dipper bowl; arrange flowers in clay. Hang on wall. Use antique dipper, if possible.

Audrey V. Craig
Divide High School
Nolan, Texas

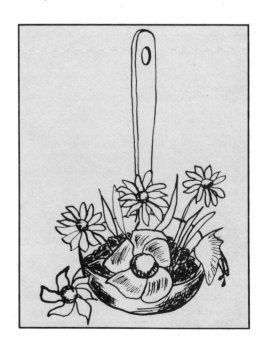

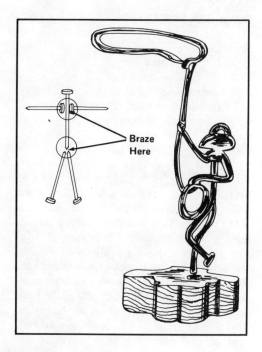

Braze Here

also be determined by size of cowboy. Nails may be bent at various angles to give each cowboy its own individual identity.

Milburn E. Wink
Hamlin High School
Hamlin, Texas

WAXLESS CANDLE

Materials:
   Brandy snifter or other glass
   Food coloring
   Vegetable oil
   1 1/8-in. thick slice cork
   Foil
   Wick or birthday candle

Fill snifter half full of water; color with food coloring. Pour 1/4 inch oil carefully on top of water. Cover cork with foil; insert wick through center of cork and foil. Float on oil. Several floating corks may be used at one time, if desired.

Vicki Rains
North Platte R-I School
Dearborn, Missouri

COWBOY STATUE

Materials:
   5 nails
   Brazing rod
   Pliers
   1 washer
   1 staple
   1 wood screw
   Vise
   Oxyacetylene welder
   Size 0 welding tip
   10 to 24 inches wire
   Wood base
   Spray varnish or plastic

Place nails together according to illustration; braze where circles are indicated. Bend washer in half with staple between; braze bent washer for head of cowboy to top nail. Braze wood screw to 1 leg of cowboy. Place tip of 1 leg in vise; heat nails in order to bend at proper places. Shape wire into form of lasso; braze lasso to arms. Mount onto base with wood screw; finish with spray varnish. Metal base may be used instead of wood; braze metal base to cowboy. Size of nails may vary from 3d to 16d, depending upon size of cowboy made; size of wire may

LAPEL PIN

Materials:
   1 small photograph or picture
   Lens from eyeglasses
   Elmer's glue
   Paper
   Safety pin

Attach small photograph to lens, using thinned glue; press from center to side to work out air bubbles. Cut strip of paper to fit bar of safety pin; glue strip over bar to hold securely to back of lens. Cut piece of paper the shape of lens; place over back. Cut slit for pin to come through. Glue securely to finish back.

Mrs. Willie Lee W. Everett
Menard High School
Menard, Texas

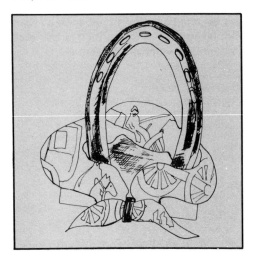

WESTERN CENTERPIECE

Materials:

Styrofoam block for base
New or clean horseshoe
Bandana handkerchief
1/2-inch washer

Cut Styrofoam block about 2 inches wider than span of horseshoe. Push horseshoe into Styrofoam to make it stand up. Cut handkerchief into a triangle; wrap around horseshoe. Pull the 2 ends of bandana handkerchief through the washer.

Mrs. William R. Taylor
East Jr. High School
Great Falls, Montana

TUNA CAN PINCUSHION

Materials:

Thin foam rubber
1 3-inch Styrofoam ball
1 tuna can with lid attached by 3/4-inch trim such as braid, rickrack or lace
Small artificial flowers

Cut 3 circles, 1 with a tail, from foam rubber. Cut 1 strip 3 1/2 x 11 1/2 inches long. Cut an 8-inch square. Cut through center of Styrofoam ball, using razor blade, then sharp knife. Whip one of the circles onto the 3 1/2 x 11-inch strip with matching thread, leaving about 1/8 inch at beginning of strip. Cut off excess, leaving 1/8 inch to whip to the other edge, up to the height of the can. Turn right side out. Fit on can with seam down center back. Clip each side at the back so you can pull edges around to the inside. Clip a little triangle off, down toward bottom of can. Place the other circle on the one with the tail. Whip together from x number 1 to x number 2. Turn right side out, place on lid with tail on inside and complete circle to the dot shown on pattern by whipping both edges of the foam under. Clip a little off the back circle at the bottom and whip to the foam at back edge of can rim, where it will be hidden by braid. Glue or baste braid in place around the top and bottom edges of the can. Top braid joins at center front and is hidden by flower decoration. The lower edge joins at center back. Sew or

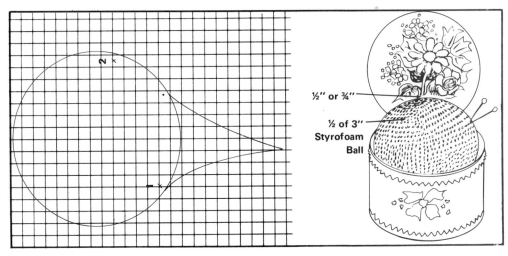

½″ or ¾″

½ of 3″
Styrofoam Ball

glue on flowers. Place 8-inch square on half ball. Pull around the edges, eliminating all gathers. Tie tightly underneath with twine. Place little scraps of leftover foam in bottom of can, then push in covered half ball, leaving at most attractive height. Thin foam rubber may be purchased at hobby shops or dime stores.

Mrs. Mildred Sanders
Clint High School
Clint, Texas

Uses For Baby Food Jars

Baby food jars are excellent for rooting cuttings in water, storing seeds, storing stray buttons, pins or snaps, or used as jelly jars. Filled with crushed mothballs, vinegar, water, florist clay and a wintry scene, jar makes a cute child's knick-knack. Nail lids to boards and nail boards in storage area. Fill jars with screws, nuts and bolts.

Mrs. Brett W. Slusser
Agra High School
Agra, Oklahoma

Carpet Spot Remover

1 qt. water
1/4 c. white vinegar
1 tbsp. shampoo

Combine all ingredients; mix well. Store in container with tightfitting lid. Use on sponge or soft cloth for spot cleaning carpets.

Blanche Young
Northeast High School
North Little Rock, Arkansas

Uses For Soda

Unplug sluggish drains by pouring a handful of soda down drain and adding 1/2 cup vinegar. Place plug in drain for several minutes. Remove plug; run hot water through drain.

Eliminate odors by placing an opened box of baking soda in refrigerator; change every 2 months.

Sprinkle baking soda in pet litter pan after washing and before adding new litter to reduce odor.

Sprinkle inside of running shoes, boots and other footwear with baking soda to eliminate odor.

Mrs. Barbara Goedicke
Lindsay Thurber Comprehensive H.S.
Red Deer, Alberta, Canada

Copper Cleaner

1 tbsp. cornmeal
1 tbsp. salt
1 to 2 tbsp. vinegar

Combine cornmeal, salt and enough vinegar to form a paste; mix well. Dip dry paper towel or rag in paste to scrub copper. Polish with dry paper towel or rag. Rinse in clear water.

Christine M. Applin
Reagan High School
Austin, Texas

Removing Ball Point Pen Ink Stain

Spray clothing stained with ink from ball point pen with hair spray and then wash, using detergent. Stain will disappear.

Mrs. Julius W. Williams
Independence School
Coldwater, Mississippi

Washing Instructions File

Keep a file box on washer with a file card for each special garment. Attach the tag of the garment with washing instructions to card.

Nadine D. Powell
Mont Harmon Jr. High School
Price, Utah

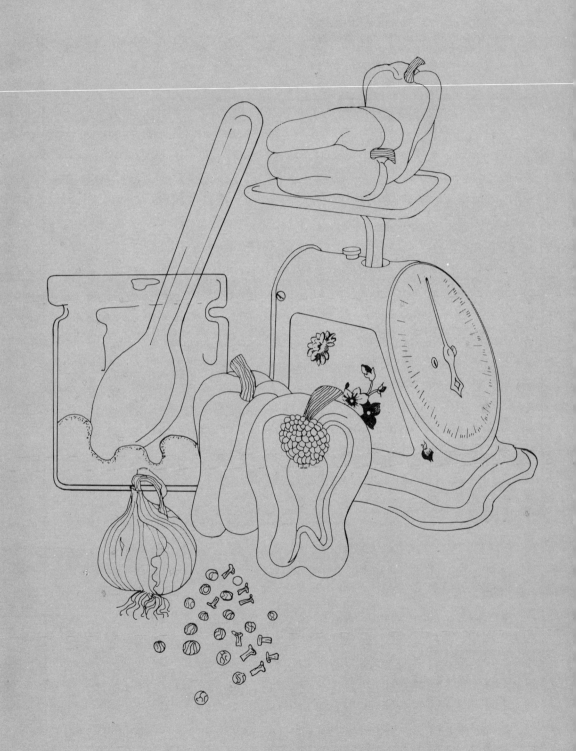

"Life-Saver"

Recipes

— It's 7 A.M. You overslept. Your family's hungry and there's no time to cook . . . you need a "life-saver"!

— Home from work, you're in a rush; the children are off to a ballgame while you and husband visit some friends . . . A warm, filling meal is a must but what can you prepare in a hurry?

Of course, there are frozen pizzas, TV dinners and instant breakfasts by the score that can be heated and served in minutes. While these may be the answer occasionally, they are just no substitute for homemade waffles, steaming biscuits or a delicious casserole. Because Home Economics Teachers know how difficult it is to find really good recipes that can be prepared quickly and easily, they invite you to try a number of excellent ones they've found can help you, round the clock.

A basic recipe, *Master Mix*, is simple to make and can be used as a starter for lots of favorite breakfast treats like pancakes, waffles, sweet breads and muffins. And — for budget-saving lunches that can be tossed together speedily, the *Old-Fashioned Egg Salad* and *Clock Watcher's Salad* recipes are sure to come in handy.

Remember — how long it takes to prepare a meal is not what's important. Instead, it's the quality of the dishes you serve that counts. For example, *Instant Potato Casserole* and *Black Bottom Cupcakes* require little preparation time yet they can be proudly served on special occasions

Today's busy wife, mother and career woman needs all the help in the kitchen she can get. Home Economics Teachers' professional ideas for quick and easy cooking are just the "lifesavers" you've been wanting!

Quick aNd Easy

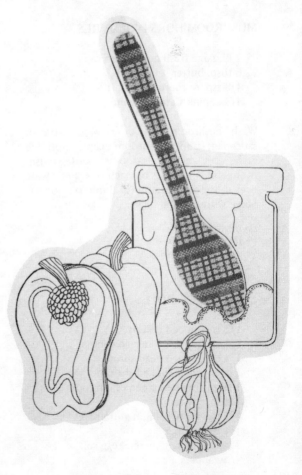

QUICK CHEESE BALLS

2 c. flour
2 c. shredded Cheddar cheese
1 c. margarine, softened
Salt and pepper to taste
2 c. Rice Krispies

Mix all ingredients well; shape into balls. Place on ungreased baking sheet; flatten slightly. Bake in preheated 350-degree oven for 10 to 12 minutes. May be frozen; place in oven for several minutes to crisp.

Mrs. Karen Oliver
University Hills Jr. High School
San Antonio, Texas

MUSHROOM HORS D'OEUVRES

1 lb. large fresh mushroom caps
6 tbsp. butter
1/8 tsp. or more garlic salt
1/3 c. pink Catawba wine

Wash mushroom caps; drain. Melt butter in saucepan; add mushroom caps. Sprinkle garlic salt over mushrooms; saute mushrooms for 4 minutes on each side. Pour wine over mushrooms; saute for 3 minutes longer. Serve with cocktail picks.

Darlene Kness
Hunter College
New York, New York

CHINESE EGG ROLLS

1/2 c. chopped onions
1/4 c. chopped water chestnuts
1/4 c. chopped bean sprouts
1 c. chopped cooked shrimp
1 tbsp. chopped green onion tops
1 tbsp. soy sauce
1/2 tsp. monosodium glutamate
1/4 tsp. pepper
3-in. square commercial egg roll
  wrappers

Mix all ingredients except egg roll wrappers. Place 1 tablespoon shrimp mixture in center

of each wrapper; roll up. Fold edges in; seal by dipping finger in water and moistening wrapper edges. Fry in deep, hot fat for 2 to 3 minutes or until golden brown; drain on paper towels. Yield: About 25 rolls.

Lenora A. Hill
CMR High School
Great Falls, Montana

CUCUMBER DIP

1 cucumber
1 3-oz. package cream cheese, softened
1/2 c. chopped nuts
Mayonnaise

Grate cucumber; drain well. Add cream cheese; mix well. Add nuts and enough mayonnaise to moisten; mix until combined.

Mrs. Jane Beery
London High School
London, Ohio

CHILI PEPPER DIP

1 can cream of chicken soup
1 can green chilies, chopped
1 c. grated Cheddar cheese
2 tsp. instant minced onion

Combine all ingredients in saucepan; stir over low heat until cheese melts. Serve with chips.

Mrs. Jess Adams
North Heights Center
Vocational Education for the Handicapped
Amarillo, Texas

MINI PIZZAS

1 can refrigerator biscuits
1 8-oz. can tomato sauce
1/4 c. finely chopped onion
1 tsp. garlic salt
1/2 tsp. salt
2 tbsp. grated Parmesan cheese
3/4 tsp. crushed oregano leaves
1 c. shredded mozzarella cheese

Flatten biscuits to small circles; place on cookie sheet. Mix tomato sauce, onion, garlic salt, salt, Parmesan cheese and oregano for sauce. Spoon about 1 tablespoon sauce on each biscuit; top with mozzarella cheese. Bake in preheated 400-degree oven for 10 minutes. Meat topping may also be used, if desired.

Sharon Dean
Dibble School
Dibble, Oklahoma

HARVEST POPCORN

1/3 c. melted butter
1 tsp. dried dillweed
1 tsp. lemon pepper marinade
1 tsp. Worcestershire sauce
1/2 tsp. onion powder
1/2 tsp. garlic powder
1/4 tsp. salt
2 qt. popped popcorn
2 c. canned shoestring potatoes
1 c. mixed nuts

Combine first 7 ingredients; mix well. Add remaining ingredients. Toss until well mixed. Spread on cookie sheet. Bake in preheated 350-degree oven for 6 to 10 minutes or until lightly browned, stirring once.

Judith Brown
Rawlins School
Rawlins, Wyoming

FAST FANTASTIC FONDUE

1 pkg. cheese sauce mix
1 c. milk
1 lg. can deviled ham

Combine cheese mix with milk; heat according to package directions. Add deviled ham; heat for several minutes, stirring occasionally. Pour into fondue pot; serve with French bread cubes.

Mary Stager
Montgomery Co. High School
Mount Vernon, Georgia

PEPPERONI BALLS

1 pkg. hot roll mix
1/4 lb. mozzarella cheese, cut in cubes
1/4 to 1/2 lb. pepperoni, thinly sliced

Prepare roll mix according to package directions, omitting egg and using 1 cup water. Dough does not need to rise. Place 1 cheese cube on 1 pepperoni slice. Pinch off piece of dough; shape carefully around cheese and pepperoni, forming a ball. Repeat until all ingredients are used. Fry in deep hot oil for about 5 minutes or until brown, turning once.

Margaret K. Shollenberger
Girard High School
Girard, Pennsylvania

RUSSIAN SPINACH SOUP

6 c. water
6 beef bouillon cubes
1 pkg. frozen chopped spinach
Sour cream
Finely sliced green onions or chopped
  chives

Combine water and bouillon cubes in saucepan; bring to a boil, stirring until bouillon cubes are dissolved. Place frozen spinach in broth; cook just long enough to thaw completely. Ladle soup into bowls. Top each serving with dollop of sour cream; sprinkle with green onions.

Olga Bier
El Cerrito High School
El Cerrito, California

MAINE CRAB MEAT SOUP

1 can tomato soup
1 can pea soup
1/2 can beef consomme
1 c. cream or milk
1/4 to 1/2 c. dry sherry
1/2 lb. crab meat

Mix all ingredients except crab meat in kettle in order listed. Heat, stirring frequently, until blended and heated through. Stir in crab meat; serve hot. Yield: 4 servings.

Mrs. Polly Webster
Mattanawcook Academy
Lincoln, Maine

Quick and Easy

ZUCCHINI SOUP

2 strips bacon
4 c. coarsely grated zucchini
1 sm. onion, chopped
2 c. beef stock
1/2 tsp. sweet basil
1 sm. clove of garlic, crushed
2 tsp. chopped parsley
1/2 tsp. salt
1/8 tsp. pepper
1/2 tsp. seasoned salt

Fry bacon until crisp; drain. Combine all ingredients in kettle; cook until zucchini is soft. Place in blender container; process until smooth. Reheat. May be frozen. Bouillon cubes may be used to prepare beef stock.

Mary Cates
Occupational Center
Milwaukee, Oregon

CHINESE EGG FLOWER SOUP

6 chicken bouillon cubes
1/2 tsp. sugar
1 tsp. salt
1/4 tsp. pepper
3 tbsp. cornstarch
2 eggs, beaten
2 or 3 green onions, thinly sliced

Bring 6 cups water to a boil in saucepan. Add bouillon cubes; heat, stirring, until dissolved. Mix 3 tablespoons water, sugar, salt, pepper and cornstarch in small bowl. Stir into boiling bouillon slowly; cook for 1 minute. Reduce heat. Pour in beaten eggs, stirring until eggs cook into shreds. Remove from heat; add green onions. Serve at once.

Olga Bier
El Cerrito High School
El Cerrito, California

HAMBURGER SOUP

1 tbsp. margarine
1 sm. onion, diced

1/2 green pepper, diced
1/2 lb. hamburger
1 pkg. frozen mixed vegetables
1 can tomato soup
1/2 c. pasta or rice
Salt and pepper to taste
1/2 tsp. sugar
Dash of Worcestershire sauce

Melt margarine in large saucepan. Add onion and green pepper; saute for 5 minutes. Add hamburger; cook, stirring, until lightly browned. Add mixed vegetables, soup and 3 soup cans water. Add any diced, leftover vegetables desired; stir in pasta. Season with salt, pepper, sugar and Worcestershire sauce; simmer until vegetables are tender and soup is thick. Yield: 4-6 servings.

Ruth M. Allard
Lyndon Institute
Lyndon Center, Vermont

FARMER'S CHOP SUEY

1 1-lb. carton cottage cheese
1 1-lb. carton sour cream
Salt
1 c. sliced unpeeled cucumbers
2 c. torn lettuce
3 green onions with tops, chopped
1/2 c. sliced radishes
1/2 c. sliced green pepper
2 hard-cooked eggs, quartered
Cherry tomatoes, halved

Combine cottage cheese, sour cream and 1 teaspoon salt; chill for 1 hour. Salt cucumber slices; chill thoroughly. Place lettuce in large salad bowl; spoon in cottage cheese mixture. Drain cucumbers. Arrange cucumbers, onions, radishes, green pepper, eggs and tomatoes on top. Toss together before serving. Yield: 7 cups.

Photograph for this recipe on page 86.

Recipe on page 90.

ETHELBURKE RABBIT SALAD

3 c. cubed cooked rabbit
1 c. finely chopped celery
2 hard-cooked eggs, finely chopped
1/2 c. sweet pickle salad cubes
2 tbsp. finely chopped green pepper
2 tbsp. finely chopped pimento
Salt to taste
Mayonnaise

Mix rabbit, celery, eggs, salad cubes, green pepper, pimento and salt; stir in enough mayonnaise to moisten. Yield: 6-8 servings.

Pauline Farrow
Greene County Central High School
Snow Hill, North Carolina

CLOCK WATCHER'S SALAD

3 c. shredded carrots
1 15 1/2-oz. can pineapple chunks, drained
2/3 c. salad dressing
1/2 c. raisins
1/2 c. sliced celery
Lettuce leaves

Combine all ingredients except lettuce; mix lightly. Chill. Serve salad in lettuce-lined bowl. Yield: 6 servings.

Dotti Andersen
Washington Park High School
Racine, Wisconsin

PISTACHIO FRUIT SALAD

1 11-oz. can mandarin oranges
1 29-oz. can sliced peaches in light syrup
1 20-oz. can pineapple chunks in natural juice, undrained
1 3 1/2-oz. package instant pistachio pudding mix

Drain oranges and peaches in colander for about 30 minutes or until well drained. Place

Recipe on page 84.

oranges, peaches and pineapple in large bowl; mix with wooden spoon. Sprinkle pudding mix over fruits; stir gently until pudding mix is moistened. Chill until ready to serve.

Karen Mae Jones
Chisholm Middle School
Newton, Kansas

MEAL-IN-ONE MEXICAN SALAD

1 lb. ground beef
1/4 c. chopped onion
2 c. cooked kidney beans
1/2 c. Catalina French dressing
1/2 c. water
1 tbsp. chili powder
4 c. shredded lettuce
1/2 c. sliced green onions
1 1/2 c. shredded Cheddar cheese

Cook ground beef until brown. Add chopped onion; cook until tender. Stir in beans, French dressing, water and chili powder; simmer for 15 minutes. Combine lettuce and green onions. Add beef sauce and cheese; toss lightly. Sprinkle lightly with additional cheese.

Mrs. LeRoy Bieber
Del Norte High School
Crescent City, California

FLUFFY GELATIN SALAD

1 10-oz. carton cottage cheese
1 recipe prepared Dream Whip
1 3-oz. package orange gelatin
1 11-oz. can mandarin oranges, drained

Mix all ingredients; serve immediately or chill overnight. Salad may be varied by using lemon or lime-flavored gelatin and pineapple or by using strawberry gelatin and frozen strawberries. One 6-ounce carton frozen whipped topping may be used instead of Dream Whip.

Edith A. Bullock
Theodore Roosevelt High School
San Antonio, Texas

TACO SALAD

1 lb. thinly sliced cooked roast beef
2 c. shredded lettuce
1 c. grated Cheddar cheese
1/2 c. sliced pickled mild cherry peppers
1 med. tomato, cut into wedges
1 med. avocado, sliced
1/4 c. sliced red onion
2 c. tortilla chips
1 c. tomato juice
2 tbsp. chili sauce
1 tbsp. salad oil
1 tbsp. vinegar
1 tbsp. chopped onion
1 clove of garlic, halved
1/4 tsp. oregano
1/3 c. chopped pickled mild cherry
    peppers

Roll roast beef into cornucopias; arrange on large plate. Mix lettuce, cheese, sliced pickled peppers, tomato wedges, avocado and onion in medium bowl. Spoon lettuce mixture into center of plate. Garnish with tortilla chips. Combine remaining ingredients except chopped pickled peppers in blender container; blend until smooth. Stir in chopped peppers. Serve dressing separately with salad.

Photograph for this recipe above.

OLD-FASHIONED EGG SALAD

1 head lettuce
6 hard-cooked eggs, sliced
1 med. onion, thinly sliced
1 1/2 tsp. salt
1/4 tsp. pepper
1/4 c. salad oil
Dash of paprika
2 tbsp. vinegar
1 tsp. Worcestershire sauce
1 tbsp. minced parsley
1/4 c. grated sharp cheese

Break lettuce into bite-sized pieces into salad bowl. Place alternate layers of eggs and onion over lettuce. Mix remaining ingredients except parsley and cheese. Add to lettuce mixture; toss lightly. Sprinkle with parsley and grated cheese; serve immediately. Salad ingredients may be prepared ahead of time; do not add dressing until time to serve. May add fresh spinach or other greens to salad for variety in flavor and color. Fresh green onions may be used instead of onion. Yield: 6 servings.

Mrs. Mary Ada Parks
Anna-Jonesboro High School
Anna, Illinois

HOT CHICKEN SALAD

2 c. diced cooked chicken
1 tbsp. lemon juice
1/2 tsp. salt
1/4 tsp. pepper
1 c. finely chopped celery
1/2 c. mayonnaise
1/4 c. bread crumbs
1/2 c. grated Cheddar or Swiss cheese

Combine chicken, lemon juice, salt, pepper and celery. Add mayonnaise; mix well. Place in buttered 1-quart casserole. Mix remaining ingredients; sprinkle over chicken mixture. Bake in preheated 350-degree oven for 30 minutes. Celery will be tender-crisp. Yield: 4-6 servings.

Mrs. William Fredd
South Brandywine Jr. High School
Coatesville, Pennsylvania

EASY POTATO SALAD

6 med. potatoes
1/4 c. oil
3/4 c. sour cream
1/2 c. salad dressing
2 hard-boiled eggs, chopped

Peel potatoes; cut into uniform cubes. Cook in boiling, salted water until just done. Drain off water; place potatoes in refrigerator until cool. Remove from refrigerator; stir in oil gently. Combine sour cream and salad dressing; add to potatoes. Add eggs; mix gently. Other ingredients may be added, if desired.

Catherine C. DiNapoli
Madison-Mayodan High School
Madison, North Carolina

RIGOLETTI SALAD

3/4 c. sugar
1/4 c. water
2 c. salad dressing
1/4 c. instant minced onion
1/2 carrot, grated
Cooked green peas to taste
Dillweed to taste
Parsley to taste
1 can Spam, cut into cubes
1 15-oz. package rigoletti noodles, cooked

Mix sugar and water in small saucepan; boil for 1 minute. Mix salad dressing, onion, carrot, peas, dillweed and parsley in bowl. Pour sugar mixture over carrot mixture; stir until well mixed. Add Spam and rigoletti; mix well. Chill.

Kay Luckow
Valders High School
Valders, Wisconsin

CREAMY FRUIT-MINT DRESSING

1 1/2 c. cottage cheese
1/4 c. pineapple juice
2 tbsp. lemon juice
3/4 to 1 env. French salad dressing mix
2 tsp. finely chopped mint

Place cottage cheese in small mixing bowl; beat with electric mixer at high speed until almost smooth. Beat in pineapple and lemon juices, salad dressing mix and mint slowly. Cover; chill. Use as dressing for fruit salads. Yield: 2 cups.

Kathleen Burchett
Assistant State Supervisor
Home Economics Education
Bristol, Virginia

CELERY SEED DRESSING

1/4 c. grated onion
1 c. sugar
2 tsp. salt
2 tsp. dry mustard
1/2 tsp. paprika
1 1/2 c. salad oil
1/2 c. vinegar
1 tsp. celery seed

Combine first 5 ingredients; mix well. Add oil and vinegar gradually, beating constantly. Add celery seed; beat well. Always add celery seed last. Yield: 1 quart.

Marie Comelius
Medford Mid High School
Medford, Oregon

OVERNIGHT FRENCH DRESSING

1 c. salad oil
1 c. catsup
1/2 c. vinegar
1/2 c. sugar
1 tbsp. grated onion
1 tsp. Worcestershire sauce
Pepper to taste
1 clove of garlic, cut in half

Place all ingredients in jar; cover. Shake well; refrigerate overnight for best flavor. Remove garlic clove before serving. Dressing may be served as soon as mixed by using garlic salt and onion salt instead of fresh garlic and onion.

Marguerite S. Darnall
Corona Sr. High School
Corona, California

BUDGET STROGANOFF

1 lb. steak
Salt and pepper to taste
1/2 c. flour
1 sm. onion, diced
1 tbsp. tomato paste
2 tbsp. soy sauce
1 6-oz. jar chopped mushrooms
1 pt. sour cream

Remove fat from steak; cut steak into 1 x 2-inch strips. Season with salt and pepper; dredge with flour. Saute onion in 2 tablespoons fat in pressure cooker until tender; remove from cooker. Cook steak strips in same fat until brown; add onion, tomato paste, soy sauce and mushrooms. Cover; cook for 15 minutes. Place cooker in cold water to lower pressure. Add sour cream to steak mixture; heat for 5 minutes. Do not boil. Serve over hot rice or mashed potatoes.

Mrs. D. H. Boyd
Moultrie Jr. High School
Moultrie, Georgia

QUICK BEEF STROGANOFF

2 tbsp. butter
2 tbsp. flour
2 c. water
3 bouillon cubes
2 tbsp. tomato paste
1 clove of garlic, finely chopped
4 c. diced cooked roast beef
1 c. drained mushrooms
Salt and pepper to taste
1/4 c. sour cream

Melt butter in saucepan. Stir in flour; cook over low heat, stirring, for 3 minutes. Do not brown. Stir in water; add bouillon cubes. Cook, stirring constantly, until thickened. Add tomato paste, garlic, beef, mushrooms, salt and pepper; mix well. Stir in sour cream; heat through. Do not boil. Serve over hot, buttered noodles or cooked rice.

Mrs. Paul Drazer
Kouts High School
Kouts, Indiana

MEAT ROLL-UPS

1 recipe Bisquick biscuit dough
2 c. ground roast beef or pork
2 eggs, beaten
Seasonings to taste
1 can cream of mushroom soup, heated

Pat out biscuit dough on floured surface into 1/2-inch thick rectangle. Mix beef with eggs and seasonings; spread over dough. Roll as for jelly roll; cut into 1/2-inch thick slices. Place slices, cut side down, in greased 9-inch square pan. Bake in preheated 350-degree oven for 30 minutes or until lightly browned. Spoon soup over each serving.

Susan Smith
Fall Mountain Regional High School
Alstead, New Hampshire

FRANKFURTERS A LA CREOLE

3 tbsp. butter
1 med. onion, minced
1 sm. clove of garlic, minced
1/2 tsp. salt
Dash of pepper
3 1/2 c. drained canned tomatoes
6 to 10 frankfurters
5 c. cooked rice

Melt butter in frying pan. Add onion and garlic; saute until tender. Add salt, pepper and tomatoes; mix well. Dice 2 frankfurters; add to tomato mixture. Cook over low heat for 15 to 20 minutes. Add remaining frankfurters; cook until frankfurters are plump and sauce is thick. Pile rice lightly on hot platter; arrange whole frankfurters on rice. Pour sauce over all; serve. One 12-ounce can tomato sauce may be substituted for tomatoes.

Mrs. Elsie Clements
Corbett High School
Corbett, Oregon

REUBEN SANDWICHES

2 1/4 c. drained sauerkraut
1/4 c. chopped sweet onion

3 tbsp. chopped parsley
Creamy Russian Dressing
16 slices rye bread
3/4 lb. sliced corned beef
3/4 lb. sliced Swiss cheese
Butter or margarine, softened

Combine sauerkraut, onion and parsley; toss until well mixed. Spread dressing on each slice of bread. Top 8 slices of bread with corned beef, cheese and sauerkraut mixture; top with remaining bread slices. Spread both sides of sandwiches lightly with butter. Grill slowly until cheese melts and bread browns.

Creamy Russian Dressing

1/2 c. mayonnaise
1/4 c. chili sauce

Combine mayonnaise and chili sauce; mix well.

Photograph for this recipe on page 85.

CAMPER'S KABOBS

3/4 c. butter or margarine
1 1/2 tsp. chili powder
3/4 tsp. salt
1/8 tsp. pepper
1/2 c. liquid drained from sweet
  gherkins
2 garlic cloves, crushed
2 12-oz. cans luncheon meat
6 ears of corn, quartered
12 lg. sweet gherkins, halved crosswise

Melt butter in small saucepan; stir in chili powder, salt, pepper, pickle liquid and garlic. Cut each piece of luncheon meat into 12 chunks. Alternate meat chunks, corn chunks and pickle halves on twelve 8-inch skewers. Place skewers on grill; brush with chili mixture. Grill about 5 inches from source of heat for 8 to 10 minutes or until corn is fork tender, turning once and basting occasionally with chili mixture. Yield: 6 servings.

Photograph for this recipe above.

EGG NOODLE DINNER SPECIAL

1   5-oz. jar dried beef, cut into
     pieces
1/4 c. butter or margarine
1 c. chopped onion
1 lg. garlic clove, crushed
1   10-oz. package frozen Italian green
     beans, thawed
1 1/2 c. milk
1   10 3/4-oz. can cream of mushroom
     soup
1   17-oz. can cream-style corn
2 tbsp. prepared mustard
Salt
1 lb. fine egg noodles

Pour enough boiling water over beef to
cover; let stand for 5 minutes. Drain. Melt
butter in large saucepan; add onion, garlic
and green beans. Saute, stirring constantly,
for about 5 minutes or until green beans are
crisp-tender. Stir in drained beef, milk, soup,
corn, mustard and 2 teaspoons salt. Heat
until just hot, stirring constantly. Do not
boil. Simmer over low heat while cooking
noodles. Add noodles and 2 tablespoons salt
gradually to 4 to 6 quarts rapidly boiling
water so that water continues to boil. Cook
uncovered, stirring occasionally, until
tender. Drain in colander. Combine hot noo-

dles with vegetable sauce in large saucepot.
Toss until well mixed. Yield: 8 servings.

Photograph for this recipe opposite.

BEEF CRESCENT LOAF

1 1/2 lb. ground beef
1 can Cheddar cheese soup
3/4 c. chopped green pepper
1/2 c. chopped onion
3/4 tsp. salt
1/4 tsp. pepper
1 tbsp. Worcestershire sauce
1   8-oz. can crescent dinner rolls
1/2 c. shredded Cheddar cheese

Saute ground beef in skillet until brown;
drain off excess fat. Add soup, green pepper,
onion, salt, pepper and Worcestershire sauce;
stir until well mixed. Separate crescent rolls
into 2 large rectangles on ungreased cookie
sheet. Overlap edges to form 1 large rectangle, pressing firmly to seal. Spoon about
2 1/2 cups meat mixture in 4-inch wide strip
down center of rectangle to within 1 inch of
ends. Fold long sides of dough over meat
mixture to center. Bake in preheated 375-
degree oven for 15 to 20 minutes or until
crust is lightly browned. Spoon remaining
meat mixture down center of crust. Sprinkle
with cheese. Bake for 5 to 10 minutes longer
or until crust is golden brown. Slice to serve.
Yield: 6-8 servings.

Dotti Andersen
Washington Park High School
Racine, Wisconsin

QUICKIE SKILLET SPAGHETTI

2 tbsp. shortening
1 lb. ground beef
1 sm. onion, chopped
1 c. spaghetti, broken in 1-in. pieces
1 clove of garlic, chopped (opt.)
1 c. catsup
1/4 tsp. pepper
1 tsp. salt
1/4 tsp. thyme
2 1/2 c. tomato juice

Melt shortening in large skillet over high heat. Add ground beef and onion. Cook, stirring, until ground beef is lightly browned. Add remaining ingredients; mix well. Cover. Bring to a rapid boil. Reduce heat. Simmer for 45 minutes without removing cover. Yield: 6 servings.

Mrs. Nadia Hamilton
Harbor Creek Jr.-Sr. High School
Harbor Creek, Pennsylvania

SPANISH RICE

2 tbsp. shortening
1/2 c. rice
1 med. onion, chopped
1/2 green pepper, chopped
1/2 lb. ground beef
3/4 tsp. salt
1 No. 2 can tomatoes

Melt shortening in skillet. Add rice, onion, green pepper and ground beef. Cook over medium heat, stirring occasionally, until rice and ground beef are lightly browned. Add 1 cup water, salt and tomatoes. Cover. Simmer for about 30 minutes or until rice is tender. Yield: 4-6 servings.

Sarah Barrett
Tuckerman High School
Tuckerman, Arkansas

HOT TAMALE PIE

1 pkg. corn chips
2 No. 303 cans chili or chili con carne
1 No. 2 can tamales
12 to 15 slices Velveeta cheese

Arrange corn chips over bottom of lightly buttered 9 x 13-inch casserole. Spread chili over chips. Slice tamales over chili. Top with cheese slices. Bake in preheated 350-degree oven for 20 to 30 minutes or until heated through and cheese is melted. Yield: 6 servings.

Marilyn Hay
Ottawa High School
Ottawa, Kansas

MEXICAN LUNCHEON

1 lb. sausage
1 c. diced onions
Diced jalapeno peppers to taste
1 c. diced green pepper
1 8-oz. package elbow macaroni
1 1-lb. can tomatoes
1 c. sour cream
1 c. milk
2 tbsp. sugar
1 tbsp. chili powder
1 tsp. salt

Saute sausage in skillet until brown; drain off excess fat. Add onions, jalapeno peppers and green pepper. Saute until onion is transparent. Add macaroni, tomatoes, sour cream, milk, sugar, chili powder and salt. Cover. Simmer for 20 to 25 minutes or until macaroni is tender. Yield: About 8 servings.

Donna Samuelson
Monahans High School
Monahans, Texas

TEXAS BURRITOS

1 lb. ground beef
1/2 c. chopped onion
1/2 tsp. cumin
1/4 tsp. garlic powder
1/4 tsp. chili powder
Salt and pepper to taste
1 tbsp. flour
1 can tomatoes
1 can chopped green chilies
l pkg. flour tortillas
1 can refried beans

Combine ground beef, onion, seasonings, flour, tomatoes and chilies. Cook until beef is almost done. Heat tortillas in dry skillet on both sides. Spread with heated refried beans; spread ground beef mixture over beans. Roll up; place, seam side down, in shallow baking dish. Cover with foil. Keep warm in oven.

Mrs. Juanita Pitts
Linden-Kildare High School
Linden, Texas

WINE-SAUCED HAMBURGER STEAK

1 1/2 lb. ground beef
1 tsp. salt
1/4 tsp. pepper
2 tbsp. butter
1/4 c. dry red wine
Lemon juice to taste
1/2 tsp. Worcestershire sauce
1 1/2 tbsp. dried parsley flakes
1 tsp. instant minced onions

Combine ground beef, salt and pepper; mix well. Shape into 4 patties about 1/2 inch thick. Melt butter in skillet over medium-high heat. Cook patties for 2 minutes on each side for medium rare or to desired doneness. Remove to warm plates. Add wine, lemon juice, Worcestershire sauce, parsley flakes and onions to skillet; heat to boiling point. Pour over patties.

Sandy Galvan
Riley Middle School
San Antonio, Texas

BEEF AND GREEN BEAN CASSEROLE

1 lb. ground beef
1 can French-style green beans
1 sm. can sliced mushrooms
1 sm. package slivered almonds
1 can cream of celery soup
1 can cream of mushroom soup
1 soup can water
1 sm. package Tater Tots

Saute ground beef in skillet until lightly browned; drain off excess fat. Toss ground beef with green beans, mushrooms and almonds. Combine soups and water in saucepan. Cook over low heat, stirring, until smooth. Pour soup mixture over green bean mixture; toss lightly. Spoon into casserole. Arrange Tater Tots over top. Bake in preheated 350-degree oven for 25 minutes or until bubbly and Tater Tots are lightly browned. Serve with garlic bread, if desired.

Mrs. Brett W. Slusser
Agra High School
Agra, Oklahoma

FIESTA MACARONI

1 lb. ground beef
1 pkg. taco seasoning mix
1 No. 303 can tomato sauce with herbs
1 can whole kernel corn, drained
1/4 c. chopped onion
1/4 c. chopped green pepper
2 c. elbow macaroni

Saute ground beef in deep skillet until brown. Add seasoning mix, tomato sauce, corn, onion and green pepper; mix well. Cook until onion is tender. Add macaroni and 2 1/2 to 3 cups water. Cover. Simmer, stirring occasionally, until macaroni is tender.

Mrs. Brett W. Slusser
Agra High School
Agra, Oklahoma

EASY LASAGNA

1 to 2 lb. ground beef
1 med. onion, chopped (opt.)
1 sm. can tomato paste
1 lg. can tomato sauce
1 sauce can water
1 pkg. spaghetti mix
1 1-lb. carton cottage cheese
2 8-oz. packages cream cheese
1 pkg. lasagna noodles

Saute ground beef and onion in skillet until ground beef is brown. Add tomato paste, tomato sauce, water and spaghetti mix; mix well. Combine cottage cheese and cream cheese. Prepare noodles according to package directions; drain. Layer 1/3 of the noodles in bottom of large baking dish. Add 1/3 of the ground beef mixture. Top with 1/3 of the cheese mixture. Repeat layers twice, ending with noodles and cheese mixture. Bake in preheated 350-degree oven for about 20 minutes or until bubbly. May be frozen and baked later.

Janice Schaffer
Hudson Sr. High School
New Port Richie, Florida

PLANET PIZZA

1 can crescent dinner rolls
1 8-oz. can tomato sauce
1/2 lb. sliced bacon, fried
Sliced mushrooms or olives to taste
Ground oregano to taste
1 c. grated mozzarella cheese

Place roll dough on cookie sheet; flatten to form rectangle. Spread tomato sauce over dough evenly; crumble bacon over tomato sauce. Sprinkle mushrooms over bacon; sprinkle oregano and cheese over mushrooms. Bake in preheated 375-degree oven for 15 minutes or until cheese is melted and bubbly.

Bonita Wiersig
Anson Jones School
Bryan, Texas

PICCOLO PIZZA

1/2 lb. bulk Italian sausage
1 tbsp. oregano
1 clove of garlic, pressed
1 10-count pkg. refrigerator biscuits
1 sm. can tomato paste
1 c. grated sharp cheese
1/4 c. grated Parmesan cheese

Cook sausage until brown; drain. Add oregano and garlic to sausage; mix well. Flatten each biscuit on greased baking sheet to 4-inch circle, leaving a rim. Fill with tomato paste; add sausage. Sprinkle with sharp cheese, then with Parmesan cheese. Bake in preheated 425-degree oven for 10 minutes.

Mary Stager
Montgomery Co. High School
Mount Vernon, Georgia

INDIVIDUAL TACOS

1 lb. ground beef
1 pkg. taco seasoning mix
1 pkg. Fritos

Shredded cheese
Chopped lettuce
Chopped onions
Chopped tomatoes
Taco sauce (opt.)

Saute ground beef in skillet until lightly browned. Drain in colander. Return to skillet. Add taco seasoning mix; cook according to package directions. Arrange layers of Fritos on individual serving plates. Spoon equal amounts of ground beef mixture over Fritos. Layer desired amounts of cheese, lettuce, onions and tomatoes over ground beef mixture. Drizzle each taco with taco sauce. Yield: Approximately 6 servings.

Mrs. Ann Hughes
Pea Ridge High School
Pea Ridge, Arkansas

TURKEY TETRAZZINI

1 1/2 c. noodles
Broth
1 1/2 c. finely chopped celery
1 tbsp. finely chopped parsley
1 tbsp. finely chopped green pepper
1/2 c. finely chopped onion
1 clove of garlic, finely chopped (opt.)
1/2 c. mushroom soup
1 c. tomato sauce
Salt and pepper to taste
1 1/2 c. diced cooked turkey or chicken
3/4 c. grated sharp cheese
2 tbsp. buttered crumbs

Cook noodles according to package directions, using broth instead of water. Cook celery, parsley, green pepper, onion and garlic in broth until tender; drain. Add noodles, soup, tomato sauce, salt, pepper and turkey; mix well. Place in casserole. Add cheese; top with crumbs. Bake in preheated 300-degree oven until lightly browned. Yield: 6-8 servings.

Mrs. Edith May Bryan
Harrisonburg School
Harrisonburg, Virginia

Quick and Easy

TURKEY-NOODLE PARTY CASSEROLE

2 c. noodles
1 10-oz. package frozen broccoli
   spears
3 tbsp. margarine
3 tbsp. flour
1 tsp. salt
1/4 tsp. prepared mustard
1/4 tsp. pepper
2 c. milk
1 c. grated American cheese
2 c. cubed cooked turkey
1/3 c. toasted slivered almonds

Cook noodles in boiling, salted water until tender; drain. Cook broccoli in boiling, salted water until tender; drain. Remove stems from broccoli tops; reserve tops. Dice stems. Melt margarine in saucepan; stir in flour, salt, mustard and pepper. Add milk; cook, stirring, until thick and smooth. Remove from heat. Add cheese; stir until cheese melts. Arrange noodles, broccoli stems and turkey in greased casserole; cover with cheese sauce. Arrange reserved broccoli tops over cheese sauce; sprinkle with almonds. Bake in preheated 350-degree oven for 15 minutes or until bubbling hot. Yield: 4-6 servings.

Dana Ray Owens
Schleicher County Independent School
Eldorado, Texas

TURKEY PIE WITH VEGETABLE SAUCE

1 6-oz. package chicken-flavored
   stuffing mix
1 3/4 c. diced cooked turkey or chicken
4 eggs, slightly beaten
1 8-oz. package frozen mixed
   vegetables with onion sauce
Milk

Prepare stuffing mix according to package directions, reducing water to 1 1/2 cups. Add turkey and eggs; mix well. Spread in greased 9-inch pie pan. Bake in preheated 375-degree oven for 30 minutes. Prepare mixed vegetables according to package direc-

tions, using milk instead of water. Serve wedges of pie topped with vegetable sauce. Yield: 6 servings.

Mrs. Virginia T. Bond
Scott High School
Madison, West Virginia

TANGY CREAMED TURKEY

2 tbsp. butter
1/4 lb. mushrooms, diced
1/4 c. diced green pepper
1/2 c. diced onion
1 c. mayonnaise
1 c. yogurt
1/2 tsp. salt
1/8 tsp. pepper
1 1/2 c. diced cooked turkey
1 c. cooked tiny green peas
1 sm. jar pimentos, drained and chopped

Melt butter in saucepan. Add mushrooms, green pepper and onion; saute until tender. Add mayonnaise, yogurt, salt and pepper; bring to a simmer. Add turkey, peas and pimentos; heat through. Serve over rice. Yield: 6 servings.

Virginia B. Collie
Tunstall High School
Dry Fork, Virginia

DEEP-DISH TURKEY PIE

6 med. potatoes, pared and quartered
6 med. carrots, pared and quartered
1 sm. onion, chopped
1/4 c. chopped green pepper
6 tbsp. butter or margarine
1 can cream of chicken soup
3 c. diced cooked turkey
1 1/2 c. sifted all-purpose flour
2 tsp. baking powder
1/2 tsp. salt
Milk

Cook potatoes and carrots in boiling, salted water in large saucepan for 15 to 20 minutes or until tender. Drain; reserve 1 cup liquid. Saute onion and green pepper in 2 tablespoons butter in medium saucepan until soft; stir in soup and reserved liquid. Spoon vegetables and turkey into 8-cup casserole; pour onion sauce over top. Bake in preheated 425-degree oven for 15 minutes. Sift flour, baking powder and salt into bowl; cut in remaining 1/4 cup butter. Add 1/2 cup milk all at once; stir until blended. Knead lightly on floured surface; roll out to 1/2-inch thickness. Cut with 2-inch biscuit cutter; brush tops of biscuits with milk. Arrange biscuits on turkey mixture; bake for 15 minutes longer or until biscuits are golden brown.

Mrs. Ruth Riale
Central Columbia High School
Bloomsburg, Pennsylvania

QUICK COMPANY CHICKEN

1/4 c. melted margarine
1 c. cracker crumbs
2 c. diced cooked chicken
1 c. sour cream
1 can cream of chicken soup
1/4 c. broth or milk
Salt and pepper to taste

Combine margarine and cracker crumbs; blend well. Spoon half the crumbs into shallow 2-quart casserole; cover with chicken. Combine sour cream, soup, broth, salt and pepper; blend well. Pour over chicken; top with remaining crumbs. Bake in preheated 350-degree oven for 20 to 25 minutes. Yield: 6 servings.

Mrs. Phil Addy
Plains High School
Plains, Georgia

CHICKEN VEGETABLE CASSEROLE

1 10-oz. package frozen green peas
1 No. 2 can potatoes, drained
Butter
Salt and pepper to taste
1 6-oz. can boned chicken
1/3 c. milk
1 can cream of chicken soup
Crushed potato chips

Cook peas according to package directions; drain. Arrange potatoes in casserole. Dot with butter; sprinkle with salt and pepper. Add peas. Break chicken into chunks; place over peas. Blend milk with soup; pour over chicken. Cover with potato chips. Bake in preheated 350-degree oven until bubbly. Yield: 6 servings.

Evelyn B. Willey
Gates County High School
Gatesville, North Carolina

FISH IN WINE SAUCE

1/2 c. margarine
2 tbsp. minced parsley
2 cloves of garlic, chopped
Flounder fillets
Italian bread crumbs
1/2 c. dry white wine

Melt margarine in heavy skillet over medium heat; add parsley and garlic. Place flounder in margarine; sprinkle generously with bread crumbs. Add wine. Reduce heat; cover skillet immediately. Cook for 4 to 10 minutes, depending on thickness of flounder. Fluke, weakfish, bluefish, striped bass, scallops, shrimp or eel may be used instead of flounder.

Jacqueline Pell Tuttle
Southampton Intermediate School
Southampton, New York

EASY TUNA CASSEROLE

1 6-oz. can tuna
1 can cream of mushroom, chicken or
celery soup
1 1-oz. bag potato chips, crushed

Place tuna in layer in casserole or loaf pan; add undiluted soup. Cover with potato chips. Bake in preheated 350-degree oven for about 20 minutes or until bubbly. Recipe may be served to large groups by increasing as many times as desired. Yield: 4 servings.

Sue Farris
Altus-Denning High School
Altus, Arkansas

BAKED TUNA CHOW MEIN CASSEROLE

1 c. chopped celery
1/4 c. finely chopped onion
2 tbsp. chopped green pepper
1 tbsp. butter
1 can cream of mushroom soup
1/4 c. milk
1/4 c. water
1 3-oz. can chow mein noodles
1 4-oz. package salted cashew nuts
1 7-oz. can tuna
1/8 tsp. pepper

Saute celery, onion and green pepper in butter until tender-crisp. Mix soup with milk and water. Reserve 1/3 cup noodles; mix remaining noodles with soup mixture, celery mixture and nuts. Stir in tuna and pepper. Place in buttered 1 1/2-quart baking dish; sprinkle with reserved noodles. Bake in preheated 350-degree oven for 30 minutes. Yield: 4-6 servings.

Mrs. Mary Ada Parks
Anna-Jonesboro High School
Anna, Illinois

QUICK TUNA CASSEROLE

1 14-oz. package macaroni and cheese
   dinner
1 sm. onion, minced
1 can cream of mushroom soup
1/2 c. milk
1 6 1/2-oz. can tuna
Butter
Crushed potato chips
2 slices American cheese, cut into
   1/2-in. strips

Prepare macaroni and cheese dinner according to package directions, adding onion while preparing. Add soup, milk and tuna; stir thoroughly. Coat casserole with butter and potato chips; add tuna mixture. Top with potato chips and cheese strips. Bake in preheated 350-degree oven for 20 minutes. Yield: 6-8 servings.

Lorene L. Arent
Wausa Public Schools
Wausa, Nebraska

ROLLED FISH FILLETS IN OLIVE-SHERRY SAUCE

1 16-oz. package frozen fillet of
   sole, thawed
1 10-oz. package frozen asparagus
   spears, cooked and drained
4 tbsp. olive or salad oil
1/2 c. chopped onion
1 lg. clove of garlic, minced
1 10-oz. package frozen peas, thawed
2 tbsp. flour
1/2 c. dry sherry
1 8-oz. can minced clams
1/2 c. sliced pimento-stuffed olives
2 tbsp. chopped parsley
Dash of pepper
3 c. hot cooked rice

Separate and drain fillets. Wrap each fillet around some asparagus spears; secure with wooden toothpicks. Heat 3 tablespoons oil in large skillet. Add fish; fry for 3 to 5 minutes or until fish is partially cooked, turning rolls carefully. Remove from skillet; drain on paper towels. Heat remaining 1 tablespoon oil in skillet. Add onion, garlic and peas; saute, stirring constantly, for about 5 minutes or until onion and peas are tender. Stir flour into sherry until smooth; stir into onion mixture. Add undrained clams, sliced olives and chopped parsley to mixture in skillet. Cook, stirring constantly, until mixture thickens and begins to boil; boil for 1 minute. Reduce heat to low; add fish rolls and pepper. Cover; cook for about 5 minutes or until fish flakes easily when tested with fork. Remove toothpicks; serve with rice. Garnish with whole pimento-stuffed olives and parsley, if desired. Two fresh sole fillets, cut in half lengthwise, may be used instead of frozen sole. Yield: 4 servings.

Photograph for this recipe on opposite page.

HADDOCK-SHRIMP BAKE

1 can shrimp, drained
2 lb. frozen haddock, thawed
1 can shrimp soup
1/4 c. melted margarine
1 tsp. grated onion
1/2 tsp. Worcestershire sauce
1/4 tsp. garlic salt
1 1/4 c. crushed Ritz crackers

Place shrimp and haddock in greased 13 x 9 x 2-inch baking dish; spread soup over top. Bake in preheated 375-degree oven for 20 minutes. Combine remaining ingredients; sprinkle over fish mixture. Bake for 10 minutes longer. Yield: 6 servings.

Mrs. Connie Phillips
4 District Industrial Training Center
Fenton, Michigan

QUICK AND EASY CURRY

1/4 c. butter or margarine
1/4 c. flour
1 tsp. salt
2 c. milk
Curry powder to taste
1 c. shrimp
1/2 c. mushrooms or green peas
3 to 4 c. cooked rice

Melt butter in saucepan. Add flour and salt; blend well. Add milk; cook, stirring, until thickened. Stir in curry powder; cook over low heat for 10 minutes. Add shrimp and mushrooms; heat through. Serve over rice. Noodles, potatoes or toast may be used instead of rice. Other meats or vegetables may be used in recipe.

June Miller
Lincoln Jr. High School
Newport, Oregon

BUFFET ASPARAGUS CASSEROLE

1 can asparagus, drained
1 can green peas, drained
1 can cream of mushroom soup
1/2 c. grated Velveeta cheese
1 c. buttered bread crumbs

Arrange asparagus evenly in large casserole. Top with peas. Spoon mushroom soup over peas. Sprinkle with cheese. Top with bread crumbs. Bake in preheated 350-degree oven for about 30 minutes or until bubbly.

Barbara Beadles
Channing High School
Channing, Texas

CURRIED MUSHROOMS

1/2 c. chopped onion
1/2 c. chopped celery
1   4-oz. can sliced mushrooms
Butter
1 can cream of celery soup
1 can cream of potato soup
1 tsp. curry powder
Toasted English muffins
6 hard-boiled eggs, sliced

Saute onion, celery and mushrooms in a small amount of butter in saucepan until onion and celery are tender. Add soups and curry powder. Cook over low heat, stirring occasionally, until heated through. Spoon over muffins. Top with egg slices.

Cheryl Fisher
Thomas Stone High School
Waldorf, Maryland

BROCCOLI GENOVESE

2   10-oz. packages frozen chopped
       broccoli
1 tbsp. vinegar
1 tsp. Dijon mustard
6 eggs, separated
2 tbsp. flour
1/4 tsp. salt
1/2 tsp. coarsely ground pepper
2 c. grated Monterey Jack cheese
1/2 c. grated Parmesan cheese

Prepare broccoli according to package directions, omitting salt. Drain. Combine vinegar and mustard; stir into broccoli. Set aside. Beat egg whites until soft peaks form. Beat egg yolks with flour and salt until thick and lemon colored. Fold egg yolk mixture into egg whites. Spoon 1/3 of the egg mixture into greased 2-quart souffle dish. Arrange 1/2 of the broccoli mixture over egg mixture. Sprinkle with 1/4 teaspoon pepper, 1 cup Jack cheese and 1/3 of the Parmesan cheese. Add 1/2 of the remaining egg mixture. Arrange remaining broccoli over egg mixture. Sprinkle with remaining 1/4 teaspoon pepper and 1 cup Jack cheese. Sprinkle 1/2 of the remaining Parmesan cheese over top. Cover with remaining egg mixture. Sprinkle with remaining Parmesan cheese. Bake in preheated 350-degree oven for about 25 minutes or until set. Serve immediately. Yield: 6-8 servings.

Margaret Ann Bruce
Redwood High School
Larkspur, California

CABBAGE AND NOODLES

1/4 c. shortening
2 med. heads cabbage, shredded
2   8-oz. packages noodles
2 tsp. salt
2 tsp. pepper

Melt shortening in large skillet. Add cabbage. Cook over medium heat, stirring occasionally, for 20 to 30 minutes or until cabbage is transparent. Prepare noodles according to package directions. Rinse with warm water;

drain. Add noodles, salt and pepper to cabbage. Simmer, stirring occasionally, until heated through. Yield: 6-8 servings.

Mildred Christofeno
Jimtown High School
Elkhart, Indiana

FRIED CAULIFLOWER

1 head cauliflower
1 egg
Milk
Cracker crumbs

Separate cauliflower into flowerets; cook in boiling salted water until tender. Drain. Beat egg with a small amount of milk. Dip cauliflower in egg mixture. Roll in cracker crumbs. Fry in deep hot fat until brown.

Mable Benge
Madison High School
Richmond, Kentucky

SCALLOPED CORN

1/4 c. chopped green pepper
Butter
2 cans cream-style corn
3 eggs, well beaten
1 tbsp. sugar
1 c. milk
1/2 tsp. salt
Cracker crumbs

Saute green pepper in a small amount of butter until lightly browned. Combine pepper, corn, eggs, sugar, milk and salt. Pour into buttered casserole. Cover. Bake in preheated 300-degree oven for 1 hour. Sprinkle with cracker crumbs. Bake, uncovered, for 15 minutes longer or until cracker crumbs are lightly browned.

Judith E. Brown
Desert High School
Wamsutter, Wyoming

INSTANT POTATO CASSEROLE

1 box instant mashed potatoes
4 oz. cream cheese, whipped

1 egg, beaten
2 tbsp. chopped parsley
2 tbsp. chopped onion
Butter
Paprika

Prepare 6 servings mashed potatoes according to package directions, omitting butter. Add cream cheese, egg, parsley and onion; mix well. Place in buttered casserole. Dot with butter. Sprinkle with paprika to taste. Bake in preheated 400-degree oven for 30 minutes or until heated through. May be prepared a day ahead.

Mrs. Jane Markham
Memorial Jr. High School
Houston, Texas

CORN WITH BRUSSELS SPROUTS

1 pt. Brussels sprouts
1 12 or 16-oz. can whole kernel corn
1/4 tsp. salt
Dash of pepper
2 tbsp. butter or margarine

Wash and prepare Brussels sprouts for cooking. Drain liquid from corn; add enough water to make 1/2 cup liquid. Cook Brussels sprouts in liquid for about 10 minutes or until tender. Add remaining ingredients; heat through. Yield: 6 servings.

Photograph for this recipe below.

BLENDER WHITE SAUCE

4 to 6 slices white bread
1 c. hot milk
Dash of salt
Dash of pepper
1 tbsp. butter

Trim crusts from bread slices; break into pieces into blender container. Process to make fine crumbs. Add remaining ingredients; process until smooth. Serve immediately. Grated cheese may be blended into white sauce to make a cheese sauce.

Mrs. Elaine Schramm
Plateau Valley School
Collbran, Colorado

TARTAR SAUCE

1/2 c. chopped dill pickle
1/4 c. chopped onion
1 c. mayonnaise
1/2 c. salad dressing
1/4 c. lemon juice
1/4 tsp. dry mustard
Pepper to taste

Mix all ingredients together thoroughly. Cover; store in refrigerator until ready to use.

Kay Caskey
Manogue High School
Reno, Nevada

FAVORITE BARBECUE SAUCE

1 bottle catsup
1/2 bottle Worcestershire sauce
1/2 c. butter
2 tbsp. brown sugar
3 or 4 drops of Tabasco sauce
1 med. onion, minced

Combine all ingredients in saucepan; simmer for 10 minutes or until flavors are blended, stirring frequently. Tomato sauce may be substituted for part of the catsup, if desired.

Mrs. Jane Beery
London High School
London, Ohio

NEVER-FAIL FLUFFY HOLLANDAISE SAUCE

1/2 c. margarine
4 egg yolks
2 tbsp. lemon juice
1/4 tsp. salt
Dash of cayenne pepper
1 tsp. prepared mustard

Melt margarine in top of double boiler over simmering water, being sure the top pan does not touch simmering water during cooking. Stir in 1/4 cup water; remove from water. Add unbeaten egg yolks, all at one time; beat with electric mixer for 2 to 3 minutes. Mix in remaining ingredients. Place over simmering water; cook until thick and fluffy, beating constantly. Remove from heat; serve immediately. Place over simmering water and stir lightly to reheat.

Mrs. Mary Ada Parks
Anna-Jonesboro High School
Anna, Illinois

SPEEDY RAREBIT

1 can Cheddar cheese soup
1/4 tsp. prepared mustard
1/4 c. milk
4 slices tomato
4 slices toast

Mix soup and mustard in saucepan until smooth; stir in milk gradually. Place over low heat, stirring frequently until heated through. Arrange tomato slices on toast; place on serving plates. Pour cheese sauce over top. Yield: 4 servings.

Mrs. Elizabeth B. Lengle
Warrior Run High School
Turbotville, Pennsylvania

MAG'S JALAPENO RICE

3 vegetable bouillon cubes
2 c. rice
1/2 c. oil
1 c. chopped onions
3 jalapeno peppers, chopped fine
Salt and pepper to taste
1/2 lb. cheese, grated
1/2 c. butter or margarine

Dissolve bouillon cubes in 4 cups boiling water. Cook rice in oil in skillet until yellow, stirring constantly; do not brown. Add onions and jalapeno peppers; stir in salt and pepper. Pour bouillon over rice; reduce heat. Cover; simmer for 20 minutes. Add cheese and butter; cover. Simmer for about 10 minutes longer.

Lynn Lankford
Taylor High School
Taylor, Texas

LOUISIANA CORN BREAD DRESSING

1/2 c. finely chopped onion
1/2 c. finely chopped bell pepper
1/2 c. finely chopped celery
1/3 c. margarine
8 c. crumbled corn bread
6 eggs, beaten
1 can cream of chicken soup
2 cans chicken broth
Salt and pepper to taste

Saute onion, bell pepper and celery in margarine until tender. Add remaining ingredients; mix well. Place in casserole. Bake in preheated 350-degree oven until medium brown.

Mrs. L. K. Rush
Louisiana Special Education Center
Alexandria, Louisiana

QUICKIE BISCUIT MIX

8 c. sifted all-purpose flour
5 tbsp. baking powder
2 tsp. salt
2 tsp. cream of tartar
3 tbsp. sugar
2 c. shortening

Sift dry ingredients together three times. Cut in shortening until mixture resembles cornmeal. Store in refrigerator in tightly covered container. Do not sift mix.

Biscuits

2 c. mix
2/3 c. milk

Combine mix and milk lightly, using fork. Knead on floured cloth 5 or 6 times. Pat out to 1/2-inch thickness; cut to desired size. Place on ungreased cookie sheet. Bake in preheated 425-degree oven for 10 to 12 minutes. Grated cheese may be added, if desired. Yield: 8-10 Biscuits.

Waffles

2 tbsp. sugar
2 c. mix
1 c. milk
1/4 c. Wesson oil
2 eggs, separated

Combine sugar and mix. Beat milk, oil and egg yolks together; stir into mix. Fold in stiffly beaten egg whites. Bake in waffle iron until golden. Yield: 4 Waffles.

Reuben Roll-Ups

1 recipe Biscuits
1 8-oz. can sauerkraut
1/4 c. Thousand Island dressing
8 thin slices corned beef
8 1/2-in. strips Swiss cheese

Pat out dough to 1/8-inch thickness; cut into eight 3 x 4-inch rectangles. Snip sauerkraut with scissors; place 2 tablespoons sauerkraut on each rectangle. Top with 1 teaspoon Thousand Island dressing, 1 slice corned beef and 1 strip cheese. Roll up as for jelly roll; place on ungreased cookie sheet. Bake in preheated 375-degree oven for 10 to 15 minutes or until golden brown. Serve hot.

Dorothy Wuertz
John Marshall High School
Los Angeles, California

COUNTRY-STYLE BISCUITS

2 c. sifted flour
4 tsp. baking powder
1 tsp. salt
1 to 1 1/4 c. whipping cream

Sift dry ingredients together in medium-large bowl. Stir in cream gradually, using fork, until mixture holds together. Turn out onto lightly floured board; knead 8 to 10 times. Roll out to 1/2-inch thickness; cut with 1 1/2 to 2-inch biscuit cutter. Place biscuits on ungreased cookie sheet about 3/4 inch apart. Bake in preheated 425-degree oven for 10 to 12 minutes or until golden. Yield: 12-16 biscuits.

Karen Mae Jones
Chisholm Middle School
Newton, Kansas

DOWN EAST BISCUITS

2 c. flour
1/4 c. (rounded) shortening
1 tsp. (rounded) soda
2 tsp. (rounded) cream of tartar
1 tsp. salt
1 c. milk

Mix flour, shortening, soda, cream of tartar and salt together. Add milk slowly; mix until dough clings together. Knead dough lightly on floured board. Pat out; cut biscuits. Heat small amount of additional shortening in 8-inch pan. Dip tops of biscuits in shortening; turn and place in pan. Bake in preheated 425-degree oven for 12 minutes or until golden brown.

Mrs. Polly Webster
Mattanawcook Academy
Lincoln, Maine

ONION-CHEESE BREAD

1/2 c. chopped onion
Butter
1 beaten egg
1/2 c. milk
1 1/2 c. biscuit mix
1 c. grated sharp cheese
2 tbsp. minced parsley

Saute onion in small amount of butter until tender but not brown. Combine egg and milk; stir into biscuit mix only until mix is moistened. Add onion, 1/2 of the cheese and parsley; mix well. Spread in greased 8 x 1 1/2-inch pan. Sprinkle with remaining 1/2 cup cheese; drizzle 2 tablespoons melted butter over top. Bake in preheated 350-degree oven until bread tests done.

Kristie Boyer
South Cobb High School
Austell, Georgia

QUICK CHEDDAR BREAD

3 1/3 c. all-purpose biscuit mix
2 1/2 c. shredded sharp natural Cheddar
    cheese

2 eggs, slightly beaten
1 1/4 c. milk

Combine biscuit mix and cheese. Combine eggs and milk; stir into cheese mixture, mixing just enough to moisten. Pour into greased and floured 9 x 5-inch loaf pan. Bake in preheated 350-degree oven for 55 minutes or until done. Remove from pan; serve warm.

Mrs. Frances R. Tharpe
North Wilkes High School
Hays, North Carolina

DOUBLE CORN BREAD

1 No. 2 can cream-style corn
1/2 c. (scant) vegetable oil
1 c. self-rising cornmeal
2 eggs, beaten
1 sm. carton sour cream

Combine all ingredients in mixing bowl; mix well. Pour into baking dish. Bake in preheated 425-degree oven for 30 minutes or until done.

Emily Rickman
State Dept. of Ed.
Danville, Virginia

SQUASH PUPPIES

1 c. self-rising cornmeal
1/2 c. self-rising flour
1/2 c. chopped onion
1 c. grated squash
1 egg, beaten
2 tbsp. (about) milk

Combine cornmeal and flour in mixing bowl; add onion and squash. Stir in egg and enough milk to make a stiff batter. Drop by spoonfuls into hot fat. Fry until brown on all sides. Drain and serve. Yield: 4-6 servings.

Jo Nell Hollingsworth
Hubbertville School
Fayette, Alabama

PANCAKE MIX

6 c. sifted flour
1 tbsp. salt
2 tbsp. baking powder
1 c. shortening

Sift flour, salt and baking powder together twice; place in large bowl. Cut in shortening with pastry blender until mixture resembles coarse meal. Store in tightly covered glass jar.

Pancakes

1 c. Pancake Mix
1 lg. egg, beaten
2/3 c. milk

Combine Pancake Mix and egg. Stir in milk; mix well. Pour batter onto hot greased griddle. Bake on both sides until golden brown.

Elsie Klassen
Georges P. Vanier School
Tohigo, Alberta, Canada

GERMAN OVEN PANCAKE

1/2 c. flour
3 eggs, slightly beaten
1/2 c. milk
2 tbsp. melted butter or margarine
1/4 tsp. salt

Beat flour and eggs together, using a rotary beater. Stir in remaining ingredients; pour into cold greased 10-inch baking dish. Bake in preheated 450-degree oven for 20 minutes. Pancake will puff into big bubbles while baking. Cut into wedges; serve with melted butter, powdered sugar and lemon. Yield: 2 servings.

Mrs. Fran Heckman
Waupaca High School
Waupaca, Wisconsin

SOFT PRETZELS

1 env. yeast
1 tbsp. sugar
2 tsp. salt
4 c. flour
1 egg yolk
Coarse salt

Dissolve yeast in 1 1/2 cups lukewarm water. Add sugar and salt; stir until dissolved. Add flour; mix well. Turn out dough on floured board; knead for about 5 minutes. Roll into thin strips; shape into pretzels. Place on well-greased cookie sheet. Beat egg yolk with 1 tablespoon water; brush on pretzels. Sprinkle generously with coarse salt. Bake in preheated 425-degree oven for 15 to 20 minutes.

Fran Banks
Freedom Jr. High School
Freedom, Pennsylvania

RAISIN-BRAN MUFFINS

1 c. bran buds
1 c. All-Bran flakes
1 c. quick-cooking rolled oats
1/2 c. Crisco oil
1 c. sugar
2 eggs
2 c. buttermilk
2 1/2 c. flour
1 tsp. salt
2 1/2 tsp. soda
1 c. raisins

Combine bran buds, All-Bran flakes and rolled oats in mixing bowl. Stir in 1 cup boiling water; let cool for several minutes. Mix oil and sugar together. Add eggs, one at a time, beating well after each addition. Stir in buttermilk. Sift flour, salt and soda together; stir into buttermilk mixture just to moisten. Stir in raisins. Pour into greased muffin tins, filling 3/4 full. Bake in preheated 400-degree oven for 15 minutes or until top springs back when touched. Any remaining batter may be stored in covered container in refrigerator. Will keep up to 1 week. Do not stir mixture before spooning into muffin tins after refrigeration. Yield: 24 muffins.

Mrs. Joy Barkowsky
Stanton Jr. High School
Hereford, Texas

WALNUT-LEMON MUFFINS

1 3/4 c. sifted all-purpose flour
1/2 c. sugar
3 tsp. baking powder
1 tsp. salt
2/3 c. chopped California walnuts
1 egg
2/3 c. milk
1/2 tsp. grated lemon peel
1 tbsp. lemon juice
1/3 c. shortening, melted
Lemon Sugar
California walnut halves or large pieces

Sift flour, sugar, baking powder and salt; add walnuts. Beat egg lightly; add milk, lemon peel, lemon juice and shortening. Add to flour mixture; stir just until all dry ingredients are moistened. Spoon into greased muffin cups. Sprinkle with Lemon Sugar; top each muffin with walnut half. Bake in preheated 400-degree oven for about 20 minutes or until browned and baked through. Let stand for 1 or 2 minutes; carefully remove from cups. Serve warm. Yield: Twelve 2 1/2-inch muffins.

Lemon Sugar

3 tbsp. sugar
1/2 tsp. grated lemon peel

Combine ingredients; mix well.

Photograph for this recipe above.

DELICIOUS ICEBOX BRAN MUFFINS

2 c. 100% bran
1 c. shortening
3 c. sugar
4 eggs, beaten
1 qt. buttermilk
5 c. all-purpose flour
5 tsp. soda
1 tsp. salt
2 c. All-Bran flakes

Pour 2 cups boiling water over 100% bran; let cool. Cream shortening and sugar together. Add eggs and buttermilk, beating constantly; stir in cooled bran. Sift flour, soda and salt together; stir into buttermilk mixture. Fold in All-Bran flakes until well mixed. Pour into four 1-quart jars; cover. Store in refrigerator until ready to use. Will keep up to 6 weeks. Stir batter down; pour into greased muffin tins. Bake in preheated 400-degree oven for 20 minutes or until muffins test done.

Mrs. Luella P. McKenzie
South Salem High School
Salem, Oregon

THIRTY-DAY BRAN MUFFIN MIX

2 c. 100% bran
4 c. All-Bran flakes
1 qt. buttermilk
1 c. shortening
2 c. sugar
6 eggs
5 c. sifted flour
5 tsp. soda
1 tsp. salt

Combine 100% bran, All-Bran flakes and 2 cups boiling water; let stand for several minutes. Stir in buttermilk. Cream shortening and sugar together. Add eggs, one at a time, beating well after each addition. Add to bran mixture; mix well. Sift flour, soda and salt together; stir into bran mixture just to moisten. Cover; store in refrigerator until needed. Will keep up to 30 days. Bake muffins in preheated 400-degree oven for 15 to 20 minutes or until done. Nuts may be added to batter before baking, if desired.

Rowa Lee
R. O. Gibson Jr. High School
Las Vegas, Nevada

MAKE-AHEAD ICEBOX BRAN MUFFINS

2 c. 100% bran
1 c. vegetable shortening
3 c. sugar

4 eggs, beaten
1 qt. buttermilk
5 c. sifted flour
5 tsp. soda
1 tbsp. salt
4 c. All-Bran flakes

Combine 2 cups boiling water and 100% bran; set aside to cool. Cream shortening and sugar together; stir in eggs, buttermilk and soaked bran. Add remaining ingredients; mix well. Store in tightly covered container in refrigerator. Will keep for 6 weeks or longer. Bake muffins as needed in preheated 400-degree oven for 15 to 20 minutes. Raisins, dates or nuts may be added to batter before baking, if desired.

Barbara Gaylor
Supvr., Consumer and Home Ec. Ed. Unit
Michigan Dept. of Ed.
Lansing, Michigan

PUMPKIN PUFFS

1 1/2 c. sifted flour
2 tsp. baking powder
3/4 tsp. salt
Sugar
1/2 tsp. cinnamon
1/2 tsp. nutmeg
1/4 c. shortening
1 egg, beaten
1/2 c. cooked pumpkin
1/2 c. milk
1/2 c. raisins (opt.)

Sift flour, baking powder, salt, 1/2 cup sugar, cinnamon and nutmeg together into mixing bowl. Cut in shortening until consistency of cornmeal. Combine egg, pumpkin and milk; add to flour mixture. Mix only until flour is moistened. Fold in raisins. Spoon into greased muffin tins, filling 2/3 full. Sprinkle each with 1/4 teaspoon sugar. Bake in preheated 400-degree oven for 15 to 20 minutes or until done.

Mrs. Phyllis Larson
Glen Crest High School
Glen Ellyn, Illinois

Quick and Easy

MASTER MIX

1/3 c. baking powder
1 tbsp. salt
1/4 c. sugar
1 tsp. cream of tartar
9 c. all-purpose flour
2 c. shortening

Sift baking powder, salt, sugar and cream of tartar into flour. Sift together twice into large mixing bowl. Cut in shortening until mixture resembles cornmeal. Store in tightly covered container at room temperature. Will keep for 6 weeks. Pile Master Mix lightly into cup; level with spatula to measure. Yield: 13 cups.

Coffee Cake

3 c. Master Mix
1/2 c. sugar
2/3 c. milk
1 egg
1/4 c. (packed) brown sugar
1 1/2 tsp. cinnamon

Combine mix and sugar. Beat milk and egg together; stir into mix. Turn into 2 greased 9-inch layer pans. Combine brown sugar and cinnamon; sprinkle over batter. Bake in preheated 400-degree oven for 25 minutes or until done.

Muffins

2 tbsp. sugar
3 c. Master Mix
1 c. milk
1 egg, beaten

Add sugar to mix. Combine milk and egg; stir into mix until flour is just moistened. Pour in greased muffin pans. Bake in preheated 425-degree oven for 20 minutes or until done. Yield: 10 muffins.

Dumplings

2 c. Master Mix
1/2 c. milk

Combine mix and milk; stir until mix is just moistened. Drop from tablespoon into hot stew, hot tomato soup or hot fruit sauce. Cover; steam without lifting cover for 12 minutes.

Orange-Raisin Cake

3 c. Master Mix
1 1/2 c. sugar
Juice of 1 orange
2 eggs, beaten
2/3 c. chopped raisins
Grated peel of 1 orange

Combine mix and sugar. Add enough water to orange juice to measure 1 cup liquid. Mix liquid and eggs together; stir 1 cup egg mixture into mix. Beat for 2 minutes. Add remaining liquid, raisins and orange peel; beat for 1 minute longer. Pour into 2 waxed paper-lined 8-inch layer pans. Bake in preheated 375-degree oven for 20 to 25 minutes or until done. Frost as desired.

Molasses Snaps

1/2 c. sugar
1 tsp. cinnamon
3/4 tsp. ginger
3/4 tsp. cloves
1/2 tsp. soda
4 c. Master Mix
1 egg
1 c. molasses

Combine sugar, spices and soda; stir into mix. Combine egg and molasses. Add to dry ingredients; mix well. Chill thoroughly. Shape in balls; roll in additional sugar. Flatten on greased cookie sheet. Bake in preheated 375-degree oven for 10 to 12 minutes. Yield: 4 dozen.

Marie Heltzel
Union County High School
Lake Butler, Florida

QUICK DOUGHNUT BALLS

3 c. pancake mix
1/3 c. sugar
1 1/2 tsp. cinnamon
1/2 tsp. nutmeg
2 eggs, beaten
3/4 c. milk
2 tbsp. vegetable oil
Confectioners' sugar

Combine pancake mix, sugar, cinnamon and nutmeg in mixing bowl. Mix eggs, milk and oil together. Stir into pancake mixture; mix well. Drop by teaspoonfuls into deep fat at 375 degrees. Fry until golden. Drain on paper toweling; roll in confectioners' sugar.

Jacqueline Witt
C-4 Iron County School
Viburnum, Missouri

CINNAMON TWIST

1/2 c. sugar
2 tsp. ground cinnamon
1 pkg. refrigerator biscuits
4 tbsp. melted margarine
2 tbsp. chopped walnuts (opt.)

Combine sugar and cinnamon. Roll biscuits into 9-inch rope. Bring ends together; pinch to seal. Dip in melted margarine; coat with sugar mixture. Twist into a figure eight; place on greased baking sheet. Sprinkle with walnuts. Bake in preheated 400-degree oven for 10 to 12 minutes or until done. Dough may be twisted into heart, shamrock or Christmas designs, if desired.

Joy N. Pool
Northlawn Jr. High School
Streator, Illinois

EASY SWEET ROLLS

1 tbsp. melted butter or margarine
1/4 c. maple syrup
1/4 c. chopped walnuts
1   10-count pkg. refrigerator biscuits
Cinnamon to taste

Combine butter and maple syrup in round 8-inch baking pan. Sprinkle in walnuts. Cut each biscuit into quarters; place close together on syrup mixture. Sprinkle cinnamon over top. Bake in preheated 400-degree oven for 10 to 15 minutes or until biscuits are golden brown. Invert pan onto large plate; serve warm.

June Dorothy Allan
Mark Twain Jr. High School
Los Angeles, California

GOOEY CINNAMON ROLLS

1 pkg. refrigerator biscuits
1/3 c. sugar
2 tsp. cinnamon
3 tbsp. melted butter or margarine
1/2 c. miniature marshmallows

Separate and flatten biscuits. Combine sugar and cinnamon. Dip biscuits into butter then into sugar mixture. Place 4 marshmallows in center of each biscuit; bring edges up to form balls. Place in greased muffin cup, seam side down. Bake in preheated 400-degree oven for 10 to 12 minutes or until done. Remove from pan immediately.

Margery Juk
Wolcott Jr. High School
Warren, Michigan

QUICK CARAMEL ROLLS

1 pkg. frozen rolls
1/2 c. (packed) brown sugar
1/2 pkg. butterscotch pudding mix
1/2 c. butter or margarine

Place rolls in greased 9-inch baking pan. Sprinkle brown sugar and butterscotch pudding mix over tops of rolls; dot with butter. Let stand overnight. Bake according to package directions.

Carmen M. Tripp
Minnesota Braille and Sight Saving School
Faribault, Minnesota

COWBOY BUTTER

1 lb. margarine, at room temperature
1/2 c. salad oil
1 c. buttermilk
Salt to taste (opt.)

Place margarine in deep 1 1/2-quart mixing bowl; break into chunks with fork. Add small amount of oil and buttermilk; beat with electric mixer at high speed. Continue beating, adding small amounts of oil and buttermilk at a time, until all oil and buttermilk have been added and mixture is fluffy. Add salt; mix well. Yield: About 1 1/2 pounds.

Mrs. Lorrayne Sutton
Williams High School
Williams, Arizona

MOCK MAPLE SYRUP

1 c. (packed) brown sugar
1/3 c. water
Pinch of salt
1/4 tsp. vanilla extract

Dissolve sugar in water in saucepan. Add salt; boil for 1 minute. Add vanilla; mix well. Serve warm.

Emely Sundbeck
Manor High School
Manor, Texas

EASY AS PUNCH

4 6-oz. cans frozen orange juice
    concentrate
3 pkg. cherry Kool-Aid
3 pkg. orange Kool-Aid
2 46-oz. cans pineapple juice
Sugar to taste
3 (or more) ripe bananas

Reconstitute orange juice according to directions. Prepare cherry and orange Kool-Aid according to package directions. Combine orange juice, pineapple juice, cherry and orange Kool-Aid in punch bowl; stir in sugar.

Place bananas in blender container; process to puree. Stir into punch just before serving. Yield: 40-50 servings.

Ruth Larson
Hickman High School
Columbia, Missouri

EASY HOT CHOCOLATE MIX

1 1-lb. can instant chocolate mix
1 8-qt. box instant nonfat dry milk
1 6-oz. jar non-dairy coffee creamer
1/2 c. confectioners' sugar

Mix all ingredients together; store in sealed container. Place 1/3 cup chocolate mixture in cup; fill with hot water. Stir until mix is dissolved. Yield: About 50 servings.

Mrs. Jan Gruetzmacher
Wilson Jr. High School
Appleton, Wisconsin

INSTANT HOT COCOA MIX

1 8-qt. box instant nonfat dry milk
1 2-lb. can Nestles quik
1 6-oz. jar non-dairy coffee creamer
1 c. confectioners' sugar

Mix all ingredients together until well blended. Store in airtight container until ready to use. Place 1/4 cup cocoa mix in cup. Fill with hot water; stir until cocoa mix is dissolved.

Mrs. Linda C. Griffin
Gayle Middle School
Falmouth, Virginia

INSTANT RUSSIAN TEA

2 c. instant tea
1 c. Tang
1 c. sugar
1 env. lemonade mix
2 tsp. cinnamon
3/4 tsp. cloves

Combine all ingredients; mix well. Store in airtight container until ready to use. Place 2 teaspoons tea mix in cup; fill with hot water. Stir until tea mix is dissolved.

Cassandra Lee
Visitation Valley Jr. High School
San Francisco, California

ORANGE FROSTED

2 12-oz. cans frozen orange juice concentrate
6 orange juice cans (scant) cold water
1 qt. vanilla ice cream, softened

Combine orange juice and water; mix well. Add ice cream; beat for 1 minute with electric beater. May process in blender, if desired. Serve in tall glasses garnished with orange slices.

Beverly Rieck
Bridgewater High School
Bridgewater, South Dakota

TROPICAL DELIGHT

2/3 c. hot water
2 env. gelatin
1/4 c. sugar
1 pkg. frozen strawberries

Combine water and gelatin in blender container; process for 40 seconds. Add sugar; process just until sugar is dissolved. Add strawberries; blend thoroughly. Serve immediately.

Elaine Schramm
Plateau Valley School
Collbran, Colorado

AFTER-DINNER MINTS

1 8-oz. package cream cheese, softened
Vanilla, mint or butter flavoring to taste
Food coloring
2 1-lb. boxes confectioners' sugar
Sugar

Combine cream cheese and flavoring. Add enough food coloring to tint desired shade. Add confectioners' sugar gradually, mixing well. Form into 1/2 to 1-inch balls. Roll in sugar. Press down with thumb. Place in container with waxed paper between layers; cover tightly. May be frozen until ready to use. Yield: About 200 mints.

Neldalea Dotray
La Grove School
Farina, Illinois

CONCORDGRAPE JELLY-LADE

1 c. Concordgrape jelly
1/4 c. orange marmalade
1 tbsp. shredded coconut

Blend all ingredients. Spread on biscuits or toasted English muffin along with cream cheese. Yield: 1 1/4 cups.

Photograph for this recipe on page 76.

GINGERED CONCORDGRAPE PRESERVES

1 c. Concordgrape preserves
1/4 c. applesauce
1 tsp. finely chopped candied ginger

Combine all ingredients. Spread on toast, muffins or toasted corn bread. Yield: 1 1/4 cups.

Photograph for this recipe on page 76.

NUTTY CONCORDGRAPE-PINEAPPLE SPREAD

1 c. Concordgrape jam
1/4 c. chopped macadamia nuts
1/4 c. crushed pineapple, well drained

Combine all ingredients. Serve with omelets or fresh hot rolls. Yield: 1 1/2 cups.

Photograph for this recipe on page 76.

CALIFORNIA-STYLE GRANOLA AND STRAWBERRIES

1 c. old-fashioned oats
1 c. wheat germ
1/2 c. graham cracker crumbs
1/2 c. flaked coconut
1/2 c. slivered blanched almonds
1 to 2 tbsp. light brown sugar
1 tsp. vanilla extract
Milk
3 pt. California strawberries

Combine oats, wheat germ, crumbs, coconut, almonds, sugar and vanilla in shallow baking pan. Bake in preheated 275-degree oven for 1 hour, stirring occasionally. Cool. Combine 1/2 cup granola, 1/2 cup milk and about 3/4 cup whole strawberries for each serving. Store granola in tightly covered container in refrigerator.

Photograph for this recipe on opposite page.

QUICK-FROSTED CHOCOLATE CAKE

1/2 c. margarine
1/2 c. shortening
3 1/2 tbsp. cocoa
2 c. sugar
2 c. flour
2 eggs
1 tsp. vanilla extract
1 tsp. soda
1/2 c. buttermilk
Frosting

Combine margarine, shortening, cocoa and 1 cup water in saucepan. Bring to a boil, stirring. Remove from heat. Add sugar and flour; mix well. Add eggs and vanilla; mix well. Stir soda into buttermilk; add to batter. Beat until well blended. Pour into greased and floured rectangular baking pan. Bake in preheated 400-degree oven for 20 minutes or until cake tests done. Spread Frosting over warm cake in pan.

Frosting

1/2 c. margarine
3 1/2 tsp. cocoa
1/3 c. milk
1   1-lb. box powdered sugar
1 tsp. vanilla extract

Combine margarine, cocoa and milk in saucepan. Bring to a boil, stirring. Remove from heat. Stir in powdered sugar and vanilla until smooth. One cup coconut or chopped pecans may be added, if desired.

Mrs. Joe Wayne Carter
Hamlin High School
Hamlin, Texas

CHOCOLATE SHEET CAKE

2 c. flour
1 tsp. cinnamon
1/2 tsp. salt
3 1/2 c. sugar
1 c. shortening
2 tbsp. cocoa
2 eggs, well beaten
1 tsp. soda
1/2 c. buttermilk
1 tsp. vanilla extract
1/3 c. butter or margarine
1/3 c. milk
1/2 c. semisweet chocolate bits

Sift flour, cinnamon, salt and 2 cups sugar together into mixing bowl. Combine shortening, cocoa and 1 cup water in saucepan. Bring to a boil, stirring. Pour over flour mixture; mix well. Combine eggs, soda, buttermilk and vanilla; mix well. Add to flour mixture. Beat until well blended. Pour into greased rectangular baking pan. Bake in preheated 350-degree oven for about 25 minutes or until cake tests done. Cool. Combine remaining 1 1/2 cups sugar, butter and milk in saucepan. Bring to a boil; boil for 30 seconds, stirring. Add chocolate bits. Beat until bits are melted and mixture is thick and smooth. Spread evenly over cooled cake in pan.

Mrs. Mary Cates
Occupational Skills Center
Milwaukie, Oregon
Mrs. Willie Lee W. Everett
Menard High School
Menard, Texas

113

SCOTTISH CHOCOLATE CAKE

2 c. flour
2 c. sugar
1 c. margarine
4 tbsp. cocoa
1/2 c. buttermilk
1 tsp. cinnamon
1 tsp. soda
2 eggs
1 tsp. vanilla extract
Icing

Sift flour and sugar together into large mixing bowl. Combine margarine, cocoa and 1 cup water in saucepan; bring to a boil, stirring to dissolve cocoa and melt margarine. Add cocoa mixture to flour mixture; mix well. Combine buttermilk, cinnamon, soda, eggs and vanilla, mixing well. Add buttermilk mixture to flour mixture. Beat until well blended. Batter will be thin. Pour into greased and floured 9 x 12-inch baking pan. Bake in preheated 350-degree oven for 30 minutes or until done. Spread Icing over hot cake in pan.

Icing

1/2 c. margarine
4 tbsp. cocoa
6 tbsp. milk
1 1-lb. box confectioners' sugar
1 c. chopped toasted pecans

Combine margarine, cocoa and milk in saucepan. Bring to a boil, stirring. Remove from heat. Stir in confectioners' sugar until smooth. Add pecans; mix well. Three-fourths cup black walnuts may be substituted for pecans, if desired.

Mrs. Judy Compton
Albany High School
Albany, Texas

WACKY CAKE

1 1/2 c. flour
1 c. sugar
1 tsp. soda
1/2 tsp. salt

3 tbsp. cocoa
6 tbsp. salad oil
1 tsp. vinegar
1 tsp. vanilla extract

Sift flour, sugar, soda, salt and cocoa together into 9-inch square baking pan. Make 3 wells in dry ingredients. Pour salad oil into first well, vinegar into second well and vanilla into third well. Pour 1 cup warm water over entire mixture. Stir with a wooden spoon until well mixed. Bake in preheated 350-degree oven for about 30 minutes or until cake tests done. Coconut or chopped nuts may be added to batter, if desired.

Betty J. Brandt
Gibbon Public School
Gibbon, Minnesota
Elizabeth V. Mullins
North Middle School
Westfield, Massachusetts

BLACK BOTTOM CUPCAKES

1 1/2 c. flour
1 1/3 c. sugar
1 tsp. soda
1/4 c. cocoa
Salt
1/3 c. oil
1 tsp. vanilla extract
1 tsp. vinegar
1 8-oz. package cream cheese
1 egg
1 c. semisweet chocolate bits

Sift flour, 1 cup sugar, soda, cocoa and 1/2 teaspoon salt together into large mixing bowl. Make a well in center. Pour oil, 1 cup water, vanilla and vinegar into well. Blend for 4 minutes at medium speed of electric mixer. Combine cream cheese, remaining 1/3 cup sugar, egg and 1/8 teaspoon salt in small mixing bowl; beat until smooth. Stir in chocolate bits. Fill greased muffin tins 1/2 full with batter. Add 1 tablespoon cream cheese mixture to each tin. Bake in preheated 350-degree oven for 30 to 35 minutes or until cupcakes test done. Yield: 3 dozen.

Rosemary Pacha
Washington Jr. High School
Washington, Iowa

MANDARIN ORANGE CAKE

2 eggs
2 11-oz. cans mandarin oranges, well drained
2 c. flour
2 c. sugar
2 tsp. soda
1/2 tsp. salt
3/4 c. (packed) brown sugar
3 tbsp. milk
3 tbsp. butter

Beat eggs in large mixing bowl until lemon colored. Add oranges. Sift flour, sugar, soda and salt together. Add to orange mixture. Beat for 4 minutes at low speed of electric mixer or until tiny flakes of oranges are showing. Pour into greased 9 x 13-inch baking pan. Bake in preheated 350-degree oven for 30 to 35 minutes or until cake tests done. Combine brown sugar, milk and butter in saucepan. Bring to a boil; pour over warm cake. Serve with whipped cream, if desired.

Mrs. Donna Rasmussen
Central Middle School
Montevideo, Minnesota

PINEAPPLE CAKE

1/2 c. melted butter or margarine
1 box white cake mix
1 20-oz. can crushed pineapple, undrained

Pour butter over cake mix in mixing bowl. Add pineapple; mix well. Pour into greased 9 x 13-inch baking pan. Bake in preheated 350-degree oven for 25 minutes or until cake tests done. May serve with ice cream or whipped topping, if desired.

Jean Mason
Hi Plains School
Seibert, Colorado

FLUFFY FROSTING

1 c. milk
1/4 c. flour
1/2 c. butter

1/3 c. shortening
1 tsp. vanilla extract
1 c. sugar
Pinch of salt

Combine milk and flour in saucepan; cook over low heat, stirring, until thick. Cream butter, shortening, vanilla, sugar and salt together until fluffy; add to milk mixture. Whip until consistency of whipped cream. Yield: Frosting for 2-layer cake.

Mrs. Cecelia Sanchez
Salina High School Central
Salina, Kansas

CARROT CAKE ICING

1 8-oz. package cream cheese
1/4 c. margarine
1 1-lb. box confectioners' sugar, sifted
1 c. chopped nuts
1 can flaked coconut
1 tsp. vanilla

Combine cream cheese and margarine in mixing bowl; blend until smooth. Add confectioners' sugar. Mix well. Stir in remaining ingredients, mixing well.

Audrey V. Craig
Divide High School
Nolan, Texas

DECORATOR CAKE FROSTING

1 1-lb. box powdered sugar
1/2 c. shortening
4 to 5 tbsp. milk or water
1 tsp. desired flavoring

Combine powdered sugar, shortening and milk in mixing bowl. Beat for 5 minutes at high speed of electric mixer. Add flavoring; mix well. Add more milk if frosting is too stiff. Food coloring may be added for colored frosting, if desired. Keeps well in refrigerator.

Mrs. Kristen Roudybush
Grand Valley Community School
Kellerton, Iowa

GLOSSY CHOCOLATE FROSTING

1/2 c. sugar
2 tbsp. cornstarch
1 sq. chocolate, cut up
1/4 tsp. salt
2 tbsp. margarine
1 tsp. vanilla extract

Combine sugar and cornstarch in 1-quart saucepan. Add 1/2 cup boiling water, chocolate and salt. Cook over medium heat, stirring, until thickened. Remove from heat. Stir in margarine and vanilla. Spread over hot cake. Yield: Frosting for 2-layer cake or 9 x 13-inch sheet cake.

Lois L. Cynewski
Portsmouth Jr. High School
Portsmouth, New Hampshire

LEMON FLUFF

1 can frozen lemonade, thawed
1 can sweetened condensed milk
1 lg. container Cool Whip
Graham cracker crumbs

Combine lemonade with condensed milk. Fold in Cool Whip. Sprinkle bottom of 8-inch square pan with part of the graham cracker crumbs. Pour lemonade mixture over crumbs. Sprinkle remaining crumbs on top. Refrigerate for at least 20 minutes. May pour into graham cracker crust, if desired.

Connie Delaney
New Providence High School
New Providence, Iowa

LEMON FRUIT DELIGHT

1 No. 2 can apricots
1 No. 2 can sliced peaches
1 No. 2 can pineapple chunks
2 pkg. instant lemon pudding mix
2 to 3 bananas, sliced
8 to 10 maraschino cherries, halved
Whipped topping (opt.)

Drain canned fruits, reserving 1 cup juice. Chop apricots and peaches. Combine pud-

ding mix and reserved juice; stir until thickened. Stir in fruits. Chill. Serve with whipped topping. Yield: 12 servings.

Ruth Riffe
Hobart High School
Hobart, Oklahoma

CHOCOLATE PUDDING DESSERT

1/2 c. melted margarine
1 c. flour
2 1/2 tbsp. sugar
1/4 c. chopped nuts
1 c. confectioners' sugar
1 c. Cool Whip
1 8-oz. package cream cheese, softened
2 pkg. instant chocolate pudding mix
3 c. milk

Combine margarine, flour, sugar and nuts in mixing bowl; mix well. Press into bottom of 9 x 13-inch baking pan. Bake in preheated 325-degree oven for 15 minutes or until lightly browned. Cool. Combine confectioners' sugar, Cool Whip and cream cheese; beat well. Spread over crust. Combine pudding mix and milk in mixing bowl; beat for 1 minute. Pour over cream cheese mixture. Chill until set. Garnish with additional Cool Whip and chopped nuts, if desired.

Janet F. Oyler
Griffith Sr. High School
Griffith, Indiana

CHOCOLATE VELVET

1 1/4 c. milk
2 env. unflavored gelatin
1 egg
1/4 c. sugar
1/8 tsp. salt
1 c. chocolate chips
1 tsp. vanilla extract
1 c. heavy cream or evaporated milk

Pour 1/2 cup milk and gelatin into blender container. Cover. Process on stir to soften gelatin. Bring remaining 3/4 cup milk to a boil; add to gelatin mixture. Process until gelatin is dissolved. Add egg, sugar and salt. Blend at high speed until well mixed. Add chocolate chips. Blend at high speed until smooth. Add vanilla, cream and 1 1/2 cups crushed ice. Blend until ice is liquefied. Pour into individual serving dishes or 5-cup mold. Chill for about 15 minutes or until firm. Garnish with whipped topping, chopped nuts or fruit. May pour into graham cracker crust or baked pastry shell, if desired. Yield: 6-8 servings.

Kay Caskey
Manogue High School
Reno, Nevada

PINEAPPLE-PISTACHIO DESSERT

    1 pkg. pistachio instant pudding and
        pie filling mix
    1 sm. can crushed pineapple
    1/2 c. chopped black walnuts
    1/2 c. miniature marshmallows
    1 pkg. Dream Whip, prepared

Prepare pudding mix according to package directions. Add pineapple, walnuts and marshmallows; mix well. Fold in Dream Whip; refrigerate until chilled. Will keep for several days. Other nuts may be substituted for black walnuts. Yield: 4-6 servings.

Jo Nell Hollingsworth
Hubbertville School
Fayette, Alabama

INSTANT PISTACHIO DESSERT

    1 lg. can crushed pineapple in own
        juice
    1 box instant pistachio pudding mix
    1 sm. carton Cool Whip

Combine all ingredients. Mix well. Pour into serving dish. Chill. Keeps well in refrigerator for several days.

Mary Frances Wilson
Cherokee County High School
Centre, Alabama

PECAN PRALINE COOKIES

    2 egg whites
    2 c. (packed) brown sugar
    2 c. chopped pecans
    1/4 tsp. salt
    2 tbsp. flour

Beat egg whites until stiff peaks form. Fold in brown sugar, pecans and salt, mixing thoroughly. Add flour; mix well. Drop by teaspoonfuls onto greased cookie sheets about 2 inches apart. Bake in preheated 325-degree oven for about 12 minutes or until lightly browned. Cool completely before removing from cookie sheets.

Mrs. Carl Ekstrom
New Prairie High School
New Carlisle, Indiana

EASY MIX COOKIE BARS

    2 c. (packed) brown sugar
    3 c. all-purpose flour
    1 tsp. cinnamon
    1 tsp. baking powder
    1 tsp. soda
    1/2 c. chopped nuts
    1 c. chopped dates or raisins
    2 eggs
    3/4 c. oil
    1 1/2 tsp. vanilla extract
    1 1/2 c. confectioners' sugar
    1 tsp. white corn syrup
    1 tsp. soft butter

Combine first 9 ingredients in mixing bowl. Add 1 teaspoon vanilla and 1 cup boiling water; beat until smooth. Pat onto jelly roll pan. Bake in preheated 350-degree oven for 20 minutes or until done. Combine confectioners' sugar, corn syrup, butter and remaining 1/2 teaspoon vanilla. Beat until smooth. Spread over cookie surface while hot. Cut into squares to serve.

Irma Haley
Castleford High School
Castleford, Idaho

OLD-FASHIONED GINGER ROLL COOKIES

1 c. sugar
1 c. butter or lard
2 eggs, slightly beaten
2/3 c. molasses
1 tsp. soda
1 tsp. ginger
6 1/2 to 7 c. flour

Cream sugar and butter together until light and fluffy. Add eggs and molasses; mix well. Dissolve soda in 3/4 cup boiling water; add to sugar mixture. Beat well. Stir in ginger and enough flour to make a soft dough. Turn out onto lightly floured surface. Roll out to 1/4-inch thickness. Cut into desired shapes with cookie cutters. Place on ungreased cookie sheets. Bake in preheated 350-degree oven just until set. Remove immediately to wire rack to cool. Frost with confectioners' sugar icing, if desired. Dough may be chilled before rolling out.

Mrs. Carol Ludtke
Morton Public School
Morton, Minnesota

GRANOLA COOKIES

1/2 c. shortening
1/4 c. peanut butter
1 c. (packed) brown sugar
1 egg
1 tsp. vanilla extract
1 c. flour
1 tsp. salt
1/2 tsp. soda
3 c. granola

Cream shortening, peanut butter, sugar, egg, 1/4 cup water and vanilla together. Add flour, salt and soda; blend well. Stir in granola. Drop by teaspoonfuls onto greased cookie sheet. Bake in preheated 350-degree oven for 12 minutes or until lightly browned. Yield: About 4 dozen cookies.

Barsha Elzey
Terra Linda High School
San Rafael, California

OH HANK BARS

2/3 c. butter
1 c. (packed) brown sugar
1/2 c. corn syrup
3 tsp. vanilla extract
4 c. quick-cooking oats
1 c. semisweet chocolate bits
1/3 c. peanut butter

Cream butter and sugar together. Add corn syrup, vanilla and oats; mix well. Pat dough into lightly greased 13 x 9-inch baking pan. Bake in preheated 350-degree oven for 15 minutes or until done. Cool slightly. Combine chocolate bits and peanut butter in saucepan; cook over low heat just until melted. Spread over top. Cut into bars to serve.

Marcia L. Strout
Timberlane Reg. High School
Plaistow, New Hampshire

FORTIFIED OATMEAL LASSES

1 1/4 c. (packed) brown sugar
1/2 c. margarine
2 lg. eggs
2 c. flour
2 tsp. baking powder
1/8 tsp. soda
1/2 c. instant nonfat milk
6 tbsp. molasses
2 c. quick-cooking oats
1 c. raisins
1 c. chopped pecans

Cream sugar and margarine together. Add eggs; beat well. Sift flour, baking powder, soda and nonfat milk together; add to creamed mixture gradually, beating well after each addition. Add molasses; mix well. Stir in oats, raisins and pecans. Drop by teaspoonfuls onto lightly greased cookie sheet. Bake in preheated 400-degree oven for about 12 minutes or until lightly browned.

Mrs. Betty Ambrose
Robert E. Lee High School
Midland, Texas

Recipe on page 139.

SOFT OATMEAL COOKIES

1 1/2 c. raisins
1 c. shortening
1/2 c. (packed) brown sugar
1/2 c. sugar
3 eggs
2 1/2 c. flour
1 tsp. soda
1/2 tsp. salt
1 c. chopped nuts
2 c. oatmeal
1 tsp. vanilla extract
Confectioners' sugar icing (opt.)

Simmer raisins in 3/4 cup water for 5 minutes. Remove from heat; cover. Cream shortening, sugars and eggs together until lemon colored. Sift flour, soda and salt together; add to creamed mixture gradually, beating well after each addition. Stir in raisins with liquid, nuts, oatmeal and vanilla. Drop by tablespoonfuls onto greased cookie sheet. Bake in preheated 350-degree oven for 15 to 20 minutes or until tops spring back when touched in center. Frost with confectioners' sugar icing while warm. Wheat germ and sunflower seeds may be added to dough, if desired.

Mrs. Millie Griswold
Lincoln School
Wyandotte, Michigan

SNICKERDOODLES

1/2 c. butter or margarine, softened
1/2 c. shortening
Sugar
2 eggs
1 tsp. vanilla extract
2 1/4 c. sifted flour
2 tsp. cream of tartar
1 tsp. soda
1/4 tsp. salt
3 tbsp. ground cinnamon

Cream butter, shortening, 1 1/2 cup sugar, eggs and vanilla together. Sift flour, cream of

Recipe on page 162.

tartar, soda and salt together. Blend into creamed mixture. Shape rounded teaspoons of dough into balls. Combine 3 tablespoons sugar and cinnamon; roll balls in sugar mixture. Place 2 inches apart on ungreased baking sheets. Bake in preheated 400-degree oven for 8 to 10 minutes or until golden brown. Remove from baking sheets; cool on racks. Yield: About 6 dozen balls.

Mrs. Margaret DeJournette
North Wilkes School
Hays, North Carolina

EASY GRAHAM CRACKER COOKIES

1/2 c. butter
1/2 c. (packed) brown sugar
2 pkg. graham crackers, broken
  into desired sizes
1/2 c. chopped nuts

Melt butter in saucepan. Add brown sugar; stir until dissolved. Place graham crackers flat in jelly roll pan. Spoon brown sugar mixture over crackers. Sprinkle with nuts. Bake in preheated 350-degree oven for about 12 minutes or until bubbly.

Mrs. Fran Heckman
Waupaca High School
Waupaca, Wisconsin

INSTANT COOKIES

1 pkg. desired flavor instant
  pudding mix
3/4 c. Bisquick
1/4 c. corn oil
1 egg

Combine all ingredients in mixing bowl; mix well. Drop by spoonfuls onto ungreased baking sheet; flatten slightly with fork tines. Bake in preheated 375-degree oven for 7 to 8 minutes or until lightly browned. Chopped nuts or colored sugar may be sprinkled on top before baking, if desired.

Mrs. Cal Fleser
Zeeland Middle School
Zeeland, Michigan

121

EASY CAKE BROWNIES
WITH FROSTING

    1 1/2 c. butter
    8 tbsp. cocoa
    2 c. flour
    2 c. sugar
    1/2 tsp. salt
    2 eggs
    1/2 c. sour cream
    1 tsp. soda
    1/4 c. milk
    1 1-lb. box confectioners' sugar
    1/2 c. chopped nuts (opt.)

Melt 1 cup butter in saucepan. Add 4 table-spoons cocoa and 1 cup water; stir until cocoa is dissolved. Sift flour, sugar and salt together; add to cocoa mixture, mixing well. Combine eggs, sour cream and soda; add to flour mixture. Blend well. Pour into greased 9 x 13-inch baking pan. Bake in preheated 375-degree oven for 15 to 18 minutes or until done. Melt remaining 1/2 cup butter in saucepan. Add remaining 4 tablespoons cocoa, milk, confectioners' sugar and nuts. Stir until smooth. Spread over slightly cooled brownies. Cut into squares to serve.

Mrs. Mary C. Belknap
Michigan Center High School
Michigan Center, Michigan

CHOCOLATE QUICKIES

    1/2 c. oil
    4 sq. chocolate
    2 c. sugar
    4 eggs
    2 tsp. vanilla extract
    2 c. flour
    2 tsp. baking powder
    1/2 tsp. salt
    Confectioners' sugar

Place oil and chocolate in saucepan over low heat; stir until chocolate is melted. Add sugar, eggs and vanilla; mix well. Sift flour, baking powder and salt together. Add flour mixture to chocolate mixture gradually, mixing well after each addition. Drop dough by teaspoonfuls into confectioners' sugar; coat well. Shape into balls. Place on lightly greased cookie sheet. Bake in preheated 350-degree oven for about 10 minutes or until done.

Helen Maxwell
Big Sandy Public High School
Big Sandy, Montana

CHOCOLATE SQUARES

    1 15-oz. can sweetened condensed milk
    2 c. graham cracker crumbs
    1 6-oz. package chocolate chips

Combine all ingredients thoroughly. Pour into greased 9-inch square pan. Bake in preheated 350-degree oven for 20 minutes or until done. Cool in pan on rack for 10 minutes. Cut in squares while warm.

Sondra Keener
Solon High School
Solon, Ohio

CHOCOLATE CHIP-SUNFLOWER
SEED COOKIES

    1/2 c. butter or margarine, softened
    1/2 c. (firmly packed) brown sugar
    1 egg
    1/2 tsp. vanilla extract
    1/2 c. sifted whole wheat flour
    1/2 c. toasted wheat germ
    1/2 tsp. soda
    1/2 tsp. salt
    1 6-oz. package chocolate chips
    1/2 c. unsalted sunflower seeds
    1/2 c. flaked coconut

Cream butter, sugar, egg and vanilla until light and fluffy. Sift flour, wheat germ, soda and salt together; add to creamed mixture. Mix until well blended. Stir in chocolate chips, sunflower seeds and coconut. Drop by rounded teaspoonfuls 2 inches apart onto greased cookie sheets. Bake in preheated 350-degree oven for 10 to 12 minutes or until edges are lightly browned. Remove with spatula to wire rack to cool.

Jeanne Williams
Custer City High School
Miles City, Montana

CALIFORNIA WALNUT BROWNIES

1 pkg. brownie mix
Chopped walnuts
1 recipe 1 or 2-egg meringue
Walnut halves

Prepare mix according to package directions, adding 3/4 cup chopped walnuts. Spread in baking pan. Top half the batter with meringue and sprinkle with chopped walnuts. Place walnut halves on remaining batter. Bake according to package directions.

Photograph for this recipe below.

OLD-FASHIONED WALNUT BALLS

1 c. butter or margarine
1/3 c. (firmly packed) brown sugar
1 tsp. vanilla extract
2 c. sifted all-purpose flour
1/2 tsp. salt
2 c. finely chopped California walnuts
Powdered sugar

Cream butter, sugar and vanilla until fluffy. Sift flour and salt together; add to creamed mixture, mixing well to make a soft dough. Stir in walnuts. Break off pieces of dough the size of a walnut and shape into balls. Place on ungreased cookie sheet. Bake in preheated 375-degree oven for 12 to 15 minutes. Remove from cookie sheet with spatula or pancake turner; cool slightly so they won't crumble when handled, then roll in powdered sugar. Yield: 4 dozen.

Photograph for this recipe below.

NO-ROLL SUGAR COOKIES

1 c. sugar
1 c. margarine
1 egg
1 tsp. vanilla extract
2 1/2 c. flour
1 tsp. cream of tartar
1 tsp. soda

Cream sugar, margarine, egg and vanilla together until light and fluffy. Sift flour, cream of tartar and soda together. Add flour mixture to creamed mixture gradually, mixing well after each addition. Pinch off dough; form into walnut-sized balls. Roll balls in additional sugar. Place on greased cookie sheet; flatten with bottom of greased or sugared glass. Bake in preheated 350-degree oven for 10 to 15 minutes or until lightly browned. Dough may be chilled before forming into balls, if desired. Yield: About 3 dozen cookies.

Mrs. Dee Ryan
Edina-West Secondary School
Edina, Minnesota

HIKER'S DELIGHT

1   6-oz. package semisweet chocolate bits
1   6-oz. package butterscotch bits
2 c. granola
1   7 1/2-oz. package salted peanuts
1 c. raisins

Combine chocolate and butterscotch bits in top of double boiler. Cook, stirring, over hot water until melted. Stir in remaining ingredients, mixing well. Drop by teaspoonfuls onto cookie sheet or waxed paper. Chill. Yield: About 4 dozen.

Midge Bean
Centennial Jr. High School
Boulder, Colorado

PEANUT BUTTER BARS

1 c. butter
1 c. peanut butter

1   1-lb. box confectioners' sugar
1/3 lb. graham crackers, crushed
1 1/4 c. semisweet chocolate bits

Combine butter and peanut butter in saucepan. Cook over low heat, stirring, until melted. Combine confectioners' sugar and cracker crumbs in mixing bowl. Add peanut butter mixture; mix well. Spread in 9 x 12-inch baking pan. Melt chocolate bits in saucepan over low heat; spread over peanut butter mixture. Cool until chocolate sets. Cut into squares to serve.

Mrs. Janet Goodwin
Schuyler R-1 Jr. High School
Queen City, Missouri

CHOCOLATE NO-BAKE COOKIES

2 c. sugar
1/4 c. cocoa
1/2 c. milk
1/2 c. butter or margarine
1/2 c. peanut butter
1/2 tsp. vanilla extract
3 c. quick-cooking oatmeal

Combine sugar, cocoa, milk and butter in saucepan. Bring to a boil; boil for 1 minute, stirring constantly. Remove from heat. Stir in remaining ingredients, mixing well. Drop by tablespoonfuls onto waxed paper. Cool.

Sondra Keener
Solon High School
Solon, Ohio

RICE KRISPIES-PEANUT BUTTER BARS

1 c. corn syrup
1 c. sugar
1/2 c. butter or margarine
1 c. peanut butter
7 c. Rice Krispies

Combine syrup, sugar and butter in saucepan; bring to a boil. Reduce heat. Add peanut butter, stirring until melted. Pour peanut butter mixture over Rice Krispies in large mixing bowl. Stir carefully until well mixed. Spread into greased 9 x 13-inch baking pan; press down lightly. Let cool. Cut into bars to serve. Coconut, nuts, chocolate bits or butterscotch bits may be added to mixture, if desired.

Carmen M. Tripp
Minnesota Braille School
Faribault, Minnesota

QUICK AND EASY BARS

1 pkg. miniature marshmallows
1 12-oz. package semisweet chocolate
    bits
1 c. peanut butter
1 c. butter or margarine

Arrange marshmallows in buttered oblong pan. Combine chocolate bits, peanut butter and butter in saucepan. Cook, stirring, over low heat until all ingredients are melted. Pour over marshmallows. Swirl chocolate mixture through marshmallows. Chill.

Betty Jean Herbel
Turtle Mountain Community School
Belcourt, North Dakota

TRAIL COOKIES

8 1/2 c. flour
1 tbsp. salt
2 tbsp. soda
8 c. quick-cooking oats
2 1/2 c. sugar
1 tbsp. ginger
2 c. melted shortening
2 c. light molasses
4 eggs, beaten
3 c. raisins
2 c. chopped nuts

Sift flour, salt and soda together. Add oats and sugar; mix well. Add remaining ingredients and 1/4 cup hot water. Mix well, using hands, if necessary, to form a stiff dough. Divide dough into 3 parts. Roll 1 part out on lightly floured surface to 1/4-inch thickness. Brush with water; sprinkle with additional

sugar. Cut into squares. Place on greased cookie sheets. Bake in preheated 375-degree oven for 8 to 10 minutes or until lightly browned. Cool. Repeat process with remaining 2 parts dough. Wrap and freeze, if desired. One teaspoon each of ginger, cloves and cinnamon may be used instead of 1 tablespoon ginger. One cup each of raisins, dried apricots and chocolate chips may be used instead of 3 cups raisins.

Mrs. Bette Cox
South High School
Denver, Colorado

GRANOLA SWEET TREAT

1/3 c. honey
1/2 c. crunchy peanut butter
1/2 c. nonfat dry milk
1 to 1 1/2 c. granola

Combine honey and peanut butter in mixing bowl until thoroughly mixed. Add milk; mix well. Stir in granola until mixture can be easily handled. Form into small balls.

Mildred B. Goe
Monument High School
Monument, Oregon

SODA CRACKER COOKIES

2 c. sugar
1/2 c. evaporated milk
1/2 c. margarine
1 tsp. vanilla
1/2 c. peanut butter
1 stack pack (or more) soda
    crackers, finely crushed

Combine sugar, milk, margarine and vanilla in saucepan. Bring to a boil; boil for 1 minute, stirring constantly. Remove from heat. Add peanut butter, stirring until melted. Stir in cracker crumbs; mix well. Drop by spoonfuls onto waxed paper. Cool.

Martha C. Chastain
Roy P. Otwell Middle School
Cumming, Georgia

QUICK PEACH COBBLER

1/2 c. soft butter
1 pkg. yellow cake mix
1/2 c. coconut
1 can sliced peaches, drained
1/2 c. sugar
1 tbsp. cinnamon
2 egg yolks
1 c. sour cream

Cut butter into cake mix and coconut until crumbly. Press into bottom of ungreased 9 x 13 x 2-inch baking pan. Bake in pre-heated 350-degree oven for about 10 minutes or until lightly browned. Arrange peaches over crust. Sprinkle with sugar and cinnamon. Blend egg yolks into sour cream. Drizzle over peaches. Bake for 20 minutes longer or until bubbly.

Mrs. Jesse Clausel
Kossuth High School
Kossuth, Mississippi

CHERRY CRUNCH

1/3 c. butter, softened
1 pkg. butter cake mix
1 can cherry pie filling
1 c. chopped nuts
1 c. whipping cream, whipped

Cut butter into cake mix until crumbly. Sprinkle half the cake mixture over bottom of greased and floured oblong baking pan. Spread pie filling over cake mixture. Sprinkle with nuts. Sprinkle remaining cake mixture over nuts. Bake in preheated 375-degree oven for 30 to 35 minutes. Cut into squares. Serve warm with whipped cream.

Mrs. Norine Edwards
Kilbourne High School
Kilbourne, Louisiana

CRUSTY CHERRY DESSERT

1/2 c. butter or margarine, softened
1 1/2 c. flour

3 tbsp. confectioners' sugar
1 3-oz. package vanilla pudding mix
1 3/4 c. milk
1 can cherry pie filling
Whipped cream or ice cream

Combine butter, flour and confectioners' sugar in mixing bowl until the consistency of cornmeal. Pat into lightly greased 9-inch square baking pan. Bake in preheated 350-degree oven for about 15 minutes or until done. Combine pudding mix and milk; cook according to package directions. Spread pudding over crust. Spread pie filling over pudding just before ready to serve. Cut into squares. Serve topped with whipped cream.

Jane Bower
Del Norte High School
Crescent City, California

BASIC PASTRY MIX

12 c. flour
2 tbsp. salt
2 tbsp. sugar
4 c. lard

Combine flour, salt and sugar in large mixing bowl. Work lard into flour mixture with pastry blender until the size of peas. Divide mixture into 3 equal parts. Place in freezer containers. Store in freezer. Add enough cold water to hold mixture together when ready to use. Yield: Dough for 3 double-crust pies.

Kay Caskey
Manogue High School
Reno, Nevada

CRUST FOR FRIED PIES

2 1/2 c. sifted flour
1/3 c. margarine
1/2 tsp. salt
2 tsp. baking powder
1 tbsp. sugar
1 egg
1 c. (scant) evaporated milk

Combine flour and margarine in mixing bowl until crumbly. Add remaining ingredients, using enough evaporated milk to hold mixture together. Turn out onto lightly floured cloth; knead lightly. Roll out to desired thickness. Cut in desired shapes. Spoon favorite filling into center of each piece. Dampen edges; fold over. Press edges together with fork tines. Prick tops. Fry in deep 350-degree oil until brown on each side, turning once. Drain on absorbent toweling.

Audrey V. Craig
Divide High School
Nolan, Texas

QUICK BLUEBERRY CHIFFON PIE

Vanilla wafers
2   3 3/4-oz. packages orange deluxe
    dessert mix
3/4 c. cold water
3/4 c. light cream
2 c. blueberries
2 egg whites
1/4 c. sugar

Line bottom and side of 9-inch pie pan with vanilla wafers. Prepare dessert mix according to package directions using water and cream. Fold in blueberries. Beat egg whites until stiff. Beat in sugar, 1 tablespoon at a time until mixture is stiff and glossy. Spoon filling into pie shell. Chill until firm.

Photograph for this recipe below.

COTTAGE CHEESE-LEMON PIE

1   12-oz. carton cottage cheese
2 c. milk
1/4 c. sugar
1 pkg. instant lemon pudding mix
1   9-in. baked pie crust

Beat cottage cheese, 1/2 cup milk and sugar together lightly. Add remaining 1 1/2 cups milk and pudding mix. Beat for 1 minute. Pour into pie crust. Chill until ready to serve.

Mrs. Rhonda Ward
Old Glory Rural High School
Old Glory, Texas

APPLE CRUMB DELIGHT

2 1/2 c. Bisquick
1/2 c. sugar
6 tbsp. soft butter
1/3 c. milk
1 can apple pie filling
1/2 tsp. cinnamon

Combine Bisquick, sugar and butter in mixing bowl until crumbly. Reserve 1 cup for topping. Add milk to remaining crumb mixture; mix well. Press dough into 8-inch pie plate. Top with pie filling. Sprinkle with cinnamon. Top with reserved crumb mixture. Bake in preheated 350-degree oven for about 15 minutes or until crumbs are lightly browned.

Maxine Cowan
Pipkin Jr. High School
Springfield, Missouri

GERMAN CHOCOLATE PIE

1 c. sugar
1 tbsp. cornstarch
2 tbsp. flour
2 tbsp. cocoa
Pinch of salt
2/3 c. milk
2 eggs, slightly beaten
3 tbsp. margarine
3/4 c. coconut
1/2 tsp. vanilla
1/3 c. chopped pecans
1 9-in. unbaked pie shell

Combine first 5 ingredients in mixing bowl; mix well. Add remaining ingredients except pecans and pie shell. Mix well. Stir in pecans. Pour into pie shell. Bake in preheated 400-degree oven for 30 minutes or until set.

Mrs. Linda C. Griffin
Gayle Middle School
Falmouth, Virginia

GRAHAM CRACKER PIE

4 egg whites
1 tsp. vanilla extract

Pinch of salt
1 c. sugar
1 c. graham cracker crumbs
1/2 c. chopped pecans
1 med. carton whipped topping

Beat egg whites, vanilla and salt with electric mixer until soft peaks form. Add sugar gradually, beating until stiff peaks form. Fold in cracker crumbs and pecans. Pour into greased and floured 9-inch pie pan. Bake in preheated 350-degree oven for 30 minutes. Cool. Spread with whipped topping.

Sandy Galvan
Riley Middle School
San Antonio, Texas

TOASTED COCONUT PIE

1 1/4 c. coconut
1/2 c. evaporated milk
1 c. sugar
1/4 c. butter
3 eggs
1 tsp. vanilla extract
1 9-in. unbaked pie shell

Combine coconut and milk in bowl, mixing well. Set aside. Cream sugar and butter until light and fluffy. Add eggs and vanilla; beat well. Add coconut mixture; mix well. Pour into pie shell. Bake in preheated 350-degree oven for 30 minutes or until set.

Mrs. Juanita Pitts
Linden-Kildare High School
Linden, Texas

MIRACLE PIE

3 egg whites
1 c. sugar
1 tsp. baking powder
1 tsp. vanilla extract
3/4 c. chopped walnuts
26 Ritz crackers, crushed

Beat egg whites until stiff peaks form. Fold in sugar, baking powder, vanilla, walnuts and cracker crumbs. Pour into buttered glass pie plate. Bake in preheated 325-degree oven for 30 minutes. Garnish with whipped cream.

Ginny Holmes
Penquis Valley High School
Milo, Maine

LEMONADE PIE

1 can frozen lemonade
1 can sweetened condensed milk
1 lg. carton Cool Whip
1 graham cracker crust

Mash lemonade with fork in mixing bowl. Add condensed milk and Cool Whip. Mix well. Pour into pie shell. Garnish with graham cracker crumbs or chopped nuts, if desired. Refrigerate until ready to serve.

Mrs. Mary E. Cantwell
Mt. Markham High School
West Winfield, New York

CRUNCHY CHEESE PUDDING

1/2 c. Grape Nuts
2 tbsp. brown sugar
2 tbsp. melted butter or margarine
1 3 3/4-oz. package instant lemon
   pudding mix
1 c. cottage cheese
2 c. milk

Combine Grape Nuts, brown sugar and butter in mixing bowl; set aside. Combine pudding mix and cottage cheese, stirring until well blended. Add milk, stirring for about 1 minute or until thickened. Place alternate layers of pudding and Grape Nuts mixture in serving dish or individual dishes. Chill. Yield: 6 servings.

Mrs. Virginia T. Bond
Scott High School
Madison, West Virginia

DADDY'S CHOCOLATE PUDDING

2/3 c. sugar
1/4 c. cocoa

6 tbsp. flour
Dash of salt
2 c. milk
2 egg yolks
2 tbsp. butter or margarine
1 tsp. vanilla extract

Combine sugar, cocoa, flour and salt in saucepan. Add enough milk to make a smooth paste. Add egg yolks; beat well. Stir in remaining milk and butter. Bring to a slow boil over medium heat, stirring constantly; boil for 2 to 3 minutes. Remove from heat. Stir in vanilla. Pour into serving dish. Chill.

Mrs. Gladys Olson
Monmouth High School
Monmouth, Illinois

BASIC PUDDING MIX

2 1/2 c. powdered skim milk or nonfat
   dry milk
1 1/2 c. sugar
1 1/4 c. flour
1 tsp. salt
1 tbsp. margarine
1 egg, well beaten
3/4 tsp. vanilla extract

Sift powdered milk, sugar, flour and salt together. May store in tightly covered container in cool place until ready to use. Combine 1 1/4 cups pudding mix and 2 1/2 cups warm water in top of double boiler. Cook over boiling water, stirring constantly, until thickened. Reduce heat. Cook over simmering water for 10 minutes longer, stirring constantly. Remove from heat. Add margarine. Stir in egg slowly. Return to heat. Cook for 1 minute longer, stirring constantly. Remove from heat. Stir in vanilla. Pour into individual serving dishes. May add 2 cups cooked rice or 1 cup flaked coconut to cooked pudding or 3/4 cup cocoa to pudding mix, if desired.

Elsie Klassen
Georges P. Vanier School
Tohigo, Alberta, Canada
Barbara H. Thompson
Tom Bean High School
Tom Bean, Texas

130

American families are becoming increasingly aware of the need to adjust their diets and eating habits to modern life. Physically, we are less active, so we cut our calorie intake. But, our bodies still require plenty of nutrition to function at their healthiest. In order to get the most nutrition from the fewest calories, menus must be planned thoughtfully.

Typically, the label "low-calorie" immediately turns people off. It brings to mind a dreadfully barren dish, with little flavor, aroma, texture or appetite appeal. But, luckily, with weight consciousness becoming so important in American life, nutritionists in the Home Economics field have devoted more time to developing delicious low-calorie dishes that are not boring or dreadful.

This has been done mostly through "de-calorizing" traditional recipes, and by taking greater advantage of the newly developed low-calorie sweeteners, margarines, cheeses, and beverages. And most importantly, these "de-calorized" recipes taste great — and in some ways, maybe better. They are lighter, and often lower in fat, cholesterol or carbohydrates.

Home Economics Teachers have developed many of these recipes personally, carefully keeping the calories low, and the taste appeal and nutrition high. For example, you can dine *delightfully* on *Indoor-Outdoor Chicken, Spinach Souffle* and *Strawberry Bavarian* for approximately 400 calories! Each of these calorie conscious recipes is a "life-saver" in every sense of the word.

Low-Calorie

LOW-CAL COTTAGE CHEESE-FRUIT SALAD

1 3-oz. package flavored gelatin
1 1-lb. can desired fruit
1 lg. carton cottage cheese
1 lg. carton Cool Whip
1/2 c. toasted slivered almonds (opt.)

Mix gelatin with undrained fruit; heat until gelatin is melted, stirring frequently. Chill until thickened. Fold in cottage cheese, Cool Whip and almonds; place in mold. Refrigerate until firm. May garnish with drained maraschino cherries or other fruits, if desired.

Mrs. Alice Applegate
Knoxville Sr. High School
Knoxville, Iowa

LOW-CALORIE MOLDED SALAD

2 env. unflavored gelatin
1 16-oz. bottle diet lemon-lime carbonated drink
1 3-oz. package cream cheese
1 tbsp. lemon juice
1/2 tsp. salt
1 c. fruit juice
2 c. chopped fruits or vegetables

Sprinkle gelatin over 1 cup carbonated drink in small saucepan. Place over low heat for about 3 minutes or until gelatin is dissolved, stirring constantly. Remove from heat. Add cream cheese; stir until smooth. Add lemon juice and salt; mix well. Add fruit juice, remaining carbonated drink and fruits; pour into mold or serving dishes. Chill until partially set; stir until mixed. Chill until firm. Carrots, celery, apples, cabbage, lettuce or other fruits or vegetables may be used in recipe.

Hazel Marsh
Marion High School
Marion, Michigan

TRIPLE BEAN SALAD
(About 61 calories per serving)

1 1-lb. can undrained French-style beans
1 1-lb. can undrained wax beans
1 1-lb. can undrained red kidney beans
1 med. onion, thinly sliced
1/4 c. chopped green pepper (opt.)
1/4 c. sugar
1 tsp. celery salt or celery seed
1/2 tsp. monosodium glutamate (opt.)
1/2 tsp. salt
1/2 tsp. pepper
3/4 c. cider vinegar
1 tbsp. soy sauce

Combine all ingredients in large mixing bowl; cover. Chill overnight. Drain well just before serving; toss lightly. Serve immediately. Yield: 10 servings.

Mrs. Larry L. Clark
Cowley County Community College
Arkansas City, Kansas

OLD-FASHIONED TUNA SALAD

1/2 7 1/2-oz. can tuna, drained and flaked
1/4 c. chopped onion
1/4 c. chopped celery
2 tbsp. capers
1 tbsp. mayonnaise
Lettuce leaves
1 med. tomato, quartered

Combine tuna, onion, celery, capers and mayonnaise in bowl; mix well. Serve on lettuce; garnish with tomato quarters. Yield: 1 serving.

Mrs. Barbara Goedicke
Lindsay Thurber Comprehensive High School
Red Deer, Alberta, Canada

SUMMER SALAD

1 box macaroni and cheese dinner
1 7-oz. can tuna or salmon, drained and flaked
1 c. diced cucumbers
1 c. shredded carrots
1/3 c. sliced ripe olives

1/4 c. finely chopped onion
1 8-oz. bottle low-calorie Thousand
Island dressing

Prepare macaroni and cheese dinner according to package directions. Add remaining ingredients; mix lightly. Chill. Serve in green peppers, if desired.

Mrs. Greg Volkmer
Hemingford High School
Hemingford, Nebraska

PICKLE-CAULIFLOWER MEDLEY
(About 28 calories per serving)

1 med. head cauliflower
1 c. dill pickle liquid
1 sm. clove of garlic, crushed
1/4 tsp. liquid artificial sweetener
1/4 c. chopped onion
4 med. dill pickles, quartered
1/4 c. sliced radishes

Separate cauliflower into flowerets; there should be about 1 quart. Cook cauliflowerets in boiling salted water for 6 or 7 minutes or until crisp-tender; drain. Blend pickle liquid, garlic, sweetener and onion in shallow dish; add cauliflower, pickles and radishes. Toss lightly until vegetables are coated. Cover; chill for at least 12 hours, turning occasionally. Drain before serving.

Photograph for this recipe on page 130.

SOUR CREAM DELIGHT

2/3 c. cottage cheese
1/4 tsp. salt
1 tsp. lemon juice
1/4 c. (about) water or buttermilk

Place all ingredients in blender container; process until smooth, adding enough water for desired thickness. May be refrigerated for 4 to 5 days.

Sherry Fay
Sycamore High School
Sycamore, Illinois

RATATOUILLE SAVANNAH

2 lg. cloves of garlic, minced
1/3 c. olive oil
1/2 tsp. marjoram
1/2 tsp. oregano
1/4 tsp. dillweed
2 tsp. salt
1/8 tsp. freshly ground pepper
Dash of Tabasco sauce
2 10-oz. packages frozen sliced yellow
    summer squash, partially thawed
1 med. eggplant, peeled and cubed
1 c. thinly sliced Bermuda onion
2 green peppers, cut in slivers
4 med. firm-ripe tomatoes, peeled and
    sliced

Combine garlic, olive oil and seasonings; let stand to blend flavors. Arrange vegetables in layers in buttered 2 1/2 or 3-quart casserole, beginning and ending with squash and sprinkling each vegetable layer with seasoning mixture. Cover. Bake in preheated 350-degree oven for 1 hour. Uncover; sprinkle with additional freshly ground pepper. Bake for 15 minutes longer. Serve hot or cold. Yield: 6 servings.

Photograph for this recipe below.

LOW-CAL ROQUEFORT DRESSING
(About 12 calories per tablespoon)

1/4 c. skim milk
1/2 sm. clove of garlic
Dash of freshly ground pepper
2/3 c. cottage cheese
1 oz. Roquefort cheese

Place all ingredients in bowl; mix well. Remove garlic clove.

Mrs. Evelyn Grabowski
Plant City Sr. High School
Plant City, Florida

LOW-CALORIE SALAD DRESSING

1 c. buttermilk
1 c. mayonnaise
1 tbsp. parsley flakes
1/2 tsp. onion powder
1/2 tsp. garlic powder
1 tsp. seasoned salt
1 tsp. monosodium glutamate
1/2 tsp. coarsely ground pepper

Combine all ingredients in small mixing bowl; beat until well blended. Refrigerate until chilled.

Pauline Brown
Western Area Vo-Tech School
Lone Wolf, Oklahoma

SLIM VEGETABLE SOUP
(About 33 calories per serving)

6 c. water
6 beef bouillon cubes
2 c. canned tomatoes
1 tsp. sugar
1/2 c. chopped onion
2 c. chopped celery
2 c. diced carrots
2 c. shredded cabbage
Salt and pepper to taste

Place water, bouillon cubes and tomatoes in kettle; bring to a boil. Add sugar and remain-
ing ingredients; bring to a boil again. Cover; reduce heat. Simmer until vegetables are tender. Yield: About twelve 1/2-cup servings.

Marjorie Harris
Greeley Public School
Greeley, Nebraska

BARBECUED CHICKEN
(277 calories per serving)

1/2 c. cold water
1 med. onion, chopped
1/4 c. catsup
2 tbsp. vinegar
1 tsp. salt
1/4 c. sugar
1 tsp. Worcestershire sauce
1 tsp. prepared mustard
1/4 tsp. pepper
1   2 1/2-lb. frying chicken, quartered

Combine all ingredients except chicken in small mixing bowl; mix well. Place chicken in shallow baking dish; pour sauce over chicken. Cover; marinate at room tempera-ture for several hours or in refrigerator over-night, turning occasionally. Remove chicken, reserving marinade; place on broiler pan, skin side up. Bake in preheated 400-degree oven for about 1 hour until tender, brushing with reserved marinade every 15 minutes. Do not turn chicken. Chicken may also be grilled over hot coals and basted with mari-nade. Yield: 4 servings.

Mrs. Larry L. Clark
Cowley County Community College
Arkansas City, Kansas

CHICKEN IN YOGURT GRAVY
(250 calories per serving)

2   15-oz. chicken breasts, split
1   4-oz. can sliced mushrooms
1/2 c. tomato puree
1/2 onion, quartered
2 tbsp. fresh parsley
1/2 tsp. thyme
1 tsp. salt

1/4 tsp. pepper
1/2 c. low-calorie yogurt

Cook chicken in Teflon skillet until brown; drain off fat. Drain mushrooms; reserve liquid. Place tomato puree, reserved mushroom liquid, onion, parsley, thyme, salt and pepper in blender container; process until onion is chopped. Add to chicken; cover. Simmer for 40 to 45 minutes or until chicken is tender, stirring occasionally. Reduce heat. Add yogurt and mushrooms; stir until heated through. Do not boil. Yield: 4 servings.

Linda McKissack
J. J. Pearce High School
Richardson, Texas

INDOOR-OUTDOOR CHICKEN

1/2 c. tomato juice
1/4 c. water
1 tsp. basil leaves
1/4 tsp. Tabasco sauce
1 tbsp. Worcestershire sauce
1 c. vinegar
1 tsp. salt
1/2 tsp. pepper
1/2 tsp. instant onion flakes
1/2 tsp. oregano
2 or 3 chicken breasts, skinned

Boil tomato juice until reduced to 1/4 cup; stir in remaining ingredients except chicken. Place chicken in shallow baking pan; pour marinade over chicken. Marinate for 2 hours. Bake chicken in marinade in preheated 425-degree oven for 1 hour or until done. Chicken may be grilled over charcoal, if desired.

Mrs. Marilyn King
Lakeside School
Norwalk, California

CREAMED TUNA AND EGGS

2 c. fine bread crumbs
1 egg, well beaten

1 tbsp. water
1 tsp. onion salt
1/2 tsp. celery flakes
2 tbsp. onion flakes
1/4 c. chopped celery
1 c. green peas
1/4 c. beef bouillon
2 c. evaporated skim milk
1   7 1/2-oz. can tuna, drained and
    flaked
3 hard-cooked eggs, chopped

Place bread crumbs, beaten egg, water, onion salt and celery flakes in bowl; mix well. Divide into 4 parts; shape each portion into 2-inch square on Teflon baking sheet. Bake in preheated 325-degree oven for 10 minutes or until lightly browned; remove from baking sheet. Combine onion flakes, chopped celery, peas and bouillon in saucepan; cook, covered, over moderate heat for 8 minutes or until vegetables are just tender. Add milk, tuna and hard-cooked eggs; cook over low heat until heated through. Spoon onto 4 serving plates; top each serving with toast square.

Mrs. Barbara Goedicke
Lindsay Thurber Comprehensive High School
Red Deer, Alberta, Canada

TUNA SNACKS

1   7-oz. can water-packed tuna
2 tbsp. finely chopped celery
2 tbsp. lemon juice
1/2 tsp. Worcestershire sauce
Salt to taste
1 tsp. finely chopped onion (opt.)
1   3-oz. package cream cheese, softened
1/2 c. finely snipped parsley

Drain and flake tuna. Add celery, lemon juice, Worcestershire sauce, salt, onion and cream cheese; blend well. Shape into small balls; roll in parsley. Cover tightly with plastic wrap; chill for about 2 hours. Serve with cocktail picks. Yield: About 40 balls.

Alicia Flores
Taft High School
Taft, Texas

BARBECUED SHRIMP KABOBS

  1 lb. shrimp in shells
  12 whole tiny onions
  4 slices bacon, quartered
  1 green pepper, cut in 1 1/2-in. squares
  Baja Barbecue Sauce

Peel shrimp, leaving last section of tail intact. Devein under cold running water. Add onions to enough boiling salted water to generously cover; bring water back to boiling point. Boil for 8 minutes. Drain onions in colander; cut off ends. Slip onions out of skins. Fold each quarter piece of bacon in half. Alternate bacon on skewers with shrimp, onions and green pepper squares. Press ends of each piece of bacon against shrimp and onion, but leave ends of skewers free of bacon because bacon tends to char. Arrange skewers on barbecue grill; brush liberally with Baja Barbecue Sauce. Broil over moderately hot coals for 5 minutes on each side, brushing frequently with sauce. Add cherry tomato to each skewer last few minutes of cooking, if desired. Yield: 4 servings.

Baja Barbecue Sauce

  1 c. catsup
  1/2 c. brown sugar
  1/2 c. beer
  1/2 c. red wine vinegar
  1/2 c. chili sauce
  1/3 c. lemon juice
  2 tbsp. dry mustard
  3 tbsp. bottled thick steak sauce
  2 tsp. coarsely ground pepper
  2 tsp. salad oil
  1 tsp. soy sauce

Combine all ingredients thoroughly. Pour into jars to store. The sauce will keep for several weeks at room temperature or several months in refrigerator. Use to baste skewered shrimp or meat. Yield: About 3 cups.

Photograph for this recipe on cover.

STARTING CHARCOAL

Charcoal fires sometimes defy even the most determined incendiary efforts. For guaranteed results when camping or barbecuing, save all used cardboard egg cartons. Place a charcoal briquette in each section of the egg carton. Squirt the charcoal with lighter fluid. Close the egg carton; place carton in grill. The lighted carton will ignite the charcoal and continue burning long enough to start all 12 pieces.

Margaret M. Ekstrom
New Prairie High School
New Carlisle, Indiana

SPINACH SOUFFLE
(115 calories)

  1 c. chopped spinach
  2 tbsp. chopped onion
  1/4 c. cottage cheese
  1 egg white, well beaten

Cook spinach and onion in saucepan over low heat until spinach is tender, stirring frequently; drain well. Stir in cottage cheese; fold in egg white. Pour into ungreased small baking pan. Bake in preheated 350-degree oven for 20 to 25 minutes or until done.

Mrs. Virginia T. Bond
Scott High School
Madison, West Virginia

LOW-CAL MEAT LOAF

  2 eggs, slightly beaten
  1 1/2 lb. lean hamburger
  1 onion, finely chopped
  1/2 c. finely chopped celery
  1/4 c. chopped dill pickle
  1/4 c. chopped parsley
  1 tsp. salt
  1/4 tsp. pepper
  1 tsp. Worcestershire sauce
  2 4-oz. cans tomato sauce

1/2 tsp. prepared mustard
2 tbsp. vinegar
1 tbsp. honey

Place eggs, hamburger, onion, celery, dill pickle, parsley, salt, pepper, Worcestershire sauce and 1 can tomato sauce in bowl; mix well. Shape into loaf; place in shallow baking pan. Mix remaining 1 can tomato sauce, mustard, vinegar and honey in bowl; pour over loaf. Bake in preheated 350-degree oven for 1 hour or until done.

Mrs. Linda Anderson
Somonauk High School
Somonauk, Illinois

STEAMED BEEF BALL FLOWERS

1 slice stale bread
1/4 c. buttermilk
2 lb. ground lean beef
1 lg. onion, chopped
1/2 c. sliced celery tops
2 tsp. dillweed
1/2 tsp. thyme
1/2 tsp. marjoram
1/2 tsp. tarragon
1 clove of garlic, crushed
2 tsp. salt
1/2 tsp. pepper

3 eggs, lightly beaten
1 head cauliflower
6 carrots
1/4 c. chopped parsley
1 tbsp. paprika

Soak bread in buttermilk. Combine beef, bread mixture, vegetables, herbs, seasonings and eggs; mix well. Shape into 6 balls. Separate cauliflower into flowerets with rather pointed stems; poke into balls to simulate small heads of cauliflower. Place in large pan; add carrots and about 3 inches boiling water. Cover; simmer for 30 minutes, adding water as needed. Sprinkle with parsley and paprika before serving. Yield: 6 servings.

Photograph for this recipe on this page.

SPANISH NOODLES
(200 calories per serving)

1 1/2 c. sliced celery
1 lb. lean ground beef
1 med. onion, finely chopped
1 green pepper, diced
1/4 lb. noodles
2 c. chopped tomatoes or tomato juice
1 8-oz. can tomato sauce
1 1/2 tsp. salt
1/4 tsp. pepper
1 tsp. seasoned salt

Cook celery in 1 cup salted water until tender-crisp; do not drain. Cook ground beef in frying pan until meat loses red color; drain off fat. Add onion, celery and green pepper; mix well. Stir in uncooked noodles, tomatoes, tomato sauce, salt, pepper and seasoned salt; cover. Cook over low heat for about 30 minutes or until of desired consistency and flavors are well blended. One-fourth cup catsup and 2/3 cup water may be substituted for tomato sauce. Yield: 6 servings.

Mrs. Gloria J. Smith
Valders High School
Valders, Wisconsin

137

CHEWY GRANOLA MUFFINS

1 c. granola
1 c. old-fashioned rolled oats
1/2 c. Bisquick
1/4 c. Sugartwin or sugar
1/2 c. raisins
1/4 c. chopped pecans or mixed nuts
1/4 c. cooking oil
2 eggs, beaten
2/3 c. milk

Mix first 6 ingredients in large bowl. Add oil, eggs and milk; stir until just moistened. Fill greased muffin tins 2/3 full. Bake in preheated 425-degree oven for 15 to 20 minutes or until done; serve warm or cold.

Carline Cuttrell
West Lamar High School
Petty, Texas

DIET APPLE PANCAKE

1 slice bread, crumbled
1 egg
1/3 c. instant nonfat dry milk
1 tbsp. water
Artificial sweetener to equal 2 tsp. sugar
Cinnamon to taste
1 apple, grated

Combine all ingredients except apple; blend until well moistened. Stir in 1/4 of the apple; pour into nonstick or seasoned cast-iron skillet. Sprinkle remaining 3/4 of the apple over batter. Cook over medium-low heat until brown. Turn; cook until brown. Serve with diet margarine and diet syrup.

Elaine Pugh
Hugoton High School
Hugoton, Kansas

APRICOT-PINEAPPLE KUCHEN
(123 calories per serving)

1   10-count pkg. flaky-style
     refrigerator biscuits
1   16-oz. can water-packed apricot
     halves, drained
1 c. unsweetened pineapple tidbits,
6 tbsp. sugar

1 tsp. grated lemon peel
1/4 tsp. ground cinnamon
3/4 c. low-calorie sour cream
1 egg, beaten

Flatten biscuits in 13 x 9 x 2-inch baking pan, sealing edges together; build up edges around pan slightly. Bake in preheated 350-degree oven for 5 minutes. Cut apricot halves into quarters. Combine apricots, pineapple, 1/4 cup sugar, lemon peel and cinnamon; toss lightly. Spoon over biscuits. Blend sour cream with egg and remaining 2 tablespoons sugar; drizzle over apricot mixture. Bake for 20 minutes longer.

Kathleen Burchett, Area Supervisor
Southwest Area of Home Economics
Jonesville, Virginia

BREAKFAST BARS
(145 calories per bar)

1/2 c. butter or margarine
3 c. miniature marshmallows
1/2 c. peanut butter
1/2 c. instant nonfat dry milk
1/4 c. orange-flavored breakfast drink
1 c. raisins
4 c. Cheerios or other breakfast cereal

Melt butter and marshmallows in large saucepan over low heat, stirring constantly; stir in peanut butter until mixed. Stir in milk and breakfast drink; fold in raisins and Cheerios, stirring until evenly coated. Place in buttered 9 x 9 x 2-inch pan; pat evenly with buttered fingers. Cool thoroughly. Cut into 1 1/2 x 1-inch bars.

Mildred B. Goe
Monument High School
Monument, Oregon

FRUIT SHERBET SURPRISE
(80 calories per serving)

1   3-oz. package fruit-flavored gelatin
1/2 c. sugar
1 1/2 c. boiling water
1 c. buttermilk
1 tsp. grated lemon rind
3 tbsp. lemon juice
1 egg white

Combine gelatin and sugar in mixing bowl. Add boiling water; stir until dissolved. Stir in buttermilk, lemon rind and lemon juice; pour into 4-cup refrigerator tray. Freeze until almost firm. Break into chunks; place in mixing bowl. Beat with electric mixer until smooth. Beat egg white until stiff peaks form; fold into gelatin mixture. Spoon back into refrigerator tray; freeze until firm.

Mrs. Fran Heckman
Waupaca High School
Waupaca, Wisconsin

BLUEBERRY-LIME IMPERIAL
(About 100 calories per serving)

1 1/2 c. reconstituted frozen limeade
1 env. low-calorie lime-flavored gelatin
1 env. low-calorie whipped topping mix
1 c. fresh or frozen unsweetened
    blueberries

Pour 1 cup limeade into saucepan; bring to a boil. Remove from heat. Dissolve gelatin in hot limeade; stir in remaining 1/2 cup limeade. Chill until slightly thickened. Place bowl in larger bowl of ice and water; beat with electric mixer until about doubled in volume. Prepare topping mix according to package directions; fold into gelatin mixture. Fold in blueberries. Turn into a lightly oiled 4 or 5-cup mold; chill until firm. Combinations of other gelatins and berries may be substituted for lime gelatin and blueberries.

Mrs. J. Hal Nave, Jr.
Fulton High School
Knoxville, Tennessee

STRAWBERRY BAVARIAN
(35 calories per serving)

1 env. low-calorie strawberry gelatin
1/2 c. hot diet Dr. Pepper
1/2 c. cold diet Dr. Pepper
1/2 c. Special Whipped Topping

Mix gelatin and hot Dr. Pepper until gelatin is dissolved; stir in cold Dr. Pepper. Chill until slightly thickened; whip until frothy. Add Special Whipped Topping; beat until well mixed. Pour into serving dishes; chill until firm. Yield: 4 servings.

Special Whipped Topping

1/2 c. cold diet Dr. Pepper
1 2 1/4-oz. envelope dessert topping mix
Vanilla extract to taste (opt.)

Pour Dr. Pepper into mixing bowl. Add dessert topping mix; stir. Beat until soft peaks form; add vanilla. May be used as substitute for whipped cream. One tablespoon is approximately 14 calories.

Mrs. Sharon A. Sharp
J. J. Pearce High School
Richardson, Texas

RUSSIAN TEA MIX
(Hot tea, 2 calories per serving; iced tea, 4 calories per serving)

1 24-oz. package unsweetened lemonade
    or orangeade soft drink mix
1 tsp. (or less) ground cinnamon
1/4 tsp. ground cloves
1/3 c. granular sugar substitute

Place all ingredients in jar; cover. Shake gently to mix thoroughly. For hot tea, place 1 rounded teaspoon mix in cup; fill with boiling water. Stir until mixed. For iced tea, place 2 rounded teaspoons mix in tall glass; fill with cold water and ice. Stir until mixed.

Kathleen Burchett
Assistant State Supervisor
Home Economics Education
Bristol, Virginia

PAMPERED AMBROSIA
(130 calories per serving)

1 1/2 c. Florida orange sections
1 1/2 c. Florida grapefruit sections
10 strawberries, cut in half
3 tbsp. shredded coconut
2 tbsp. honey

Combine all ingredients in crepe pan or skillet; mix gently. Warm over Sterno canned heat for 3 to 5 minutes. Yield: 4 servings.

Photograph for this recipe on page 119.

In this modern age of instant communication and instant transportation, no one appreciates "instant" more than a busy homemaker — especially when it comes to preparing meals. Every homemaker has dreamed of the day when she could serve her family delicious, well-balanced meals without spending hours cooking over a hot stove. Now, thanks to the microwave oven, you don't have to dream anymore.

One of the most time and energy-saving devices on the market today, the microwave oven, has opened the door to carefree cooking in minutes. And, there's no limit to the number of truly delicious dishes that can be prepared in it. Everything from appetizers to desserts and omelets to casseroles come out looking and tasting as if they took hours to prepare and cook when they required only minutes.

Because microwave cooking is such a relatively new way of preparing food, more recipes are being developed everyday. Home Economics Teachers are constantly researching and after testing many of these recipes in their own kitchens, have selected those perfected for homemakers like you.

Recipes such as *Basic Meat Loaf* that is done in 15 to 17 minutes and *Easy Microwave Fudge* that's ready to eat in 2 minutes are just two examples of what this category has to offer. *Banana-Raspberry Flambe, Fun-Do-Fondue* and *Delicious Stuffed Fish* — the list goes on and on.

To be sure, a microwave oven cannot possibly meet all of your cooking needs. But, as a supplementary cooking utensil, it is very desirable. Why not let these microwave oven recipes come to your rescue today!

MICROWAVE OVEN

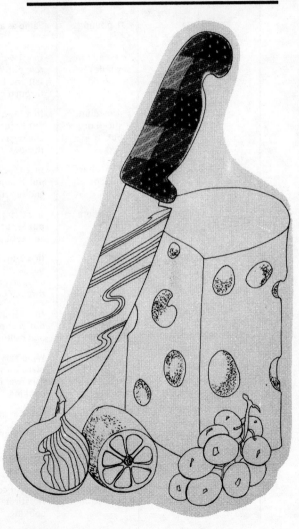

FRESH VEGETABLE COOKING CHART

Vegetable	Amount	Procedure for Cooking	Time
Asparagus	16 (4") pieces	In a 1½-qt. covered casserole put ½ cup water, ½ tsp. salt and asparagus. Stir once halfway through cooking.	6 to 9 min.
Beans, wax green	1 pound 1 " pieces	In a 1½-qt. covered casserole put ½ cup water, ½ tsp. salt and beans. Stir once halfway through cooking.	9 to 11 min.
	2 pound 1 " pieces	Same as above except increase water to ¾ cup.	15 to 20 min.
Lima Beans	1 pound	Same as above.	7 to 8 min.
Beets	4 medium whole	In a 1½-qt. covered casserole put ½ cup water, ½ tsp. salt and beets. Stir halfway through cooking.	15 to 17 min.
Beets	4 medium sliced or cubed	In a 1½-qt. covered casserole put ½ cup water, ½ tsp. salt, and beets. Stir once halfway through cooking.	7 to 10 min.
Broccoli	1 medium bunch	In a 1½-qt. covered casserole put ½ cup water, ½ tsp. salt, and broccoli.	8 to 10 min.
Cabbage	1 medium head	In a 1½-qt. covered casserole put ½ cup water, ½ tsp. salt, and cabbage.	8 to 10 min.
Carrots	6-8 sticks	In a 2-qt. covered casserole put ¼ cup water, ½ tsp. salt, and carrots. Stir halfway through cooking.	10 to 15 min.
Cauliflower	1 medium head	In a 1½-qt. covered casserole put ½ cup water, ½ tsp. salt, and cauliflower.	10 to 12 min.
Corn on the Cob	2 ears	Wrap ears in plastic wrap and place on shelf of oven. Turn ears over halfway through cooking.	4 to 6 min.
	4 ears	Same as above.	6 to 8 min.
Eggplant	1 (14 to 16 oz.) whole, not pared	Wrap eggplant in plastic wrap and place on oven shelf. Turn eggplant over halfway through cooking.	8 to 10 min.
Onions	4 medium, quartered	Place in covered casserole to fit, stir halfway through cooking.	11 to 13 min.
Peas	2 pounds, shelled	In a 1½-qt. covered casserole put ¼ cup water, ¼ tsp. salt, and peas. Stir halfway through cooking.	7 to 10 min.

FRESH VEGETABLE COOKING CHART

Vegetable	Amount	Procedure for Cooking	Time
Potatoes		See recipe this section.	
Spinach	1 pound	Put spinach in a 2-qt. covered casserole. Stir halfway through cooking.	6 to 8 min.
Squash		See recipe this section.	
Squash, Summer Zucchini and etc.	1 pound, sliced or cubed	In a 1½-qt. covered casserole put ¼ cup water, ½ tsp. salt, and 2 tbsp. butter.	10 to 14 min.

FROZEN VEGETABLE COOKING CHART

Vegetable	Quantity	Container	Special Instructions	Time
Asparagus	10 oz.	1-qt. glass casserole	Separate after 3 min., casserole should be covered.	5 to 6 min.
Broccoli	10 oz.	1-qt. glass casserole	Separate after 4 min., casserole should be covered.	8 to 9 min.
Beans, green cut, or wax French cut	10 oz.	1-qt. glass casserole	Add 2 tsp. hot water, stir, and cover.	7 to 8 min.
Beans, lima fordhook	10 oz.	1-qt. glass casserole	Add ¼ cup hot water, stir after 5 minutes in covered casserole.	7 to 8 min.
Cauliflower	10 oz.	1-qt. glass casserole	Add 2 tbsp. hot water, cook covered.	5 to 6 min.
Corn, cut	10 oz.	1-qt. glass casserole	Add ¼ cup hot water, cook covered.	4 to 5 min.
Corn, cob	2 ears	1-qt. glass casserole	Add ¼ cup hot water, turn after 3 minutes, cook covered.	5 to 6 min.
Mixed Vegetables	10 oz.	1-qt. glass casserole	Add ¼ cup hot water, cook covered.	6 to 7 min.
Okra	10 oz.	1-qt. glass casserole	Add 2 tbsp. hot water, cook covered.	6 to 7 min.
Peas, green	10 oz.	1-qt. glass casserole	Add 2 tbsp. hot water, cook covered.	4 to 5 min.
Peas & Carrots	10 oz.	1-qt. glass casserole	Add 2 tbsp. hot water, stir after 3 minutes, cook covered.	5 to 6 min.
Spinach	10 oz.	1-qt. glass casserole	Use covered casserole.	4 to 5 min.

MEAT CHART

Kind of Meat	Time Per Pound	Internal Temperature After Standing Time
Beef Rolled Rib, Rump or Sirloin Tip	Rare: 6½ minutes Medium: 7½ minutes Well Done: 8½ to 9 minutes	140 degrees 160 degrees 170 degrees
Standing Rib	Rare: 5½ minutes Medium: 6½ minutes Well Done: 7½ to 8 minutes	
Pork Cured Precooked Ham Fresh Loin Roast	5 minutes 5 minutes Well Done: 10 minutes	170 degrees 150 degrees 170 degrees
Chicken, Turkey or Duck	7 minutes	190 degrees
Veal All Roasts	Medium: 8 to 8½ minutes Well Done: 9 to 9½ minutes	170 degrees 170 degrees
Lamb Rolled Bone-In Shoulder Leg	Well Done: 9 minutes Well Done: 9 minutes Pink: 6½ minutes Well Done: 9½ minutes	180 degrees 180 degrees 180 degrees 180 degrees

CHEESE NACHOS

1 can bean dip
1 pkg. taco chips
Grated Cheddar cheese

Spread small amount of dip on each taco chip; place on paper plate. Sprinkle with grated cheese. Cook in microwave oven for 35 seconds or until cheese has melted.

C. Lee
Visitation Valley Jr. High School
San Francisco, California

CHEESY CRACKERS

1   4-oz. package grated Cheddar cheese
1 sm. jar pimentos
1 tsp. oregano
1 tbsp. mayonnaise
Desired variety of crackers

Combine all ingredients except crackers; mix well. Top crackers with mixture. Heat in microwave oven for 1 minute or until bubbly on top. Serve immediately.

Jean McOmby
Spring Lake High School
Spring Lake, Michigan

FUN-DO FONDUE

Caramel ice cream sauce
Fudge ice cream sauce
Strawberry preserves
Sprinkles
Chopped nuts

Miniature or regular-sized marshmallows
Toothpicks

Remove caps from ice cream sauces and preserves; place jars in microwave oven for about 2 minutes. Pour sauces and preserves in custard cups for easy dipping. Place remaining ingredients in bowls. Place marshmallows on toothpicks; dip marshmallows in desired sauces, then in sprinkles or nuts. Great after-school treat.

Joan Stebel
Springfield High School
Holland, Ohio

HOT CREAM CHEESE DIP

1 lg. package cream cheese, softened
1/4 c. sour cream
2 tbsp. milk
1 jar dried beef, chopped
1/4 c. chopped nuts
2 tbsp. chopped green pepper
2 tbsp. chopped onion
1 tsp. pepper

Beat cream cheese until smooth; blend in sour cream and milk. Add remaining ingredients; mix well. Place in microwave oven for 5 minutes or until bubbly.

Mrs. Stacie O. Houser
Sun Valley High School
Monroe, North Carolina

FRANKS CON QUESO

Frankfurters
Monterey Jack cheese
Canned green chilies
Taco sauce or mustard
Frankfurter buns

Make lengthwise slit in each frankfurter, being careful not to cut through. Place thin piece of cheese and a strip of green chili in slit. Spread taco sauce on frankfurter bun; place frankfurter in bun. Wrap bun in paper towel or napkin. Heat for 45 seconds. Add 45 seconds more for each additional frankfurter placed in oven at same time. Double cooking time if frankfurter and buns are frozen.

BASIC MEAT LOAF

1 1/2 lb. ground beef chuck
2 tbsp. instant minced onion
1/2 c. fine dry bread crumbs
1 egg
2 tbsp. catsup
1/2 c. milk
1 tsp. salt
1/8 tsp. pepper
1/8 tsp. thyme
1/8 tsp. dry mustard
1/8 tsp. paprika

Combine all ingredients; mix well. Shape into a rounded flat loaf. Place in 9-inch pie plate. Cover with waxed paper. Place loaf in microwave oven. Cook for 15 to 17 minutes, turning 1/4 turn every 4 minutes. Let stand for at least 5 minutes before slicing. Yield: 6 servings.

Mrs. Mary J. Higgins
East Cobb Middle School
Marietta, Georgia

LET'S PRETEND FILETS

1 1/2 lb. ground beef
4 bacon slices
Broiled Steak Seasoning
2 tbsp. Worcestershire sauce
2 tbsp. water
Mushroom slices and pieces (opt.)

Shape 4 patties of ground beef; wrap with bacon, securing with toothpicks. Sprinkle with Seasoning. Preheat browning skillet for 4 to 5 minutes. Place patties in preheated skillet. Microwave on cook or high, if available, for 2 minutes. Turn patties over; microwave for 2 minutes longer. Combine Worcestershire sauce and water; pour over patties. Microwave for 2 minutes longer. Turn patties over. Add 3 tablespoons mushrooms to top of each patty. Microwave for 2 minutes.

Janet N. Morgan
Premont High School
Premont, Texas

MEATBALLS IN DILL SAUCE

1 egg
1/2 c. milk
2 slices bread, crumbled or torn
3/4 lb. ground beef
3/4 lb. ground pork
1 med. onion, grated
1 tsp. salt
1/4 tsp. pepper
1 tsp. fresh dill, minced or 1/2 tsp.
   dillweed

Beat egg; add milk and bread. Mix well. Add remaining ingredients; knead until mixture holds together. Shape into 1-inch balls; place in large baking dish. Microwave for 3 minutes. Remove from oven; turn meatballs. Return to oven; microwave for 3 to 5 minutes longer.

Dill Sauce

1 c. brown stock or beef broth
1/4 c. flour
2 tsp. fresh minced dill
1 c. heavy cream or evaporated milk
1/4 c. sour cream

Combine stock, flour, dill and milk in saucepan; bring to a boil, stirring constantly. Pour over meatballs. Microwave for 3 minutes or until boiling. Remove from oven; add sour cream. Serve immediately over cooked noodles or rice. All beef may be used for meatballs, if desired.

Mrs. Alma Wells
South Salem High School
Salem, Oregon

LEMONY COUNTRY-STYLE SPARERIBS

1 lg. onion, finely chopped
1 lemon, thinly sliced
3 lb. country-style spareribs
1/3 c. honey
1/2 c. soy sauce
1/4 c. lemon juice
1 tsp. grated fresh ginger

1 clove of garlic, pressed
1 tbsp. cornstarch
1 tbsp. water

Arrange onion and lemon in 10-inch square baking dish; top with spareribs. Cover. Cook in microwave oven on regular power setting for 10 minutes. Combine honey, soy sauce, lemon juice, ginger and garlic; pour over spareribs. Cover; cook on low power/defrost setting for 45 minutes to 1 hour or until spareribs are tender, turning once. Lift out spareribs; skim off and discard fat from drippings. Combine cornstarch with water; add to drippings. Cook, uncovered, on regular powder setting for 4 to 5 minutes or until thickened, stirring once or twice. Return spareribs to sauce; reheat, if necessary. Yield: 4 servings.

OVEN-BARBECUED SPARERIBS

1 side of spareribs snipped apart
   between bones
2 tbsp. lemon juice
2 1/2 tbsp. chili sauce or catsup
1/2 tsp. prepared horseradish
1 1/2 tsp. Worcestershire sauce
1/4 tsp. salt
1/4 tsp. paprika
1/4 c. orange juice
1 tsp. dry mustard
2 tbsp. (firmly packed) brown sugar
1 sm. clove of garlic, minced
1 lemon, sliced

Snip spareribs apart between bones; arrange in 7 x 11-inch baking dish with large ends toward edges of dish and meatiest sides down. Cover lightly with paper towels. Cook in microwave oven for 7 minutes, turning ribs over once; drain off and discard fat. Combine lemon juice, chili sauce, horseradish, Worcestershire sauce, salt, paprika, orange juice, mustard, brown sugar and garlic; pour over ribs. Cook, lightly covered, for 20 minutes, turning ribs and repositioning them in the dish every 5 minutes. Place lemon slices between ribs before serving. Yield: 2 servings.

SPICY ORANGE-GLAZED HAM

1/3 c. orange marmalade
1 1/2 tbsp. Dijon mustard
1/8 tsp. ground cloves
1 1 1/2 lb. canned fully cooked ham

Mix marmalade, mustard and cloves. Remove ham from can; place in 7 x 11-inch baking dish. Brush about half the marmalade mixture evenly over top and sides of ham; cover lightly. Cook in microwave oven for about 4 minutes. Turn ham over; brush with more marmalade mixture. Cook, uncovered, for 5 minutes or until heated through. Let stand, covered, for 5 minutes. Stir any remaining glaze into pan drippings; serve with ham. For canned hams weighing more than 2 pounds but less than 5 pounds, double the glaze recipe and allow 6 minutes cooking time per pound. For hams over 5 pounds, triple the glaze recipe and allow 7 minutes cooking time per pound.

MEXICAN CHICKEN KIEV

4 whole chicken breasts, halved, boned
   and skinned
3 tbsp. butter
3 tbsp. sharp cheese spread
2 tsp. instant minced onion
1 tsp. salt
1 tsp. monosodium glutamate
2 tbsp. chopped green chilies
1/4 c. melted butter
1 c. crushed Cheddar cheese crackers
1 1/2 tbsp. taco seasoning mix
Shredded lettuce
Diced tomatoes
Chopped ripe olives

Pound each chicken piece with mallet. Combine butter and cheese spread; beat until well blended. Mix in onion, salt, monosodium glutamate and chilies. Divide mixture into 8 portions, placing one portion in center of each chicken piece. Roll up each piece; tuck ends in and fasten with toothpicks. Dip each roll in melted butter until well coated, then roll in mixture of cheese crackers and taco seasoning mix. Arrange rolls in 12 x 8 x 2-inch pan. Cover with waxed paper. Place in microwave oven. Cook for 10 to 12 minutes. Serve on bed of lettuce and diced tomatoes. Top with chopped olives.

Mrs. Ray R. Robertson
Madison High School
Madison, Nebraska

BAKED CHICKEN

1 c. cheese crackers
1 1/2 tsp. taco seasoning
Boned chicken pieces

Crush crackers in plastic bag; add taco seasoning. Shake to mix. Drop chicken in bag, one piece at a time; shake until coated. Place in baking dish; cover with Saran Wrap. Bake 2 pieces in microwave oven for 3 to 4 minutes, adjusting baking time for more pieces.

Mrs. Ella Jo Adams
Allen Sr. High School
Allen, Texas

CHEDDAR CHICKEN WITH CRACKED WHEAT

2 tbsp. butter or margarine
1/4 lb. mushrooms, thinly sliced
1/2 c. bulgur wheat
2 tbsp. instant minced onion
1/2 tsp. dry rosemary, crumbled
1 1/2 c. chicken broth
3 1/2 to 4 c. cooked cubed chicken
Garlic salt and pepper to taste
1 1/2 c. shredded Cheddar cheese
Paprika

Melt butter in shallow baking dish or casserole; add mushrooms. Cook, uncovered, in microwave oven for 2 minutes. Stir in bulgur wheat, onion, rosemary and 1 1/4 cups chicken broth. Cover dish; microwave for about 8 minutes or until wheat is tender. Stir in chicken; season with garlic salt and pepper. Sprinkle cheese over top; garnish with paprika. Cook, uncovered, for 2 to 3 minutes or until cheese is melted. May substitute rice or barley for wheat and turkey for chicken. Yield: 4 servings.

Margaret Ann Bruce
Redwood High School
Larkspur, California

147

FRUITED CHICKEN BREASTS

1/2 tsp. finely grated orange peel
1/2 c. orange juice
1 tbsp. sliced green onion
1 tsp. instant chicken bouillon granules
3 med. chicken breasts, split and
    skinned
Salt, pepper and paprika to taste
1 tbsp. cornstarch
1/2 c. seedless green grapes, halved

Combine orange peel, juice, green onion and bouillon granules in glass baking dish. Add chicken; sprinkle with salt, pepper and paprika. Cover dish with waxed paper. Cook in microwave oven for 12 minutes. Remove chicken to warm platter; keep warm. Measure juice in pan; add enough water to measure 3/4 cup liquid. Blend cornstarch with 1 tablespoon cold water; stir into juices. Cook in microwave oven for 2 minutes or until thick, stirring after 1 minute. Add grapes; cook for 30 seconds longer. Spoon sauce over chicken. Garnish with orange slices and grape clusters. Yield: 6 servings.

Gladys H. Dabbs
Oak Grove High School
Bessemer, Alabama

CHICKEN WITH WILD RICE

1 6-oz. package brown and wild rice
    mix
1/4 lb. mushrooms, sliced
1 1/3 c. hot water
1/4 c. dry sherry or water
2 lb. chicken breasts and thighs
Paprika

Combine rice and all but 1 tablespoon of rice seasoning mix in a 7 x 11-inch baking dish; add mushrooms, water and sherry. Cover and cook in microwave oven for 15 minutes. Rub remaining seasoning mix over chicken pieces. Stir rice; arrange chicken, skin side up, in a single layer over top. Sprinkle with paprika. Cover; cook for 12 to 15 minutes or until meat is no longer pink near bone, turning dish once or twice. Let stand, covered, for about 5 minutes.

CHICKEN DIVAN

2 whole chicken breasts
1 pkg. frozen broccoli, cooked
1   10 1/2-oz. can cream of chicken soup
1/2 c. salad dressing
1 tbsp. lemon juice
1/2 tsp. curry powder
1   4-oz. package shredded Cheddar
    cheese

Simmer chicken in small amount of water until tender. Cool and remove meat from bones. Arrange broccoli in 12 x 7-inch baking dish. Place chicken over broccoli. Combine soup, salad dressing, lemon juice and curry powder; pour over chicken. Sprinkle with cheese. Cover with waxed paper. Cook in microwave oven for 5 minutes; turn dish around. Cook for 5 minutes longer.

Peggy Munter
Moore High School
Moore, Oklahoma

TURKEY-SPAGHETTI CASSEROLE

2 tbsp. margarine
1 med. onion, finely chopped
1 clove of garlic, minced
1   1-lb. can tomatoes, chopped
1 can mushroom stems and pieces
1 tsp. salt
1/4 tsp. pepper
1/4 tsp. cayenne pepper
1 1/2 c. diced cooked turkey
1   8-oz. package spaghetti, cooked
1/2 to 1 lb. Cheddar cheese, grated

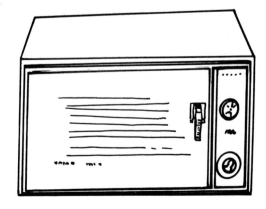

Place margarine in 3 or 4-quart glass casserole; cover. Microwave for about 1 minute and 30 seconds to 2 minutes or until melted. Add onion and garlic; cover with glass lid or plastic wrap. Microwave for about 4 minutes or until onion is almost done, using high setting if available. Add remaining ingredients except spaghetti and cheese; mix well. Cover. Microwave on cook or high for about 8 to 10 minutes or until heated through, stirring once. Stir in spaghetti, mixing well. Top with cheese; cover. Microwave on roast or cook for about 4 to 6 minutes or until cheese is melted and mixture is heated through. Cook spaghetti on top of stove while preparing turkey mixture.

Mrs. Janet N. Morgan
Premont High School
Premont, Texas

APRICOT-GLAZED DUCKLING

    1 5-lb. ready-to-cook frozen
       duckling, thawed
    Pepper
    1/2 c. apricot jam
    1/3 c. chicken broth
    1 tbsp. soy sauce
    1 tbsp. dry mustard
    1 tsp. grated orange peel
    1 tsp. cornstarch
    1 tsp. water

Remove giblets and neck from duck cavity; reserve for future use, if desired. Rinse duck well; pat dry. Prick skin in several places with a fork; sprinkle cavity and skin lightly with pepper. Secure wings akimbo-style; fasten skin across neck opening to back with wooden pick. Place duck, breast side down, on nonmetallic rack or inverted saucer in 7 x 11-inch baking dish. Cook, uncovered, in microwave oven for 10 minutes; turn dish once or twice. Mix jam, broth, soy sauce, mustard and orange peel until well blended. Drain drippings from baking dish into 2-cup glass measure. Brush jam mixture generously over duck; cook, uncovered, for 10 minutes, turning dish once or twice. Tip dish and drain cavity juices into baking dish, using 2 forks to support duck; turn duck breast side

up. Cook, uncovered, for 10 minutes, turning dish once or twice. Drain drippings from baking dish into the glass measure. Baste duck with remaining jam mixture; cook, uncovered, for 10 minutes longer or until leg joint moves easily. Drain juices from cavity into baking dish. Place duck on serving platter; keep warm. Combine all drippings in the glass measure; discard fat. Blend cornstarch and water; stir into drippings. Cook, uncovered, for 1 minute or until bubbly. Serve with duck.

PEACHY ROCK CORNISH HENS

    2 Rock Cornish game hens, thawed
    1 6-oz. package chicken-flavored
       rice mix
    Butter
    1 1-lb. can cling peach halves
    2 tbsp. honey
    1 tbsp. dry mustard
    1/4 tsp. curry powder
    Paprika

Remove giblets from game hens; save for other uses. Split hens in half with poultry or kitchen shears. Rinse well; pat dry. Combine seasoning in rice package with water and butter called for on package in 7 x 11-inch baking dish. Cook, uncovered, in microwave oven for about 1 minute or until hot; stir in rice. Cover; cook for 2 minutes longer. Arrange hen halves in dish, skin side down, with meaty portions near edges of dish. Cover; cook for 10 minutes, turning dish 2 or 3 times. Drain peach halves, reserving 2 tablespoons syrup. Set peaches aside. Combine reserved syrup, 1 tablespoon butter, honey, dry mustard and curry powder in a small bowl. Cook, uncovered, for about 45 seconds or until bubbly. Lift out hen halves; stir rice well. Return hens to dish, skin side up. Brush skin evenly with honey mixture; cook for 10 minutes longer or until meat near bone is no longer pink. Arrange peach halves around poultry; brush with any remaining honey mixture. Cook, covered, for about 45 seconds. Sprinkle paprika over poultry and peaches. Let stand, covered, for 5 minutes before serving. Yield: 4 servings.

SPECIAL SALMON RING

3 eggs, beaten
2 c. red salmon, drained and flaked
1 c. fine dry bread crumbs
1/2 c. chopped celery
1/4 c. chopped green pepper
2 tsp. instant minced onion
1 tbsp. lemon juice
3/4 c. milk
Creamed peas

Combine all ingredients except peas in 1 1/2-quart casserole; mix well. Move mixture from center; place glass custard cup in center to make ring. Cook, uncovered, in microwave oven for 8 minutes or until mixture around glass is set. Remove glass. Fill center with creamed peas. Yield: 6 servings.

Catherine A. Carter
Consultant, Consumer and Homemaking
Dept. of Adult, Voc. and Tech. Education
Illinois Office of Education
Springfield, Illinois

DELICIOUS STUFFED FISH

1   1 1/2-lb. dressed fish
1/4 c. butter
1 tsp. salt
1/2 tsp. onion salt
2 c. day-old bread cubes
2 tbsp. chopped onion
1 tbsp. chopped parsley
1 tbsp. chopped celery
1/2 tsp. poultry seasoning
1/4 c. hot water
3/4 tsp. paprika

Wash fish and dry with paper towel. Place butter in glass bowl; cover with waxed paper. Heat in microwave oven for 1 minute. Brush inside of fish with half the butter. Sprinkle cavity with salt and onion salt. Combine remaining butter with bread cubes, onion, parsley, celery and poultry seasoning; toss until blended. Add water; toss lightly. Fill fish cavity with stuffing. Sew sides of fish together. Place fish in shallow baking dish. Sprinkle with paprika. Bake in microwave oven for 6 minutes and 30 seconds to 7 minutes or until fish flakes easily. Let stand for 5 minutes. Garnish with lemon wedges.

Clara May Charlesworth
Northeast High School
Pasadena, Maryland

MICROWAVE SHRIMP

1 lb. medium shrimp

Arrange shrimp in a single layer on a large flat round plate with tails to center. Cook, uncovered, in microwave oven for 3 1/2 to 4 1/2 minutes or until shrimp turn pink, turning plate twice. Cool for about 5 minutes. Shell and devein. Use as appetizers or in salads or casseroles.

SHRIMP CREOLE

2/3 c. peanut or vegetable oil
1/2 c. flour
10 to 20 green onion bulbs, minced
1 rib celery, chopped fine
1 sm. yellow onion, peeled, chopped fine
1 green pepper, chopped fine
2 cloves of garlic, crushed
1   16-oz. can whole Italian tomatoes, drained
1   8-oz. can tomato sauce
12 sprigs of parsley, minced
1 tbsp. minced olives
1/4 c. dry red wine
4 bay leaves, crushed
6 whole allspice
2 whole cloves
1 tsp. cayenne pepper
1/4 tsp. chili powder
1/4 tsp. mace
1/4 tsp. dried basil
1/2 tsp. dried thyme
Juice of 1 lemon, strained
2 c. water
Salt to taste
Freshly ground pepper to taste
2 lb. fresh shrimp, peeled and deveined

Mix oil and flour together in a large 6 to 8-quart glass bowl. Place in microwave oven, uncovered, for 2 minutes. Add vegetables and parsley. Stir well. Return to microwave for 2 minutes. Stir in remaining ingredients except shrimp; cook for 15 minutes longer, stirring every 5 minutes. Add shrimp; microwave for 3 to 4 minutes or until pink. Yield: or until pink. Yield: 6 servings.

Wanda Stacke
Marshfield Sr. High School
Marshfield, Wisconsin

SHRIMP JAMBALAYA

2 tbsp. butter or margarine
1 lg. onion, chopped
1/3 c. chopped green pepper
1 clove of garlic, minced or pressed
1   1-lb. can tomato wedges in tomato juice
1   14-oz. can chicken broth
1 c. diced cooked ham
2 tbsp. chopped parsley
1 linquisa sausage, chopped
3/4 tsp. salt
1/4 tsp. thyme leaves, crumbled
Dash of pepper
1 bay leaf
2 c. quick-cooking rice
1 lb. medium shrimp, shelled and deveined

Melt butter in a 3-quart casserole in microwave oven for 1 minute or until bubbly. Stir in onion, green pepper and garlic; cover and cook for 7 minutes or until vegetables are limp. Stir in tomatoes and liquid, broth, ham, parsley, sausage, salt, thyme, pepper, bay leaf and rice. Cover; cook for 12 to 14 minutes or until rice is nearly tender, stirring 2 or 3 times. Arrange shrimp over top of rice; cover. Cook for 3 to 4 minutes or until shrimp turn pink. Let stand, covered, for 5 minutes. Remove bay leaf; stir well. Serve in shallow soup bowls. Yield: 4 to 6 servings.

SHRIMP FOO YUNG

2 tbsp. butter or margarine
4 eggs, well beaten
1/2 lb. fresh bean sprouts, rinsed and drained
1/3 c. thinly sliced green onions

1 c. small cooked shrimp
1/4 tsp. salt
1/8 tsp. pepper
1/8 tsp. garlic powder
1/4 tsp. hot pepper sauce

Place butter in 9-inch glass pie plate; melt in microwave oven for 30 seconds. Tip and tilt dish to spread evenly. Combine eggs, bean sprouts, onions, shrimp, salt, pepper , garlic powder and hot pepper sauce; add to butter. Cook, uncovered, for 5 minutes or until set, stirring every minute by pushing cooked mixture toward center so liquid can flow to bottom and side of dish. Serve with soy sauce. May substitute crab or chicken for shrimp, if desired.

STACKED ENCHILADAS

1/2 c. finely chopped onion
2 tbsp. lard
1 tbsp. flour
1/2 c. milk
1   4-oz. can chopped green chilies, drained
1/2 tsp. salt
2 c. diced cooked beef
2 med. tomatoes, peeled and chopped
8 corn tortillas
1/4 c. cooking oil
1 c. shredded Monterey Jack cheese or Longhorn cheese

Cook onion in skillet in lard until tender but not brown. Blend in flour. Add milk, chilies and salt. Cook, stirring constantly, until thick and bubbly. Stir in beef and tomatoes; heat through. Keep warm. Heat tortillas in small skillet, one at a time, in hot oil until limp or about 15 seconds on each side. Drain on paper toweling. Place 1 hot tortilla in a baking dish. Top with meat mixture and small amount of cheese. Repeat with remaining tortillas, beef mixture and cheese to make a stack. Top with cheese. Place in microwave oven for 5 minutes or until hot. Yield: 4 servings.

Suzzan Nutting
Salome High School
Salome, Arizona

MICROWAVE LASAGNA

1 lb. ground beef
1 tbsp. dried parsley
2 1/2 tsp. salt
1 clove of garlic, pressed
1 tbsp. basil
1 1-lb. can tomatoes
2 6-oz. cans tomato paste
2 c. ricotta cheese
1/4 c. grated Parmesan cheese
2 eggs, beaten
1/2 tsp. pepper
12 lasagna noodles, cooked
1 lb. mozzarella cheese, grated

Combine ground beef, parsley, 1 1/2 teaspoons salt, garlic and basil in glass dish. Cook in microwave oven for 4 minutes. Stir in tomatoes and tomato paste. Return to oven; cook for 4 minutes longer. Combine ricotta cheese, Parmesan cheese, eggs, pepper and remaining 1 teaspoon salt. Spread 1/2 cup meat sauce in baking dish; cover with 4 noodles. Spread half the ricotta mixture over noodles; sprinkle with half the mozzarella cheese. Repeat layers, ending with meat sauce. Bake in microwave oven for 10 minutes.

Wanda Miller
Sahuarita High School
Sahuarita, Arizona

BEEF-TORTILLA CASSEROLE

6 flour tortillas, cut into 1-in.
   squares
2 to 3 c. cooked and shredded roast beef
Salt to taste
1/2 c. sour cream
1/2 c. chopped green onions
1 c. grated Monterey Jack or Cheddar
   cheese
1/2 to 1 c. canned green chili salsa

Fry tortillas in hot oil until crisp; drain. Mix beef, salt, sour cream, onions and cheese together. Place half the tortilla chips in casserole; cover with meat mixture. Cover with remaining chips. Top with chili salsa. Bake, uncovered, in microwave oven for 4 minutes.

Top with guacamole and sour cream, if desired. May bake in oven at 350 degrees for 20 minutes, if desired. Yield: 3-4 servings.

Carol Shaw
Hilltop High School
Chula Vista, California

BEEF AND TATER CASSEROLE

1 lb. ground beef
2 tsp. instant minced onion
1 lb. frozen Tater Tots
1 10 1/2-oz. can cream of chicken soup
1 10 1/2-oz. can cream of celery soup
Paprika

Crumble ground beef into 2-quart casserole; cook for 5 minutes in microwave oven, stirring and turning dish twice. Top with minced onion and Tater Tots. Add soups; sprinkle with paprika. Bake for 15 minutes longer, turning dish every 5 minutes.

Peggy O. Munter
Moore High School
Moore, Oklahoma

FULL OF BOLONEY

1 1/2 c. diced potatoes
1 1/2 c. cubed bologna
2 tbsp. minced green pepper
1 10 1/2-oz. can cream of celery soup
2 lg. slices cheese, quartered

Combine all ingredients except cheese in 1 1/2-quart glass casserole. Bake, covered, in microwave oven for 15 minutes. Remove cover; top with cheese. Bake for 30 seconds longer or just until cheese melts. Yield: 4 servings.

Mrs. Esther Wonderlich
Mount Pleasant Jr. High School
Mount Pleasant, Iowa

FRESH CORN ON COB

1 ear . . . . 2 to 2½ minutes
2 ears . . . . 3 to 4 minutes
3 ears . . . . 5 to 6 minutes

4 ears	6 to 7 minutes
6 ears	8 to 9 minutes

Wrap each ear of corn in waxed paper; arrange in circular fashion in microwave oven. Cook according to above schedule. Unwrap; may be seasoned with butter, salt, seasoned salt, pepper, chives or mixture of dry onion soup mix and butter.

Anna Bryant, Instr.
Savannah Area Voc-Tech School
Savannah, Georgia

FAVORITE CORN ON THE COB

Corn on the cob

Remove husks and silks from corn. Dip corn in water; wrap each ear in plastic wrap. Cook in microwave oven until the plastic starts to expand. Allow to cool for about 5 minutes before unwrapping.

Margaret Maletor
Goodrich HS
Goodrich, Michigan

PARSLEY RICE

1 c. long grain rice
2 c. hot water
1 tsp. margarine
1 tsp. salt
1/2 tsp. dried parsley

Combine all ingredients except parsley in 3-quart casserole; cover. Microwave for 12 to 13 minutes. Remove from microwave oven; let stand, covered, for 5 minutes. Sprinkle with parsley; serve hot. Yield: 3 cups rice.

Anna Bryant, Instr.
Savannah Area Voc-Tech School
Savannah, Georgia

LARRY'S OMELET FOR TWO

1 tbsp. butter
6 thin slices Cheddar cheese
3 eggs

2 tbsp. honey
Salt and pepper to taste
3 to 4 tbsp. half and half

Place butter in 1-quart casserole; microwave for 1 minute or until butter is melted. Swirl to coat casserole evenly. Line casserole with half the cheese. Heat in microwave oven until cheese is slightly melted. Combine eggs, honey, salt, pepper and half and half; beat well. Pour into casserole. Microwave for 1 minute and 30 seconds. Remove from oven; top with remaining cheese. Return to microwave oven for 2 minutes and 30 seconds. Serve immediately.

Jean McOmber
Spring Lake High School
Spring Lake, Michigan

CARAMEL-BAKED APPLES

4 lg. tart apples
1/2 c. (firmly packed) brown sugar
1 tbsp. raisins (opt.)
1 tbsp. chopped nuts (opt.)
Ground cinnamon
1/3 c. whipping cream

Core apples; peel off skin from top half of each apple. Arrange in 8-inch round baking dish. Partially fill center of each apple with brown sugar; stuff with raisins and nuts. Add enough brown sugar to fill centers; spoon any remaining brown sugar into bottom of dish. Sprinkle each apple lightly with cinnamon. Drizzle cream over apples slowly, pouring some over brown sugar in each core. Cook, uncovered, in microwave oven for 8 to 10 minutes or until apples are tender when pierced with fork, turning dish 2 or 3 times. Transfer apples to individual serving dishes. Cook remaining brown sugar mixture, uncovered, for 1 1/2 to 2 minutes or until mixture boils vigorously; stir well. Spoon sauce evenly over each apple; serve warm. Cinnamon-baked apples may be prepared by filling center of each apple with 1 tablespoon red cinnamon candies. Cook, uncovered, in microwave oven for 2 to 3 minutes or until apples are tender when pierced.

153

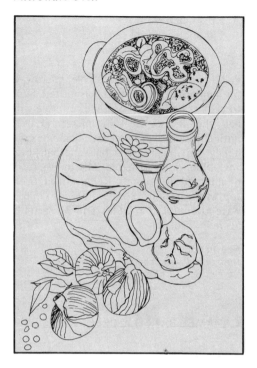

APPLESAUCE

6 c. peeled, cored and diced apples
2 tbsp. water
3/4 c. sugar

Combine apples and water in large glass bowl; cover with plastic wrap. Cook in microwave oven until soft and fluffy. Remove from oven; stir in sugar. Be careful when removing plastic wrap as the steam may burn you. This is an excellent way to make rhubarb sauce but increase the sugar.

Margaret Moletor
Goodrich High School
Goodrich, Michigan

BANANA-RASPBERRY FLAMBE

1 10-oz. package frozen red
 raspberries, thawed
2 tbsp. sugar
2 tbsp. butter
1 tbsp. brown sugar
4 med. bananas, sliced
3 tbsp. brandy or orange liqueur
Vanilla ice cream

Place raspberries and sugar in blender container; cover and blend until smooth. Sieve to remove seeds; set aside. Melt butter in 12 x 7 1/2 x 2-inch baking dish in microwave for 30 to 40 seconds. Stir in brown sugar until dissolved. Add raspberry mixture and bananas, stirring to coat all banana slices. Cook, covered, in microwave oven for 3 minutes and 30 seconds or until heated through and bananas are cooked to desired doneness, stirring twice. Place brandy in 1-cup glass measuring cup; heat in microwave oven for 30 seconds. Do not overheat. Transfer brandy to ladle; ignite. Pour over fruit. Serve over ice cream.

Mary Ellen Trawbridge
North Thurston High School
Lacey, Washington

BASIC BREAD PUDDING

4 c. (lightly packed) bread cubes
2 c. milk
1/4 c. butter
2 eggs, beaten
1/2 c. (packed) brown sugar
1/4 tsp. salt
1/2 c. raisins

Spread bread cubes evenly in 8-inch round dish. Measure milk into 1-quart measuring cup; add butter. Place in microwave oven on high power. Cook for 2 minutes or until butter is melted and milk is warm. Stir a small amount of warm milk into eggs. Stir egg mixture into milk. Add brown sugar, salt and raisins; mix well. Pour over bread cubes. Place dish in oven; cook on defrost for 4 minutes. Remove from oven. Stir mixture well, mashing bread cubes. Return to oven; continue cooking on defrost for 4 to 7 minutes. Center may be slightly soft but it will get firm as pudding sets.

Mrs. Mary J. Higgins
East Cobb Middle School
Marietta, Georgia

CATHEDRAL WINDOW CANDY

2 tbsp. butter
1 c. chocolate chips
1 egg, beaten

154

1 c. powdered sugar
3 c. colored marshmallows

Place butter and chocolate chips in medium-sized heat resistant mixing bowl. Heat, uncovered, in microwave oven for 4 minutes or until melted. Combine egg and sugar; add slowly to chocolate mixture. Stir in marshmallows until well coated. Pour onto waxed paper; form into 18-inch long log. Refrigerate; slice when ready to serve.

Opal Schubert
Western High School
Buda, Illinois

CHOCOLATE-COVERED PEANUTS

1 12-oz. package chocolate bits
1 12-oz. can dry-roasted peanuts

Place chocolate bits in china or plastic bowl. Heat in microwave oven for about 2 minutes or until chocolate is melted. Stir until creamy. Add peanuts; stir until coated with chocolate. Drop from teaspoon onto waxed paper or teflon-coated pan. Chill until firm.

Mrs. Betty G. Brant
Shanksville-Stonycreek School
Shanksville, Pennsylvania

EASY MICROWAVE FUDGE

1 lb. powdered sugar
1/2 c. cocoa
1/4 c. milk
1/2 c. butter
1 tbsp. vanilla extract
1/2 c. chopped nuts

Blend sugar and cocoa together in glass bowl; add milk and butter. Do not mix. Cook for 2 minutes in microwave oven. Remove from oven; stir. Add vanilla and nuts. Stir until blended. Pour into greased container; place in freezer for 20 minutes or refrigerate for 1 hour. Cut and serve.

Kathleen Williams
North Lamar High School
Powderly, Texas

MILK CHOCOLATE ALMOND BARS

1/2 c. softened butter or margarine
1/2 c. (firmly packed) brown sugar
1 1/4 c. flour
1/4 tsp. salt
1 6-oz. package milk chocolate morsels
1/2 c. chopped almonds

Combine butter and sugar until creamy. Sift flour and salt together; blend into butter mixture. Press evenly into 13 x 9 x 2-inch baking dish. Bake in microwave oven for 4 to 5 minutes, turning dish 180 degrees after 2 minutes. Sprinkle milk chocolate morsels over top. Return to microwave oven for 1 minute to soften morsels. Spread evenly over top. Sprinkle with almonds. Cool. Cut into 2 x 1-inch bars.

Mrs. Sharon A. Sharp
J. J. Pearce High School
Richardson, Texas

GERMAN CHOCOLATE CAKE

1/2 c. margarine
2/3 c. milk
1 pkg. coconut-almond-pecan frosting
  mix
1 pkg. German chocolate cake mix
1 1/2 c. water
2 eggs

Melt half the margarine in each of two 8-inch round glass layer baking dishes; stir 1/3 cup milk into each dish. Sprinkle half the dry frosting mix into each dish. Combine cake mix with water and eggs, beating for 4 minutes after all ingredients are moistened. Remove 1 1/4 cups batter; pour remaining batter into the 2 baking dishes. Microwave, one layer at a time, for 6 minutes or until toothpick inserted in center comes out clean. Cool for 5 minutes; invert over cake plate. Remove any frosting that sticks in pan with spatula; spread on cake. Cool; stack layers. Make cupcakes with remaining batter.

Anna Bryant, Instr.
Savannah Area Voc-Tech School
Savannah, Georgia

155

FESTIVE CHOCOLATE TORTE

2 c. unsifted all-purpose flour
1 1/2 c. sugar
2 tsp. baking powder
1 tsp. salt
1/4 tsp. soda
1/4 c. shortening
1 1/4 c. milk
1 tsp. vanilla extract
1 tsp. creme de cacao (opt.)
2 eggs
4 1-oz. squares unsweetened
  chocolate, melted
1 c. finely chopped walnuts
Whipped cream

Combine flour, sugar, baking powder, salt, soda, shortening, milk, vanilla and creme de cacao in large bowl. Blend on low speed of mixer, then beat at medium speed for 2 minutes. Add eggs and chocolate; beat for 2 minutes longer at medium speed. Stir in walnuts. Pour batter into greased 9 x 13-inch baking pan. Place in microwave oven; cook for 13 to 15 minutes or until toothpick comes out clean, giving dish 1/2 turn every 4 minutes. Cool. Cut into 3 equal pieces; cut each piece in half crosswise to make 2 thin layers. Spread whipped cream between layers and over top. Garnish with chocolate bits. Refrigerate for several hours or overnight. Yield: 12 servings.

Margaret Morgan
Austin High School
Austin, Minnesota

INDIVIDUAL CHEESECAKES

3 tbsp. butter or margarine
1/2 c. graham cracker crumbs
Sugar
1 8-oz. package cream cheese,
  softened
1 egg
1 tsp. vanilla extract
6 tsp. berry or fruit jam

Place butter in glass mixing bowl; melt for 1 minute in microwave oven. Blend in cracker crumbs and 1 1/2 teaspoons sugar. Line 6 glass custard cups with paper baking cups; spoon crumbs equally into each cup. Press crumbs firmly over bottoms and up sides with a spoon. Combine cream cheese and 1/4 cup sugar; beat until smooth. Add egg and vanilla; mix well. Spoon mixture equally into cups. Cook, uncovered, for 1 1/2 to 2 minutes, shifting inside cups to outside positions after 1 minute. Chill, uncovered, for 1 hour. Spoon 1 teaspoon jam onto each tart before serving.

GLAMOROUS CHERRIES JUBILEE

1 16-oz. bag frozen pitted dark sweet
  cherries
1 tbsp. cornstarch
1/3 c. currant jelly
2 tbsp. sugar
1/4 c. kirsch
1 1/2 pt. vanilla ice cream

Pierce top of bag of cherries with a fork in several places; cook in microwave oven for 3 minutes. Let stand for 5 to 10 minutes. Drain juices into 1 1/2 to 2-quart serving dish. Add cornstarch; mix until smooth. Add jelly and sugar. Cook, uncovered, for 2 1/2 minutes or until thickened and clear, stirring 2 or 3 times. Stir in cherries and any additional juice. Cook, covered, for 3 minutes or until cherries are heated through. Pour kirsch into glass measuring cup; cook for 25 seconds. Pour over hot cherry sauce; ignite. Stir until flames subside. Spoon hot cherries over ice cream. Yield: 6 servings.

FRENCH APPLE PIE

1/2 c. all-purpose flour
1/3 c. (firmly packed) brown sugar
6 tbsp. butter
6 c. peeled and thinly sliced tart
  apples
1 tbsp. lemon juice
3/4 c. sugar
2 tbsp. quick-cooking tapioca
1 tsp. cinnamon
1/4 tsp. nutmeg
1 baked 9-in. pastry shell

Combine flour and brown sugar; cut in 4 tablespoons butter until crumbly. Place in large pie plate. Cook, uncovered, in microwave oven for 2 1/2 to 3 minutes or until bubbly, turning dish 2 or 3 times. Cool slightly; mix with fork. Set aisde. Combine apples, lemon juice, sugar, tapioca, cinnamon and nutmeg in a 11 x 7-inch baking dish, mixing lightly. Let stand for at least 10 minutes. Cook, uncovered, in microwave oven for 10 to 12 minutes, stirring 3 times. Remove from oven; stir in remaining 2 tablespoons butter. Cool for 30 minutes. Spoon into pie shell. Sprinkle top with brown sugar mixture.

ONE-CRUST FRESH GLAZED STRAWBERRY PIE

1 1/2 qt. fresh strawberries
1 1/2 c. sugar
1 tsp. lemon juice
1/2 c. water
3 tbsp. cornstarch
1   9-in. baked pie shell

Place 1 pint cleaned strawberries in 1-quart glass casserole. Mash strawberries; add 1 cup sugar, lemon juice, water and cornstarch. Mix well. Cover; cook in microwave oven for 5 minutes, stirring at the end of each minute. Cool thoroughly. Clean remaining strawberries and slice large strawberries. Add remaining 1/2 cup sugar; mix well. Combine with cooled strawberries; pour into baked pie shell. Garnish with whipped cream, if desired.

Mrs. Sharon A. Sharp
J. J. Pearce High School
Richardson, Texas

TANGY LEMON MERINGUE PIE

1 1/2 c. water
Sugar
7 tbsp. cornstarch
1/4 tsp. salt
3 eggs, separated
3 tbsp. butter or margarine
2 tsp. grated lemon peel
1/2 c. lemon juice

1 baked 9-in. pastry shell
1/4 tsp. cream of tartar
1/2 tsp. vanilla extract

Cook water in microwave oven for 2 to 3 minutes or until simmering. Blend 1 1/2 cups sugar, cornstarch and salt in glass quart measure. Pour hot water into sugar mixture gradually, stirring until smooth. Cook, uncovered, for 4 minutes or until thick and bubbly, stirring 7 or 8 times. Beat egg yolks lightly in small bowl. Stir about 3 tablespoons hot mixture into egg yolks gradually; stir back into hot mixture. Cook, uncovered, for 1 minute longer, stirring once. Blend in butter, lemon peel and lemon juice; cool. Spoon into pastry shell. Beat egg whites and cream of tartar with electric mixer until frothy. Beat in 6 tablespoons sugar, 1 tablespoon at a time, until stiff peaks form; do not underbeat. Beat in vanilla. Place meringue over pie filling, touching crust all around. Cook, uncovered, for 3 minutes, turning pie 4 times to cook evenly: Cool away from draft; refrigerate, if desired. One teaspoon lemon juice may be substituted for vanilla.

QUICK AND EASY BAKED CUSTARD

1 3/4 c. milk
3 eggs
1/4 c. sugar
1/8 tsp. salt
1/2 tsp. vanilla extract

Pour milk into glass measure; heat, uncovered, in microwave oven for 2 minutes. Beat eggs with sugar, salt and vanilla; add scalded milk slowly, stirring constantly. Pour into 4 custard cups. Cook, uncovered, for 4 to 4 1/2 minutes or until just set when shook; stir each cup 4 times during cooking and reposition cups for more even cooking. Cool, then chill, uncovered, for 1 hour. Cover and chill if stored longer. May be garnished with dash of ground nutmeg or cinnamon, sprinkling of toasted coconut, sliced sweetened strawberries or raspberries, sliced peaches, banana slices rolled in orange juice and chopped nuts or whipped cream.

There are times when even the best homemaker wonders if she can plan another week's menu or even cook one more meal. Just the idea of preparing or serving that same meat loaf, those same peas and that tiresome pie for dessert make her almost desperate for new ideas. When this happens, what a "life-saver" a new selection of recipes can be!

That is why the Home Economics Teachers wanted to include this All-Purpose section in the "Life-Saver" Cookbook. They have known for a long time that the same foods, when prepared in a new and different way, add a new dimension to eating for both the homemaker and her family.

In this section you will find new ways to enhance chicken, meat loaf, and some deliciously different salads and vegetables. Home Economics Teachers are known for their fantastic dessert and confection recipes — and you'll find some of the best right here. There is even one for *Fried Ice Cream!*

There are also plenty of "life-saver" household hints in this section that will help you make the most of your time, money and food. Then, to keep the "hum-drum" out of economizing everyday, add a few *free* flourishes every now and then. For example, on your family's most unpopular night of the week, prepare a picnic meal and eat outside. If the weather is bad, spread TV tables in the den and have an indoor picnic. For a dramatic change at breakfast, serve strawberry or blueberry shortcake with ice cream.

Always let your imagination be your guide and it will become your best homemaking "life-saver."

All-Purpose

All-Purpose

DILL PICKLES

Sm. or med. cucumbers
Dillseed
Garlic cloves
1 qt. vinegar
2 qt. water
1 c. plain salt

Wash cucumbers; pack in clean 1-quart jars. Place 1 tablespoon dillseed and 2 or 3 garlic cloves on top of cucumbers in each quart; place jars in warm water. Mix vinegar, water and salt in saucepan; bring to a boil. Pour over cucumbers; seal jars. Process in hot water bath for 10 minutes to complete seal. Let stand for 4 to 5 weeks before using. May add a pod of pepper to each jar, if desired.

Vivian Crane
Hayden School
Hayden, Alabama

CHILI CHEESE SQUARES

1 lb. sharp Cheddar cheese, grated
1 can chopped green chilies
6 eggs
Paprika to taste

Sprinkle half the cheese in bottom of greased 8-inch square baking dish. Drain chilies, reserving liquid. Sprinkle green chilies over cheese. Add remaining cheese. Add reserved liquid to eggs; beat well. Pour over cheese. Sprinkle with paprika. Bake in preheated 350-degree oven for 35 to 40 minutes. Cut in small squares; spear with toothpicks to serve. May be frozen and reheated.

Mrs. Jess Adams
North Heights Center
Voc. Ed. for the Handicapped
Amarillo, Texas

BAR CHEESE

1 lb. American cheese, grated
1 lb. sharp cheese, grated
2 cloves of garlic, pressed
3 tbsp. Worcestershire sauce
1/2 tsp. salt

2 tsp. dry mustard
1/8 tsp. cayenne pepper
1 tsp. liquid smoke
1 c. (about) warm beer

Combine cheeses and garlic in mixing bowl. Add remaining ingredients except beer; mix well with wooden spoon. Add enough beer slowly, blending to a smooth paste. Store, covered, in crock in refrigerator. Serve at room temperature.

Mrs. Shirley S. Allen
Redford High School
Franklin Village, Michigan

ZUCCHINI RELISH

10 c. ground zucchini
4 c. ground onions
1 green bell pepper, ground
1 red bell pepper, ground
5 tbsp. salt
2 1/4 c. vinegar
4 c. sugar
2 tsp. celery seed
1 tsp. nutmeg
1 tsp. turmeric
1/2 tsp. dry mustard
1 tbsp. cornstarch

Mix zucchini, onions, green pepper, red pepper and salt; let stand overnight. Drain. Rinse with cold water; drain well. Add vinegar, sugar, celery seed, nutmeg, turmeric, mustard and cornstarch; mix well. Cook for 30 minutes; place in clean, hot jars. Seal. Process in hot water bath for 10 minutes to complete seal. Yield: About 6 pints.

Mrs. Bette Cox
South High School
Denver, Colorado

DEVILED TURKEY BONBONS

1 c. cooked finely chopped turkey
1 c. finely chopped nuts
1 tbsp. chopped onion
2 tbsp. chopped pimento
1/4 tsp. salt

Tabasco sauce to taste
1/4 c. cream of mushroom soup

Combine turkey and 1/2 cup nuts. Add remaining ingredients; mix well. Form into balls. Roll in remaining 1/2 cup nuts. Chill until ready to serve.

Stacie O. Houser
Sun Valley High School
Monroe, North Carolina

FINGER DRUMSTICKS

3 lb. chicken wings
1/2 c. sugar
3 tbsp. cornstarch
1 tsp. salt
1/2 tsp. ground ginger
1/4 tsp. pepper
3/4 c. water
1/3 c. lemon juice
1/4 c. soy sauce

Cut off wing tips; discard. Cut each wing in half; place in single layer on rack in broiler pan. Bake in preheated 400-degree oven for 30 minutes, turning once. Mix sugar, cornstarch, salt, ginger and pepper in small saucepan; stir in water, lemon juice and soy sauce. Bring to a boil; cook, stirring constantly, for 3 minutes or until thickened. Brush over chicken wings; bake, turning and brushing wings several times with remaining sauce mixture for 40 minutes or until well glazed. Place in chafing dish or hot server; garnish with ring of thin lemon slices, if desired.

Marilyn J. Fleener
Lakeview High School
Decatur, Illinois

SALMON PATE

1 7 3/4-oz. can red salmon, drained
1 8-oz. package cream cheese, softened
1 tbsp. finely chopped onion
2 tbsp. chopped parsley
1 tbsp. lemon juice
1 tsp. Worcestershire sauce

Dash of Tabasco sauce
Dash of garlic powder

Combine all ingredients, mixing well. Place in small waxed paper-lined container. Chill for several hours. Unmold. Garnish with parsley. Serve with crackers.

Mrs. Millie Griswold
Lincoln School
Wyandotte, Michigan

SALTED PUMPKIN SEEDS

Pumpkin seeds
Cooking oil
Salt to taste

Clean pumpkin seeds until no film remains. Place a small amount of oil in bottom of shallow pan. Place seeds in oil. Season with salt. Bake in preheated 350-degree oven until lightly toasted, adding more oil, if needed. Stir occasionally to keep the seeds from sticking together. Cool. Store in covered container. Use as substitute for salted peanuts.

Mrs. Marian Baker
Sycamore High School
Sycamore, Illinois

SPINACH BALL

3 pkg. frozen chopped spinach, thawed
1 c. finely chopped onion
1 1/2 c. mayonnaise
1/2 c. chopped parsley
1 1/2 tsp. salt

Squeeze as much liquid from spinach as possible. Add remaining ingredients; mix well. Let stand in refrigerator for several hours before serving. Shape into ball. Serve with bacon-flavored crackers. May be served as a salad, if desired.

Mrs. John C. Griswold
Carrollton Community Unit Dist. No. 1
Carrollton, Illinois

161

All-Purpose

SWISS FONDUE

4 c. shredded Swiss cheese
1/4 c. all-purpose flour
1 clove of garlic, halved
2 c. sauterne
1/2 tsp. salt
1/2 tsp. Worcestershire sauce
Dash of ground nutmeg

Toss cheese and flour together. Rub inside of 3-quart saucepan with garlic; discard garlic. Add sauterne; heat until bubbles rise. Reduce heat to medium low. Add cheese, 1/2 cup at a time; stir until cheese is melted after each addition. Add salt, Worcestershire sauce and nutmeg. Transfer to fondue pot. Serve with cubes of French bread, vegetable or fruit dippers, cooked ham cubes or cooked shrimp. Tomato juice or white grape juice may be substituted for sauterne. One teaspoon crushed basil leaves may be substituted for nutmeg, if desired. Yield: 3 1/2 cups.

Photograph for this recipe on page 120.

GROUND BEEF SOUP

1/4 c. margarine
1 c. flour
1 lb. ground beef
1 c. chopped onions
1 c. shredded carrots
1 c. thinly sliced celery
2 c. frozen mixed vegetables
1 16-oz. can whole tomatoes
Salt to taste
2 tbsp. beef bouillon
1 tsp. pepper

Melt margarine in large kettle. Stir in flour to make a smooth paste. Add 8 cups water slowly, stirring until smooth. Saute ground beef in frypan until well browned. Add ground beef and remaining ingredients to flour mixture. Bring to a boil; reduce heat. Simmer until vegetables are tender. May be frozen for future use. Yield: 10-12 servings.

Mary M. Yevin
Granite City Sr. High School South
Granite City, Illinois

CRAN-APPLE CREAM SALAD

1 3-oz. package cherry gelatin
1/2 c. orange juice
1 8-oz. package cream cheese, softened
1 8-oz. can whole berry cranberry sauce
1/2 tsp. orange rind
1/4 tsp. salt
3 c. chopped unpeeled red apples
1 c. cottage cheese

Dissolve gelatin in 1 cup boiling water. Stir in orange juice. Beat cream cheese in small mixing bowl until soft and creamy. Beat in cranberry sauce until smooth. Add orange rind and salt; beat well. Add gelatin mixture gradually, beating well. Chill until thickened. Fold in 2 cups apples. Pour into 4-cup ring mold. Chill until firm. Unmold onto lettuce-lined plate. Combine cottage cheese and remaining 1 cup apples. Spoon into center of mold.

Kathleen Burchett
Asst. State Supvr.
Home Ec. Ed.
Bristol, Virginia

PARTY SALAD

1 3-oz. package lime gelatin
1 4 1/2-oz. can crushed pineapple
1/2 c. cottage cheese
1 c. prepared Dream Whip
1/4 c. chopped maraschino cherries
1/4 c. chopped blanched almonds

Dissolve gelatin in 1 cup boiling water. Drain pineapple, reserving 1/2 cup syrup. Add syrup to gelatin mixture; mix well. Chill until thickened. Fold in cottage cheese, Dream Whip, pineapple, cherries and almonds. Pour into 9 x 5 x 3-inch loaf pan or individual molds. Chill until firm. Unmold. Serve on lettuce leaf with mayonnaise and shredded cheese, if desired.

Sister Marionita Gergen, OSF
Ryan High School
Omaha, Nebraska

162

CRANBERRY QUEEN SALAD

3 egg whites
1/2 c. sugar
1 can cranberry sauce
1 carton Cool Whip

Beat egg whites until stiff peaks form. Fold in sugar. Add cranberry sauce and Cool Whip; beat well. Pour into chilled mold. Freeze. Serve directly from freezer.

Sister Margaret Mary Clarke
O'Gorman High School
Sioux Falls, South Dakota

FROZEN FRUIT SALAD

1 8-oz. carton sour cream
1 8-oz. package cream cheese, softened
1/4 c. sugar
1 No. 2 can fruit cocktail, well drained
2 c. miniature marshmallows
1 banana, peeled and sliced

Cream sour cream, cream cheese and sugar together until smooth and fluffy. Fold in fruit cocktail, marshmallows and banana. Pour into 8-inch square dish. Freeze until firm. Remove from freezer 15 to 20 minutes before ready to serve. Cut into squares. Serve on lettuce leaves, if desired.

Addie Johnson
Bunker High School
Bunker, Missouri

PINK FRUIT FREEZE

1 8-oz. package cream cheese, softened
1 qt. strawberry ice cream, softened
1/2 c. mayonnaise
2 16-oz. cans fruit cocktail, drained
1/3 c. chopped pecans

Combine cream cheese, ice cream and mayonnaise; blend well. Fold in fruit cocktail and pecans. Pour into 9-inch square pan. Freeze until firm. Place in refrigerator 15

minutes before ready to serve. Cut into squares. Garnish with mint leaves and cherries, if desired.

Mrs. Elmer L. Walton
Holy Name High School
Reading, Pennsylvania

SANTA CLAUS PINEAPPLE DELIGHT SALAD

2 c. cooled cooked rice
1 c. crushed pineapple
1/2 c. sugar
3/4 c. grapes, cut in halves
1 c. chopped red apple
1/2 lb. miniature marshmallows
Maraschino cherries to taste
1 c. whipping cream, whipped

Combine all ingredients except whipped cream in mixing bowl; mix well. Fold in whipped cream. Place in refrigerator for at least 2 hours before serving. Spoon into individual serving dishes. Serve immediately.

Denise Archer
Delta C-7 High School
Deering, Missouri

SAUERKRAUT SALAD

2 cans sauerkraut, drained
1 sm. onion, diced
1 c. celery, diced
1 sm. green pepper, diced
1 sm. jar pimentos, chopped
1 1/2 c. sugar
1/4 c. oil
1/2 c. vinegar

Place sauerkraut in colander; rinse with cold water. Drain well. Combine sauerkraut, onion, celery, pepper and pimentos in large bowl; mix well. Combine sugar, oil, vinegar and 1/4 cup water; mix well. Pour over sauerkraut mixture. Toss well. Cover. Refrigerate overnight. Drain off excess dressing. Serve. Keeps well.

Mrs. Joy Cully
Laurel Highlands Sr. High School
Uniontown, Pennsylvania

All-Purpose

FRESH SPINACH SALAD

1 bag fresh spinach
1 bunch green onions
1 16-oz. can bean sprouts, drained
4 to 6 slices bacon
2 or 3 hard-boiled eggs, sliced
1 c. salad oil
3/4 c. sugar
1/3 c. catsup
1/4 c. vinegar
1 tbsp. Worcestershire sauce

Wash spinach and onions; drain well. Tear spinach leaves into large salad bowl. Reserve 2 or 3 onions. Slice remaining onions and stems; add to spinach. Add bean sprouts. Refrigerate. Fry bacon until crisp; drain and crumble. Add bacon to spinach mixture. Toss. Arrange sliced eggs over top. Refrigerate. Combine oil, sugar, catsup, vinegar and Worcestershire sauce; mix well. Chop remaining onions and stems; stir into oil mixture. Chill for 2 to 3 hours. Serve over spinach salad. One can Chinese mixed vegetables may be substituted for bean sprouts, if desired.

Mrs. Mary Ada Parks
Anna-Jonesboro High School
Anna, Illinois

ZUCCHINI TOSSED SALAD WITH GARLIC DRESSING

1 sm. head romaine
1 sm. head Boston lettuce
3 med. zucchini, washed and thinly
    sliced
1 c. sliced radishes
3 tbsp. sliced green onions
1/4 c. salad oil
2 tbsp. tarragon vinegar
2 tsp. salt
1/8 tsp. pepper
1 clove of garlic, crushed

Wash and dry salad greens; refrigerate. Combine zucchini, radishes and onion in large bowl. Cover. Refrigerate for about 1 hour. Combine remaining ingredients in jar with tightfitting lid. Shake well; chill. Tear romaine and lettuce into bite-sized pieces; add to zucchini mixture. Toss with garlic dressing.

Mrs. Vera S. Smith
Strong High School
Strong, Arkansas

TWENTY-FOUR HOUR SALAD

1 10-oz. package frozen peas
1/2 lb. bacon, diced
1/2 head lettuce, cut in 1/2-in. slices
1/2 c. chopped celery
1/2 c. chopped green pepper
1/2 c. chopped onion
1 1/2 c. mayonnaise
1 tbsp. sugar
1/2 c. grated Parmesan cheese
1/2 c. shredded Cheddar cheese

Cook peas in water to cover until crisp-tender; drain. Fry bacon until crisp; drain. Layer lettuce, peas, celery, pepper and onion in large bowl. Combine mayonnaise and sugar. Pour over top. Sprinkle with cheeses. Top with bacon. Cover. Chill overnight.

Mrs. Barbara Baker
Fort Gratiot School
North Street, Michigan

MARY'S SALAD

10 lg. potatoes
1 lg. onion, minced
Celery salt to taste
Salt and pepper to taste
2 tbsp. mustard
1 qt. mayonnaise or salad dressing

Boil unpeeled potatoes until tender. Peel hot potatoes; cut into cubes. Add onion, celery salt, salt and pepper; mix well. Stir in mustard. Add enough mayonnaise to moisten; mix well. Chill well before serving.

Ellin Weaver
Winola High School
Viola, Illinois

164

WESTERN DRESSING MIX

2 tbsp. salt
2 tsp. monosodium glutamate
2 tsp. dehydrated parsley flakes
1 tsp. garlic powder
1 tsp. pepper
1/2 tsp. onion powder
1 c. mayonnaise or salad dressing
1 c. buttermilk

Combine first 6 ingredients, mixing well. Store in airtight container until ready to use. Combine 3 1/2 teaspoons dressing mix with mayonnaise and buttermilk. Mix well. Refrigerate for 24 hours before using.

Bonita Wiersig
Anson Jones School
Bryan, Texas

SEASONED SALT

6 boxes salt
1/2 c. pepper
1/4 c. white pepper
1 tbsp. cayenne pepper
1/4 c. ground ginger
1 c. chopped garlic

Combine all ingredients in large mixing bowl. Let stand, uncovered, for at least 6 hours or overnight. Store in airtight containers.

Emely Sundbeck
Manor High School
Manor, Texas

BEEF BARBECUE

1 4 to 5-lb. chuck roast
Flour
2 tbsp. cooking oil
1 lg. onion, sliced
1 c. vinegar
1 1/2 tsp. dry mustard
2 tbsp. brown sugar
1 tbsp. Worcestershire sauce
3 tsp. prepared mustard
1 c. catsup
1 lg. clove of garlic, crushed

1 tsp. salt
1/4 tsp. pepper

Dredge roast with flour. Brown in oil in Dutch oven. Add onion and 1/2 cup water. Simmer, covered, for about 2 hours or until tender, adding more water if necessary. Remove roast from pan; reserve juices. Slice roast thinly, discarding fat and bones. Return to Dutch oven with juices. Combine remaining ingredients in saucepan; bring to a boil. Pour over roast. Simmer, covered, for 1 hour and 30 minutes longer. Serve on toasted hamburger buns.

Ingrid Nagy
Dunckel Jr. High School
Farmington Hills, Michigan

QUICK BEEF CASSEROLE

1 1/2 lb. stew beef, cut in sm. cubes
1 can golden mushroom soup
1/2 c. sherry or wine
1 can mushrooms (opt.)

Place beef in bottom of casserole. Cover with soup and sherry. Sprinkle mushrooms over top. Bake, covered, in preheated 300-degree oven for 1 hour and 30 minutes. Serve on noodles or rice.

Ina M. Huffman
William Ruffner Jr. High School
Roanoke, Virginia

EASY BEEF STEW

1 lb. stew beef, cut in sm. cubes
1 can onion soup
1 can beef consomme

Brown beef in small amount of fat. Combine browned beef, onion soup and beef consomme in saucepan. Cook over low heat for 1 hour and 30 minutes to 2 hours or until beef is tender. Serve over rice.

Mrs. Margaret W. Lyles
Westminster High School
Westminster, South Carolina

HUNGARIAN GOULASH

    4 lb. beef, cut in 2-in. pieces
    2 strips bacon, chopped
    6 med. onions, chopped
    3 tbsp. paprika
    1 1/2 tsp. salt
    2 med. green peppers, chopped

Brown beef slowly in own fat in large skillet. Transfer to Dutch oven. Add 1 cup water to skillet; stir. Add to beef. Cover. Cook over low heat. Fry bacon in skillet until crisp-tender; add onions. Cook until onions are lightly browned. Stir in paprika and salt. Add to meat. Stir in green peppers. Simmer for about 2 hours or until meat is tender. Serve on hot rice or buttered noodles.

Sally T. Accetta
Birch Run Jr. High School
Birch Run, Michigan

ZESTY BEEF CUBES ON NOODLES

    Flour
    1 1/2 tsp. salt
    Dash of pepper
    2 lb. beef chuck, cut in 1-in. cubes
    1 tbsp. cooking oil
    1 c. chopped onions
    1 tbsp. beef bouillon
    1 1/2 tsp. Worcestershire sauce
    3 tbsp. horseradish
    1 c. buttermilk
    1 8-oz. package noodles, cooked and
       drained

Combine 1/4 cup flour, salt and pepper. Add beef cubes; mix until well coated. Fry in hot oil in heavy skillet until brown on all sides. Add onions; cook until soft. Dissolve bouillon in 1/2 cup water. Add bouillon mixture, Worcestershire sauce and horseradish to skillet; mix well. Cover. Simmer for 1 hour and 30 minutes or until beef is tender. Stir 2 tablespoons flour into buttermilk; add to beef mixture. Stir until thickened. Serve over hot noodles.

Ruth M. Robare
North Albany Jr. High School
Albany, Oregon

FOUR-HOUR STEW

    6 to 8 med. potatoes, cut into cubes
    2 c. celery, cut into 1-in. pieces
    14 carrots, cut into 1-in. pieces
    8 med. onions
    1/2 green pepper, chopped
    4 to 5 lb. beef stew meat, cut into
       cubes
    1 tbsp. salt
    Pepper to taste
    3 tbsp. sugar
    6 tbsp. Minute tapioca
    2 28-oz. cans tomatoes
    2 cans peas or green beans, drained

Place potatoes, celery, carrots, onions and green pepper in large greased roaster; place meat over vegetables. Sprinkle with salt and pepper. Mix sugar, tapioca and undrained tomatoes; pour over meat. Cover. Bake in pre-heated 350-degree oven for 4 hours. Add peas; stir. Heat through. May be frozen. Yield: 10-12 servings.

Mrs. Jan Gruetzmacher
Welson Jr. High School
Appleton, Wisconsin

SPANISH BEEF STEW WITH OLIVES

    2 tbsp. olive or salad oil
    3 1/2 lb. beef stew meat
    1 tsp. salt
    1/8 tsp. pepper
    2 med. onions, sliced
    2 lg. cloves of garlic, crushed
    2 c. beef bouillon
    2 c. dry red wine
    4 tomatoes, peeled and quartered
    1 bay leaf
    4 parsley sprigs
    1/2 tsp. thyme leaves
    1 1/2 c. Spanish pimento-stuffed green
       olives
    2 1/2 lb. potatoes, peeled and halved
    2 tbsp. flour

Heat oil in large kettle or Dutch oven. Add meat, a few pieces at a time; brown well on all sides. Remove meat; season with salt and pepper. Drain off drippings in kettle if too brown and add additional 2 tablespoons oil. Add onions; cook until tender and lightly brown. Add garlic, bouillon, wine and 1 tomato. Tie bay leaf, parsley and thyme in cheesecloth bag; add to kettle. Add browned meat; bring to a boil. Cover; simmer for 2 hours or until meat is tender. Add olives and potatoes; continue cooking for 30 minutes. Remove meat and vegetables to serving dish; keep warm. Drain cooking liquid into saucepan; skim off fat. Bring to a boil. Blend flour with 3 tablespoons water; stir into boiling liquid. Cook, stirring, until thickened. Add remaining tomatoes; simmer for 10 minutes. Pour liquid over meat and vegetables. May bake at 350 degrees for 2 hours before adding olives and potatoes, if desired. Yield: 8-10 servings.

Photograph for this recipe on page 2.

SIX-HOUR BEEF STEW

    1 No. 2 can cut green beans, drained
    1 No. 2 1/2 can whole tomatoes
    2 lb. cubed stew beef
    5 potatoes, cut in bite-sized pieces
    6 carrots, cut in bite-sized pieces
    5 stalks celery, diced
    1/2 c. tapioca
    1/2 tsp. salt
    1/4 c. diced onion

Drain beans and tomatoes, reserving juice. Combine first 6 ingredients in large casserole. Combine reserved juices with remaining ingredients. Pour over meat and vegetables; toss lightly. Cover. Bake in preheated 275-degree oven for 6 hours. Do not lift lid until done.

Mrs. Marjorie Petefish
Holbrook Public Schools
Holbrook, Nebraska

MARIE'S BEEF STEW

    2 lb. chuck stew meat, cut into 1-in.
      cubes
    1/4 c. shortening

    1 bay leaf
    1 tsp. salt
    1 tbsp. Season-All
    1/4 tsp. pepper
    1/2 tsp. marjoram leaves
    1/8 tsp. tarragon leaves
    1/2 tsp. parsley flakes
    2 tsp. beef base
    2 c. water
    4 carrots
    4 potatoes
    1 onion, chopped
    1/4 c. flour

Cook stew meat in hot shortening until brown. Add seasonings and water; cover. Simmer for 1 hour and 30 minutes or until meat is almost tender. Peel carrots; cut into 1-inch pieces. Peel and quarter potatoes. Add carrots, potatoes and onion to stew; cook for 30 minutes or until vegetables are tender. Mix flour and 1/4 cup water until smooth; stir into stew. Cook, stirring occasionally, until thickened. Yield: 4 servings.

Marie Cornelius
Medford Mid High School
Medford, Oregon

PENNY-SAVER BARBECUED STEAK

    1 3/4 to 1 1/2-in. thick round or
      chuck steak
    1/2 c. vinegar
    1/2 c. cooking oil
    1/2 c. chili sauce or catsup
    1/2 tsp. paprika
    1/4 tsp. chili powder
    1/4 tsp. garlic salt or 1 clove of
      garlic, minced
    1 tsp. Tabasco sauce
    1 tsp. Worcestershire sauce

Score top of steak diagonally. Place in large shallow pan. Combine remaining ingredients; mix well. Pour over steak. Marinate in refrigerator overnight. Cook steak over hot coals to desired doneness.

Mrs. Barbara Goedicke
Lindsay Thurber Comprehensive High School
Red Deer, Alberta, Canada

All-Purpose

MOM'S SWISS STEAK

1 c. flour
1 1/2 lb. steak
Salt and pepper to taste
1 lg. onion, chopped
2 tbsp. cooking oil
8 carrots, sliced
1 No. 2 can tomatoes

Pound flour into steak using meat mallet. Season both sides with salt and pepper. Saute onion in hot oil. Add steak; brown on both sides. Place meat and onion in casserole; add carrots. Beat tomatoes with electric mixer. Pour over carrots. Cover. Bake in preheated 350-degree oven for 1 hour and 30 minutes. Serve over rice.

Jerrie L. Evans
Vallivue High School
Caldwell, Idaho

MEAT LOAF WELLINGTON

1 1/2 lb. ground chuck
1 c. bread crumbs
3/4 c. chopped onions
1/2 c. tomato sauce
3 eggs
1 tbsp. chopped parsley
1 clove of garlic, minced
2 tsp. salt
1/4 tsp. pepper
1 loaf frozen white bread dough

Combine ground chuck, bread crumbs, onions, tomato sauce, 2 eggs, parsley, garlic, salt and pepper. Mix thoroughly. Form into rectangle. Place in 8 1/2 x 4 1/2 x 2 1/2-inch loaf pan. Bake in preheated 375-degree oven for 1 hour. Remove from pan; drain and cool. Thaw bread dough. Roll out to 16 x 7-inch rectangle. Brush with remaining beaten egg. Place meat loaf in center of dough. Fold dough over meat loaf; pinch edges to seal. Place on greased cookie sheet. Let stand for 30 minutes. Brush with egg. Prick sides of dough with fork. Return to oven. Bake for 30 minutes longer or until

golden brown. Slice to serve. Yield: 8 servings.

Glenda Muller
Ballard High School
Huxley, Iowa

SPAGHETTI SURPRISE

1 lb. ground beef
1 c. soft bread crumbs
1 egg
2 1/4 c. milk
2 tbsp. grated onion
1/2 tsp. salt
2 tbsp. butter
1 clove of garlic, minced
3/4 c. green pepper strips
3 tbsp. all-purpose flour
1 tsp. oregano leaves
1 tsp. sugar
1/2 tsp. onion salt
1/4 tsp. celery salt
1 2-oz. can mushrooms
1 6-oz. can tomato paste
1/2 c. crumbled blue cheese
Spaghetti
Melted butter

Mix beef, bread crumbs, egg, 1/4 cup milk, onion and salt lightly. Shape mixture into 18 meatballs. Melt butter in large skillet; brown meatballs on all sides. Remove from skillet; place in a preheated 325-degree oven while preparing sauce. Add garlic and green pepper to skillet; saute for 5 minutes. Stir flour, oregano, sugar, onion salt and celery salt into drippings in skillet; remove from heat. Stir in remaining 2 cups milk gradually. Add mushrooms with liquid. Cook over medium heat, stirring constantly, until thickened. Cook 2 minutes longer. Stir in tomato paste and blue cheese; reduce heat to low. Heat to serving temperature. Cook spaghetti according to package directions; toss with melted butter. Remove meatballs from oven; place in sauce. Serve meatballs and sauce with spaghetti. Yield: 6 servings.

Photograph for this recipe on page 169.

CHICKEN BREASTS AND RICE

3/4 c. rice
1 can cream of chicken soup
1 can cream of celery soup
1 can cream of mushroom soup
1 c. white wine or sherry
1 sm. can whole mushrooms
1 sm. jar pimento strips, drained
1/2 green pepper, chopped
1/2 onion, chopped
1 can water chestnuts, drained and
 sliced
8 to 12 chicken breast halves
Grated Parmesan cheese

Sprinkle rice evenly into 9 x 13-inch baking pan. Mix remaining ingredients except chicken and Parmesan cheese; pour 1/3 of the mixture over rice. Arrange chicken breasts over soup mixture; cover with remaining soup mixture. Cover with Parmesan cheese. Bake in preheated 350-degree oven for about 2 hours. May be prepared ahead of time and refrigerated before baking; may be frozen.

Mrs. Phyllis Larson
Glen Crest Jr. High School
Glen Ellyn, Illinois

BAKED CHICKEN PARMESAN

1/4 c. fine bread crumbs
4 tbsp. grated Parmesan cheese
1/4 tsp. crushed oregano leaves
Dash of garlic powder
Dash of pepper
2 lb. chicken parts
1 can cream of mushroom soup
1/2 c. milk
Paprika

Combine crumbs, 2 tablespoons Parmesan cheese, oregano, garlic powder and pepper. Roll chicken in cheese mixture; arrange in 2-quart shallow baking dish. Bake in preheated 400-degree oven for 20 minutes. Turn chicken; bake for 20 minutes. Blend soup and milk; pour over chicken. Sprinkle with paprika and remaining 3 tablespoons

cheese. Bake for 20 minutes longer or until chicken is tender. Arrange chicken on platter. Stir sauce; pour over chicken. Yield: 4 servings.

Neldalea Dotray
LaGrove School
Farina, Illinois

CLARA'S CHICKEN PILAU

1/4 c. shortening
1 lb. onions, finely chopped
1 lg. can tomatoes
1/2 tsp. sugar
1 tsp. salt
Pepper to taste
Dash of hot pepper sauce
1/2 tsp. thyme
1 lg. frying chicken, cut into serving
 pieces
1 lb. long grain rice
2 c. water

Melt shortening in Dutch oven. Add onions; cook over low heat for 10 minutes, stirring frequently. Add tomatoes, sugar, salt, pepper, pepper sauce and thyme; cook until thick. Add chicken; mix well. Simmer for 20 minutes. Add rice and water; cover. Simmer for 45 to 60 minutes, stirring once with kitchen fork. Remove from heat; keep warm for flavors to blend. Serve hot.

Mrs. Ruby R. Cannon
Royal Palm School
West Palm Beach, Florida

SMOKED PORK WITH KRAUT

1 tbsp. flour
1 3-lb. smoked boneless pork shoulder
 butt
1 27-oz. can Libby's sauerkraut, well
 drained
1/4 c. (firmly packed) light brown sugar
1 med. apple, pared and diced
1/2 to 3/4 tsp. caraway seed
1/4 tsp. pepper

Place flour in a 14 x 20-inch oven cooking bag; shake to coat inside. Place pork in bag; close bag with a twist tie. Puncture 6 small slits in top of bag. Place in 9 x 13 x 2-inch baking pan. Bake in preheated 350-degree oven for 2 hours. Remove from oven; open bag. Combine remaining ingredients; spoon over and around pork. Retie bag. Bake for 40 minutes longer. Yield: 6 servings.

Photograph for this recipe on page 158.

TUNA-ASPARAGUS CASSEROLE

    1 can cream of mushroom soup
    1 can cream of chicken soup
    1/3 c. mayonnaise or salad dressing
    1   8-oz. can sliced mushrooms
    1/2 green pepper, chopped
    2   6-oz. cans tuna
    1 c. fine noodles, cooked
    1   16-oz. can chopped asparagus,
        drained
    1 c. grated American cheese

Combine soups, mayonnaise, mushrooms and juice and green pepper in saucepan. Cook over low heat just until heated through. Place alternate layers of tuna, noodles, asparagus and cheese in casserole. Pour soup mixture over top. Bake in preheated 350-degree oven for 45 minutes or until bubbly. Two cups chopped cooked turkey or chicken may be substituted for tuna.

Jill Kralicek
Oak Park High School
Kansas City, Missouri

FIESTA CORN

    2 eggs
    1 c. cornmeal
    1   1-lb. 1-oz. can cream-style corn
    1/4 c. milk
    1/3 c. melted margarine
    1/2 tsp. soda
    1 tsp. salt
    2 c. grated Cheddar cheese
    1   4-oz. can green chilies, chopped

Beat eggs lightly in mixing bowl. Stir in cornmeal. Add corn, milk, margarine, soda and salt; mix well. Pour half the corn mixture into greased 6-cup casserole. Sprinkle with 1 cup cheese and chilies. Add remaining corn mixture. Sprinkle with remaining 1 cup cheese. Bake in preheated 350-degree oven for about 45 minutes or until set. Cut into wedges to serve. Yield: 6 servings.

Mrs. Virginia T. Bond
Scott High School
Madison, West Virginia

LUSCIOUS POTATOES

    1   2-lb. package hashed brown potatoes
    2 cans cream of potato soup
    1 pt. sour cream
    Salt and pepper to taste
    2 c. grated Cheddar cheese

Combine all ingredients except cheese in large casserole; mix well. Sprinkle with cheese. Bake in preheated 350-degree oven for 1 hour.

Mrs. Phyllis Larson
Glen Crest Jr. High School
Glen Ellyn, Illinois

BUTTERNUT SQUASH CASSEROLE

    2 c. drained, mashed butternut squash
    6 tbsp. margarine
    1 c. sugar
    1 c. milk
    3 eggs
    1/2 tsp. ginger
    1/2 tsp. coconut flavoring

Combine all ingredients; place in greased casserole. Place casserole in pan of water. Bake in preheated 350-degree oven for about 45 minutes or until knife inserted in center comes out clean.

Mrs. Margaret W. Lyles
Westminster High School
Westminster, South Carolina

YELLOW SQUASH CASSEROLE

4 c. sliced yellow squash
1 med. onion, sliced
2 med. carrots, grated
1 8-oz. package Pepperidge Farm herb
   stuffing mix
1 c. sour cream
1/2 c. milk
Salt and pepper to taste
1/2 c. melted margarine

Cook squash and onion in boiling water until tender; drain and mash. Add carrots, 1/2 of the stuffing mix, sour cream and milk; mix well. More milk may be added if mixture is too thick. Season with salt and pepper. Mix remaining stuffing mix with margarine. Line rectangular casserole with stuffing mixture, reserving 1 cup to sprinkle on top. Add squash mixture to casserole; sprinkle with reserved stuffing mixture. Bake in preheated 350-degree oven for 30 to 40 minutes or until heated through and brown.

Elizabeth Green
Loretto High School
Loretto, Tennessee

SPICY BEETS

1 c. vinegar
1 c. water
1 bay leaf
6 peppercorns
6 whole cloves
1/4 c. granulated artificial sweetener
1 16-oz. can sliced beets, drained

Mix vinegar, water, bay leaf, peppercorns and cloves in saucepan; bring to a boil. Remove from heat; stir in sugar. Add beets; refrigerate overnight.

Cathy Lobe
North Central School
Spokane, Washington

YUMMY EGGPLANT

1 lg. eggplant, peeled and cubed
1 jar spaghetti sauce

1 onion, diced
3 eggs, slightly beaten
1/4 c. grated Parmesan cheese
1 c. grated Cheddar cheese
Oregano to taste

Boil eggplant in water to cover until tender; drain and mash. Add remaining ingredients; mix well. Pour into greased casserole. Bake in preheated 350-degree oven for 45 minutes or until bubbly.

Louise Gurley
Sun Valley High School
Monroe, North Carolina

MACARONI AND COTTAGE CHEESE CASSEROLE

Salt
4 to 5 qt. boiling water
3 c. elbow macaroni
6 eggs
3 c. reconstituted nonfat dry milk
1/8 tsp. pepper
1/4 tsp. thyme leaves, crushed
1 1/2 tsp. oregano leaves
1 tsp. Worcestershire sauce
1 lb. creamed cottage cheese
1/4 c. margarine
1 clove of garlic, crushed
1 c. chopped onion
1 c. chopped celery
1/4 c. chopped parsley
1/4 c. chopped pimento

Add 1 1/2 tablespoons salt to rapidly boiling water. Add macaroni gradually so water continues to boil. Cook, uncovered, stirring occasionally, until tender. Drain in colander. Combine eggs, milk, 2 teaspoons salt and seasonings in large bowl; beat well. Stir in cottage cheese and macaroni. Melt margarine in large skillet over medium heat; add garlic, onion and celery. Saute until tender. Stir in parsley and pimento; add to macaroni mixture, stirring until combined. Pour into greased shallow 3-quart casserole; cover. Bake in preheated 350-degree oven for 1 hour; uncover. Bake for 10 to 15 minutes longer or until casserole is set in center.

Photograph for this recipe on page 173.

All-Purpose

SPAGHETTI DELICADO

1 lb. spaghetti
Salt
4 to 6 qt. boiling water
2 1/2 c. milk
2/3 c. sliced pimiento-stuffed olives
2 c. grated Swiss cheese
Pepper to taste

Add spaghetti and 2 tablespoons salt gradually to rapidly boiling water so that water continues to boil. Cook uncovered, stirring occasionally, until just tender. Drain in colander. Bring milk to boiling point in kettle. Add spaghetti; cook over medium heat for 5 minutes. Add olives and cheese; toss carefully. Cook until cheese melts and sauce thickens slightly. Season with salt and pepper to taste. Turn into warm serving dish; serve immediately. Yield: 4-6 servings.

Photograph for this recipe on page 1.

DIRTY RICE

2 or 3 chicken gizzards
2 or 3 chicken livers
1/4 c. butter or margarine
1 bunch green onions, finely chopped
3 med. onions, finely chopped
1 c. chopped celery
1/2 c. chopped green pepper
1/4 c. parsley flakes
3 buds garlic, crushed
1/2 lb. ground beef
Pinch of thyme
Red pepper to taste
Salt to taste
4 c. cooked rice

Cook gizzards in water to cover until almost done. Add livers; cook until tender. Chop. Heat butter in large skillet. Add green onions, onions, celery and green pepper. Cook over low heat until vegetables are soft. Add parsley flakes, garlic, giblets and ground beef. Cook over low heat for about 20 minutes, stirring until well blended. Add thyme, salt and pepper. Add rice; mix well. Spoon

into casserole. Bake in preheated 325-degree oven for about 20 minutes or until bubbly.

Audrey V. Craig
Divide High School
Nolan, Texas

WILD RICE CASSEROLE

1 c. wild rice
1 can beer
6 slices bacon
1/2 c. chopped celery
1 onion, chopped
1 can beef broth
1 can cream of mushroom soup
1 can mushrooms
Pinch of salt
Pepper to taste
Butter

Soak rice in beer overnight. Drain. Fry bacon until crisp; reserve drippings. Drain on paper toweling. Saute celery and onion in bacon drippings. Add crumbled bacon, celery and onion to rice. Stir in beef broth and soup. Add mushrooms. Season with salt and pepper. Mix well. Pour into large casserole. Dot with butter. Bake, covered, in preheated 350-degree oven for 1 hour and 30 minutes to 2 hours or until rice is done.

Genevieve Kramer
East Chain High School
Blue Earth, Minnesota

DELICIOUS CRUMPETS

1 pkg. dry yeast
1 tsp. sugar
1/3 c. milk
1 egg
1/4 c. (about) melted butter
1 c. unsifted flour
1/2 tsp. salt

Combine yeast and sugar in small bowl; add 1/4 cup hot water. Let soften for 5 minutes. Add milk, egg and 1 tablespoon butter; mix well. Add flour and salt; mix until smooth. Cover. Let stand in warm place for about 45

174

minutes or until almost doubled in bulk. Brush bottom of heavy griddle and insides of 3-inch rings with butter. Heat rings over low heat. Spoon 3 tablespoons batter into each ring. Cook for about 7 minutes or until bubbles appear and tops become dry. Remove rings. Turn with spatula. Cook for about 2 minutes longer or until lightly browned. Repeat with remaining batter. May add raisins or dates to batter, if desired. Yield: 7-8 crumpets.

Jeanne Williams
Custer County High School
Miles City, Montana

JALAPENO CORN BREAD

1 1/2 c. yellow cornmeal
3 tsp. baking powder
1/2 tsp. salt
3 eggs
1 c. sour cream
1 c. grated Cheddar cheese
1 sm. can cream-style corn
1/2 c. jalapeno peppers, seeded and
    chopped
1/2 c. corn oil

Sift first 3 ingredients together into mixing bowl. Add remaining ingredients; beat slightly. Pour into greased baking pan. Bake in preheated 450-degree oven for 30 to 40 minutes or until done.

Linda Jaramillo
Escalante High School
Tierra Amarilla, New Mexico

BASIC WHEAT BREAD

2 c. flour
2 pkg. dry yeast
1 c. milk
1/4 c. cooking oil
1/4 c. honey
1 tbsp. salt
1 egg at room temperature
4 to 4 1/2 c. whole wheat flour

Combine flour and yeast in large mixing bowl. Combine milk, 1 cup water, oil, honey and salt in saucepan. Cook over low heat just until warm. Add milk mixture to flour mixture. Beat at medium speed of electric mixer for about 3 minutes or until smooth. Add egg; mix well. Stir in enough whole wheat flour to make a moderately stiff dough. Turn out onto lightly floured surface. Cover with bowl; let rest for 10 minutes. Knead for 5 to 10 minutes or until smooth and satiny. Cover. Let rest for 20 minutes. Divide dough in half. Shape into 2 loaves. Place in 2 greased loaf pans. Brush with additional oil. Let rise in warm place for about 1 hour or until doubled in bulk. Bake in preheated 400-degree oven for 35 to 40 minutes or until done.

Martha C. Chastain
Otwell Middle School
Cumming, Georgia

FRENCH BREAD

1 pkg. dry yeast
1 tbsp. salt
6 to 6 1/2 c. all-purpose flour
Cornmeal

Sprinkle yeast over 2 cups warm water in large mixing bowl. Add salt and 4 cups flour; beat until well mixed. Add enough remaining flour to make a stiff dough. Turn out onto floured board. Knead until smooth. Place dough in bowl; cover with damp cloth. Let rise in warm place for about 2 hours and 30 minutes or until tripled in bulk. Punch down. Let rise for 35 to 40 minutes longer or until doubled in bulk. Divide dough into 4 equal parts. Roll each part in 15-inch length with palms of hands. Sprinkle cookie sheet with cornmeal. Place rolls over cornmeal. Make 1/2-inch deep cut down center of each roll. Let rise for 2 hours. Bake in preheated 400-degree oven for 40 to 45 minutes or until done.

Frances Summers
Claremore High School
Florence, Oklahoma

All-Purpose

COFFEE CAN BREAD

4 c. flour
1 pkg. dry yeast
1/4 c. sugar
1/2 c. margarine
1 tsp. salt
1/2 c. milk
2 eggs, slightly beaten
Cinnamon to taste
Raisins (opt.)
Chopped nuts (opt.)

Measure 2 cups flour into large mixing bowl. Sprinkle with yeast. Combine 1/2 cup water, sugar, margarine and salt in saucepan. Cook over low heat, stirring, until margarine is melted. Stir in milk. Add milk mixture and eggs to flour mixture, stirring until yeast is dissolved. Add remaining flour; mix well, adding more flour if mixture is too sticky. Turn out onto lightly floured board. Knead until soft and elastic. Divide dough in half. Pat each portion into 9 x 12-inch rectangle. Sprinkle each with cinnamon and desired amounts of raisins and nuts. Roll up as for jelly roll. Drop into oiled coffee cans. Cover with aluminum foil. Let rise until foil rises 1 inch from tops of cans. Bake in preheated 400-degree oven for 20 minutes. Remove foil. Bake for 10 to 15 minutes longer or until golden brown. Cool for about 15 minutes before removing from cans. Rolled dough may be cut in 1-inch pieces and placed in mixture of 3 tablespoons melted butter, 3 tablespoons corn syrup and 1/3 cup packed brown sugar in bottom of baking pan; bake in preheated 375-degree oven for 25 minutes. Invert onto plate.

Mrs. Marian S. Holcombe
Enfield Jr. High School
Oreland, Pennsylvania

ONE-RISE MIXER BREAD

1 pkg. dry yeast
2 1/3 c. flour
2 tbsp. sugar
1 tsp. salt
1/4 tsp. soda
1 c. sour cream
1 egg

Dissolve yeast in 1/4 cup hot water. Add 1 1/3 cups flour and remaining ingredients. Beat at low speed of electric mixer for 30 seconds. Beat at high speed for 2 minutes. Stir in remaining flour. Place in well-greased loaf pan. Let rise until almost doubled in bulk. Bake in preheated 350-degree oven for 25 to 30 minutes or until done. Cool on wire rack. Freezes well.

Mrs. Jane Markham
Memorial Junior High School
Houston, Texas

CINNAMON CRUNCH WALNUT LOAF

1 1/2 c. coarsely chopped California
   walnuts
1 tbsp. melted butter
1 c. sugar
2 tsp. cinnamon
3 c. sifted all-purpose flour
4 1/2 tsp. baking powder
1 1/2 tsp. salt
1/4 c. shortening
1 egg
1 1/4 c. milk

Toss walnuts with melted butter. Add 1/4 cup sugar and cinnamon; mix until walnuts are well coated. Set aside. Resift flour with remaining 3/4 cup sugar, baking powder and salt. Cut in shortening. Beat egg lightly; combine with milk. Stir into dry mixture just until all of flour is moistened. Reserve 1/4 cup of the spiced walnuts for top of loaf. Add remaining walnut mixture to batter; mix lightly. Spoon into greased 9 1/4 x 5 1/4 x 2 3/4-inch loaf pan. Sprinkle with reserved walnut mixture. Let stand for 15 minutes. Bake in preheated 350-degree oven for about 1 hour and 10 minutes or until loaf tests done. Let stand for 10 minutes, then turn out on wire rack. Cool.

Photograph for this recipe on page 177.

PEANUT CANDY

2 1/2 c. sugar
3/4 c. light corn syrup
1 c. half and half
3 c. raw peanuts
1/4 c. butter or margarine
1 tsp. vanilla extract
Red food coloring

Combine sugar, syrup, half and half and peanuts in saucepan. Cook over low heat for 55 to 60 minutes or to hard-ball stage. Remove from heat. Add butter, vanilla and desired amount of food coloring. Beat until mixture loses gloss. Drop by tablespoonfuls onto buttered cookie sheet.

Audrey V. Craig
Divide High School
Nolan, Texas

KARO CRUNCH

2 qt. popped popcorn
1 1/3 c. chopped pecans
2/3 c. slivered almonds
1 1/3 c. sugar
1 c. butter or margarine
1/2 c. Karo syrup
1 tsp. vanilla extract

Combine popcorn, pecans and almonds on cookie sheet, mixing well. Combine sugar, butter and syrup in saucepan. Bring to a boil over medium heat; boil, stirring occasionally, for 10 to 15 minutes or until mixture turns caramel color. Remove from heat. Stir in vanilla. Pour over popcorn mixture; mix to coat well. Cool. Store in airtight container.

Beatrice Trites
Glasgon Sr. High School
Glasgon, Montana

GRANOLA MIX

1 lb. old-fashioned oats
1 c. wheat germ
1 c. hulled sunflower seeds
1 c. coarsely chopped nuts
1 c. coconut

1/2 c. honey
1/2 c. vegetable oil
1/2 c. (packed) brown sugar
2 tsp. vanilla extract
1 1/2 c. golden raisins

Combine oats, wheat germ, sunflower seeds, nuts and coconut in large mixing bowl; mix well. Combine honey, oil, brown sugar, 1/3 cup cold water and vanilla in small saucepan. Cook over low heat just until heated through. Do not boil. Pour over oats mixture. Stir until dry ingredients are thoroughly moistened and mixture is well blended. Spread evenly into 2 large shallow oiled baking pans. Bake in preheated 350-degree oven for 1 hour to 1 hour and 30 minutes, stirring after 30 minutes and at 15-minute intervals. Remove from oven. Stir in raisins. Cool. Store in airtight containers.

Mildred B. Goe
Monument High School
Monument, Oregon

NEVER-FAIL COLORED POPCORN BALLS

1 3-oz. package gelatin
Few drops of food coloring
1 c. sugar
1 c. light corn syrup
7 to 8 qt. popped popcorn

Combine gelatin, food coloring, sugar and syrup in saucepan. Bring to a rolling boil. Pour over popcorn, mixing to coat thoroughly. Cool. Butter palms of hands. Shape popcorn mixture into balls. Let dry. Wrap in plastic sandwich bags, if desired.

Mrs. Marian Baker
Sycamore High School
Sycamore, Illinois

BIRD'S NEST CAKE

3 c. flour
1 tsp. soda
2 c. sugar
1 tsp. cinnamon
1/2 tsp. salt

1 1/4 c. cooking oil
1 tsp. vanilla extract
1 c. crushed pineapple
3 eggs, slightly beaten
1/4 c. applesauce
2 c. thinly sliced bananas
1 c. chopped nuts (opt.)

Sift flour, soda, sugar, cinnamon and salt into large mixing bowl. Make a well in center. Pour remaining ingredients into well. Mix with a spoon until well combined. Pour into greased and floured bundt pan. Bake in preheated 350-degree oven for 1 hour and 15 minutes or until cake tests done. May sprinkle with confectioners' sugar while warm, if desired.

Sharon Turini
Norwalk High School
Norwalk, Ohio

CRAZY CHOCOLATE CAKE

2 1/2 c. flour
2 c. sugar
2 tsp. soda
3/4 c. cocoa
1 tsp. salt
2 tsp. vanilla extract
2 tbsp. vinegar
10 tbsp. salad oil

Combine all ingredients with 2 cups cold water in large mixing bowl. Beat for about 2 minutes or until smooth. Pour into 9 x 13-inch greased pan. Bake in preheated 350-degree oven for 35 to 40 minutes or until toothpick inserted in center comes out clean.

Mary F. Yost
Cairo-Durham Central School
Cairo, New York

BLACK MAGIC CAKE

2 c. flour
2 c. sugar
3/4 c. cocoa
2 tsp. soda
1 tsp. baking powder

Salt
2 eggs
1 c. black coffee
Milk
1/2 c. salad oil
3 tsp. vanilla extract
1/4 c. butter
2 c. confectioners' sugar

Sift flour, sugar, cocoa, soda, baking powder and 1/2 teaspoon salt together into large mixing bowl. Add eggs, coffee, 1 cup milk, salad oil and 2 teaspoons vanilla. Blend until smooth. Batter will be thin. Pour into greased 9 x 13-inch pan. Bake in preheated 350-degree oven for about 35 minutes or until done. Cream butter until soft. Stir in confectioners' sugar, 1/8 teaspoon salt and 3 tablespoons milk. Add remaining 1 teaspoon vanilla; beat until smooth and creamy, adding more milk if necessary. Spread over warm cake.

Mrs. Elizabeth B. Lengle
Warrior Run High School
Turbotville, Pennsylvania

EASY APPLE-DATE CAKE

1 c. sugar
1/2 c. shortening
1 egg
1 c. flour
1/4 tsp. salt
1 tsp. soda
1 tsp. cinnamon
2 c. chopped peeled apples
1/2 c. chopped dates
1/2 c. chopped nuts

Cream sugar and shortening together until fluffy. Add egg; mix well. Sift flour, salt, soda and cinnamon together. Add flour mixture to sugar mixture alternately with apples, mixing well after each addition. Stir in dates and nuts. Pour into 8-inch square pan. Bake in preheated 350-degree oven for 35 to 40 minutes or until done.

Wanda Miller
Sahuarita High School
Sahuarita, Arizona

FAVORITE NO-FROST CAKE

1 c. sugar
1/2 c. shortening
2 eggs
1 c. milk
1 tsp. vanilla extract
2 c. flour
1 tbsp. baking powder
1/2 tsp. salt
1/2 c. (packed) brown sugar
2 tbsp. melted butter
3/4 c. chopped nuts
1 c. miniature marshmallows

Cream sugar and shortening together until light and fluffy. Beat in eggs. Add milk and vanilla; mix well. Sift flour, baking powder and salt together. Add to sugar mixture a small amount at a time, beating well after each addition. Pour into greased and floured baking pan. Combine brown sugar and butter; mix well. Stir in nuts and marshmallows. Sprinkle over batter. Bake in preheated 350-degree oven for 35 to 40 minutes or until cake tests done.

Mrs. LeRoy Bieber
Del Norte High School
Crescent City, California

SOUR CREAM-COCONUT CAKE

1 c. butter, softened
2 c. sugar
4 eggs, at room temperature
3 c. all-purpose flour
3 tsp. baking powder
1 tsp. salt
1 c. milk, at room temperature
2 tsp. vanilla extract
Filling

Cream butter and sugar together until light and fluffy. Add eggs 1 at a time, beating well after each addition. Sift flour, baking powder and salt together; sift 2 more times. Add flour mixture alternately with milk to sugar mixture, beating just until blended. Add vanilla; blend well. Pour into 2 greased and floured 10-inch cake pans. Bake in preheated

350-degree oven for 30 to 35 minutes or until toothpicks inserted in centers come out clean. Cool. Split layers. Spread Filling between layers and over top and side of cake. Place in airtight container. Refrigerate for 3 days before serving.

Filling

2 8-oz. cartons sour cream
2 c. sugar
1 16-oz. package frozen coconut
1/4 tsp. salt

Combine all ingredients in mixing bowl. Stir until well blended. Let stand for 1 hour.

Mrs. Claire H. Shaw
Neal School
Durham, North Carolina

DUMP CAKE

1 box butter cake mix
3/4 c. melted butter or margarine
1 lg. can crushed pineapple
1 can cherry pie filling
1 c. chopped nuts

Combine cake mix and butter until crumbly. Stir in pineapple and pie filling. Pour into greased oblong baking pan. Bake in preheated 350-degree oven for 35 minutes. Remove from oven. Sprinkle with nuts. Bake for 15 minutes longer or until nuts are lightly toasted.

Emily J. Rickman
State Dept. of Ed.
Danville, Virginia

SOUR CREAM POUND CAKE

1 c. butter or margarine, softened
2 3/4 c. sugar
6 eggs
3 c. sifted cake flour
1/4 tsp. soda
1 c. sour cream
1 tbsp. vanilla extract
1 tbsp. lemon extract

Cream butter and sugar together until light and fluffy. Add eggs 1 at a time, beating well after each addition. Sift flour and soda together 3 times. Add flour mixture to sugar mixture alternately with sour cream, beating until smooth. Blend in extracts. Pour into greased and floured 9-inch tube pan. Bake in preheated 350-degree oven for 1 hour and 20 minutes or until toothpick inserted in center comes out clean. Turn out on wire rack to cool. Store in airtight container.

Mrs. Gretel L. Anderson
Clifton Forge High School
Clifton Forge, Virginia

WATERGATE CAKE

1 box white cake mix
2 pkg. instant pistachio pudding mix
3 eggs
1 c. cooking oil
1 c. Seven-Up
1 c. chopped nuts
2 pkg. Dream Whip
1 1/2 c. milk

Combine cake mix, 1 package pudding mix, eggs, oil and Seven-Up in mixing bowl. Mix well. Stir in 1/2 cup nuts. Pour into greased loaf pan. Bake in preheated 350-degree oven for 35 to 40 minutes or until toothpick inserted in center comes out clean. Combine Dream Whip, remaining package pudding mix and milk. Blend until creamy. Stir in remaining 1/2 cup nuts. Spread over cool cake. Cake must be refrigerated.

Maxine King
Unity High School
Mendon, Illinois

BANANA SPLIT CAKE

2 c. graham cracker crumbs
Butter
2 tsp. sugar
2 eggs
1 1-lb. box confectioners' sugar
1 lg. can crushed pineapple, drained
5 bananas, peeled and halved lengthwise
1 9-oz. carton Cool Whip
1 c. chopped pecans
1 sm. bottle maraschino cherries

Combine cracker crumbs, 1/2 cup melted butter and sugar; mix well. Pat into 9 x 13-inch baking pan. Bake in preheated 300-degree oven for 10 minutes. Cool. Cream eggs, confectioners' sugar and 1 cup softened butter together until light and fluffy. Pour over crust. Spread pineapple over top. Arrange banana halves over pineapple. Spread Cool Whip over bananas. Sprinkle with pecans. Indent lightly into sections. Place 1 cherry in center of each section. Chill thoroughly. A layer of strawberries may be placed over bananas for variation, if desired.

Vivian Crane
Hayden Home Ec. Dept.
Hayden, Alabama

ARKANSAS CHEESECAKE

2/3 lb. graham crackers, finely crushed
1 c. melted butter or margarine
1 8-oz. package cream cheese, softened
1 c. sugar
1 3-oz. package red gelatin
1 lg. can evaporated milk
2 tbsp. lemon juice

Combine cracker crumbs and butter; mix well. Reserve 1/2 cup for topping. Pat remaining crumb mixture into bottom of 11 x 14-inch baking pan. Combine cream cheese and sugar, stirring until well mixed. Add 1 cup boiling water to gelatin; stir until dissolved. Pour evaporated milk into ice tray; freeze until crystals form around edges of tray. Whip milk until soft peaks form; stir in lemon juice. Add gelatin mixture slowly; beat until well mixed. Add cream cheese mixture 1 tablespoon at a time, mixing well after each addition. Pour into crust. Sprinkle with reserved crumbs. Chill until firm. Garnish with strawberries or cherries, if desired.

Sue Farris
Altus-Denning High School
Altus, Arkansas

181

All-Purpose

EASY TIME HOLIDAY SQUARES

1 1/2 c. sugar
1 c. butter or margarine
4 eggs
2 c. flour
1 tbsp. lemon juice
1 can cherry or blueberry pie filling
Confectioners' sugar

Cream sugar and butter together until light and fluffy. Add eggs 1 at a time, beating well after each addition. Stir in flour gradually. Add lemon juice; mix well. Spread over 15 x 10 x 1-inch jelly roll pan evenly. Mark into 20 squares with knife or spatula. Place 1 heaping tablespoon pie filling in center of each square. Bake in preheated 350-degree oven for 40 to 45 minutes or until done. Sprinkle with confectioners' sugar while warm.

Mrs. Fran Heckman
Waupaca High School
Waupaca, Wisconsin

TWIST OF LEMON CHEESE BARS

1 pkg. lemon frosting mix
2 c. flour
2/3 c. melted butter or margarine
1 c. finely chopped nuts
1 c. sour cream
1   8-oz. package cream cheese, softened
1/2 tsp. vanilla
1 egg

Reserve 1/2 cup frosting mix. Combine remaining frosting mix, flour and butter in mixing bowl; beat at low speed of electric mixer until crumbly. Stir in nuts. Press into bottom of ungreased 9 x 13-inch baking pan. Combine reserved frosting mix and remaining ingredients in mixing bowl; beat at medium speed until smooth. Spread over crust. Bake in preheated 350-degree oven for 30 to 35 minutes or until firm. Chill. Cut into bars. Store in refrigerator.

Sharon Turini
Norwalk High School
Norwalk, Ohio

BREAKFAST YEAST COOKIES

2 pkg. yeast
3/4 c. butter or margarine
3 c. flour
1/2 tsp. salt
1 c. quick-cooking oatmeal
1 c. coconut
1/2 c. sugar
Favorite flavor jam

Dissolve yeast in 2/3 cup warm water. Beat butter with electric mixer until creamy. Add flour and salt; beat until well mixed. Add oatmeal and coconut. Mix until dough is crumbly. Add yeast mixture; stir until well blended. Chill overnight. Roll dough into walnut-sized balls. Roll each ball in sugar. Place on greased cookie sheet. Flatten slightly. Fill centers with jam. Bake in preheated 350-degree oven for about 15 minutes or until done. Chopped nuts may be substituted for jam, if desired.

Sondra Keener
Solon High School
Solon, Ohio

FORGOTTEN COOKIES

2 egg whites
1/2 tsp. vanilla extract
1 tsp. vinegar
2/3 c. sugar
1 c. semisweet chocolate bits
1 c. chopped walnuts

Remove oven racks and cover with aluminum foil. Preheat oven to 350 degrees. Combine egg whites, vanilla, vinegar and sugar in large mixing bowl; beat until stiff peaks form. Fold in chocolate bits and walnuts. Drop by teaspoonfuls onto aluminum foil-covered racks. Return racks to oven. Turn off heat. Leave cookies in oven for at least 5 hours or overnight.

Mary E. Harrington
Doherty Memorial High School
Worcester, Massachusetts
Kathleen Varvel
Heinold Junior High School
Cincinnati, Ohio

FRIED ICE CREAM

1 pt. ice cream
1 pound cake
1/2 pt. whipping cream
1 egg

Slice ice cream into 1-inch thick pieces. Place on jelly roll pan. Place in freezer. Grate cake into fine crumbs. Combine whipping cream and egg, mixing well. Dip ice cream slices into cream mixture. Coat with cake crumbs. Refreeze. Fry in deep hot oil for 1 minute. Drain. Serve immediately.

Mrs. Mary Ann Parks
Lakeview High School
Decatur, Illinois

CHOCOLATE ICE MILK

5 1/3 c. nonfat dry milk
2 17 1/2-oz. cans prepared chocolate
   pudding
1/2 tsp. mint flavoring
1 c. finely chopped chocolate bits

Dissolve milk in 6 cups water. Pour pudding into freezer container; add milk, flavoring and chocolate bits. Cover. Fill with ice and rock salt. Freeze according to manufacturer's directions. May substitute desired pudding and flavoring for chocolate pudding and mint flavoring, adding fruits or nuts to complement pudding, if desired.

Ora Goodrich
Coudersport Area High School
Coudersport, Pennsylvania

FROZEN CHIFFON

1 egg, at room temperature
1/3 c. powdered milk
1/4 c. sugar
1/2 tsp. vanilla or almond extract

Combine egg, milk and 1/3 cup ice water in mixing bowl. Whip at high speed of electric mixer until stiff peaks form. Add sugar; beat well. Stir in flavoring. Pour into plastic containers. Cover. Freeze until firm.

Mrs. Rhonda Ward
Old Glory Rural High School
Old Glory, Texas

BLENDER CUSTARD PIE

1 13-oz. can evaporated milk
3 tbsp. flour
3 eggs, slightly beaten
1 c. sugar
3 tbsp. cooking oil
1/2 tsp. vanilla extract
Nutmeg to taste

Combine milk, flour, eggs, sugar, oil and vanilla in blender container. Blend until well mixed. Pour into greased and floured 10-inch pie plate. Sprinkle with nutmeg. Bake in preheated 325-degree oven for 35 to 40 minutes or until knife inserted in center comes out clean.

Florence W. Ponder
Mendenhall School
Mendenhall, Mississippi

GLAZED PEACH PIE

6 c. pared sliced peaches
1 c. sugar
3 tbsp. cornstarch
1/4 tsp. ground cinnamon
1/2 c. orange juice
1 baked pie shell
Whipped cream

Mash enough peaches to measure 1 cup. Reserve remaining sliced peaches. Combine sugar, cornstarch and cinnamon in saucepan. Stir in orange juice and mashed peaches. Bring to a boil over medium heat, stirring constantly. Boil, stirring, for 1 minute. Spread half the glaze over bottom and side of pie shell. Spoon reserved peach slices over glaze. Spread remaining glaze evenly over peaches. Chill for at least 3 hours. Serve topped with whipped cream.

Margaret De Journette
North Wilkes School
Hays, North Carolina

PERFECT PEACH COBBLER

1/2 c. butter or margarine
1 c. sugar
1 c. flour
1 tsp. baking powder
2/3 c. milk
1 qt. sliced fresh or canned peaches

Melt butter in 9 x 13-inch baking pan. Combine sugar, flour, baking powder and milk in mixing bowl; mix well. Pour melted butter over sugar mixture. Do not stir. Arrange peach slices evenly in baking pan. Pour sugar mixture over top. Bake in preheated 325-degree oven for 30 minutes or until done.

Mrs. Don Haring
Argentine Middle School
Kansas City, Kansas

CHOCOLATE CHESS PIE

1 1/2 c. sugar
1 5 1/3-oz. can evaporated milk
1/2 c. melted butter
2 eggs
3 1/2 tbsp. cocoa
1 tbsp. vanilla extract
1 unbaked 9-in. pie crust

Combine all ingredients except pie crust in mixing bowl; beat for 1 minute. Pour into pie crust. Bake in preheated 350-degree oven for 1 hour.

Mrs. Jan W. Magee
Mendenhall High School
Mendenhall, Mississippi

LEMON BLENDER PIE

1 c. evaporated milk
1 c. lemonade concentrate
1 8-oz. package cream cheese, cut
   into chunks
1 pkg. instant lemon pudding mix
1 graham cracker crust

Combine evaporated milk and lemonade concentrate in blender container. Add cream cheese chunks, 1 at a time, blending until smooth after each addition. Add pudding mix; blend until smooth. Pour into pie crust. Garnish with lemon twists. Chill.

Beverly Nixon
Vega High School
Vega, Texas

UNCOOKED LEMON PIE

1 1/4 c. vanilla wafer or graham
   cracker crumbs
1/3 c. melted butter
Sugar
2 lg. eggs, separated
Juice of 2 lg. lemons
1 can sweetened condensed milk

Combine crumbs, butter and 1 teaspoon sugar; mix well. Pat over bottom and side of pie plate. Combine egg yolks, lemon juice and milk; beat by hand until thick. Pour into crust. Beat egg whites and 4 tablespoons sugar together until stiff peaks form. Spread over pie, sealing to edge. Bake in preheated 350-degree oven for 15 minutes or until lightly browned. Chill before serving.

Mrs. Juanita Pitts
Linden-Kildare High School
Linden, Texas

QUICK ICEBOX PIE

1 can sweetened condensed milk
1/3 c. lemon juice
1 lg. carton Cool Whip
1 10-oz. carton frozen strawberries,
   thawed
1 c. chopped pecans
2 graham cracker crusts

Combine milk, lemon juice and Cool Whip in mixing bowl; mix thoroughly. Fold in strawberries and pecans. Pour into crusts. Chill until ready to serve. May substitute other frozen fruits for strawberries, if desired.

Mrs. Fran Dobbs
Bonham High School
Bonham, Texas

BREAD PUDDING

4 c. milk, scalded
3/4 c. sugar

1 tbsp. butter or margarine
1/4 tsp. salt
1 1/2 tsp. vanilla extract
4 eggs, slightly beaten
6 slices bread, torn into sm. pieces
Nutmeg to taste

Combine milk, sugar, butter, salt and vanilla; stir until butter is dissolved. Add eggs; mix well. Arrange bread pieces in shallow 8 x 12-inch pan. Pour milk mixture over bread. Sprinkle with nutmeg. Bake in preheated 350-degree oven for 40 minutes or until set.

Mrs. Betty Ambrose
Robert E. Lee High School
Midland, Texas

SNOW PUDDING WITH CUSTARD SAUCE

1 tbsp. unflavored gelatin
1/4 c. lemon juice
1 1/4 c. sugar
Salt
3 eggs, separated
2 c. skim milk, scalded
1/2 tsp. vanilla extract

Soften gelatin in 1/4 cup cold water; dissolve in 1 cup boiling water. Add lemon juice, 1 cup sugar and 1/8 teaspoon salt; mix well. Cool until syrupy. Beat until fluffy. Beat egg whites until stiff peaks form. Fold into gelatin mixture. Fill individual serving dishes 2/3 full. Refrigerate. Beat egg yolks in top of double boiler. Add remaining 1/4 cup sugar and 1/8 teaspoon salt; mix well. Stir in scalded milk slowly. Add vanilla; mix well. Cook over hot water until thickened, stirring constantly. Cool. Serve over pudding.

Mrs. Eunice Cole Salomonson
Conrad Ball Junior High School
Loveland, Colorado

RHUBARB PUDDING

1 lb. frozen rhubarb
8 slices bread, cubed and toasted

3 eggs
3/4 c. sugar
1/2 tsp. cinnamon
1/4 tsp. salt
1 c. milk, scalded
1/4 c. melted butter
1/4 c. (packed) brown sugar

Thaw rhubarb; drain, reserving syrup. Place bread cubes in bottom of 1 1/2-quart casserole. Combine eggs, sugar, cinnamon, salt, milk, butter and reserved rhubarb syrup; mix well. Pour over bread cubes. Let stand for 5 minutes. Arrange rhubarb over milk mixture. Sprinkle with brown sugar. Bake in preheated 375-degree oven for about 40 minutes or until set. Remove from oven. Let stand at room temperature for 5 to 10 minutes. Serve with cream, if desired.

Mable Whisnant
East Lincoln Senior High School
Denver, North Carolina

Hint For Making Jam and Jelly

Add a heaping teaspoon margarine to jam and jelly mixture after it has come to a boil. This eliminates skimming off foam and improves the flavor.

Phyllis T. Krumrine
Susquehannock High School
Glen Rock, Pennsylvania

Freezer Beef Broth For Soup

Pour 1 cup water into broiler pan after broiling steaks and no gravy is to be made. Stir to loosen browned bits. Pour into soup jar; freeze. Add to it to equal 1 quart broth. Canned vegetable liquids may also be accumulated. An inexpensive and delicious use of food that may often be thrown away is pan broiled meats.

Mrs. Laurissa Rawlings
Brady High School
Brady, Texas

185

How To Soften Avocado Overnight

Wash avocado; dry well. Place in flour cannister, being sure avocado is completely covered; let stand overnight.

Jacquelyn Sanders
Taft High School
Taft, Texas

Storing Spices

Store spices and seasonings in alphabetical order on cupboard shelf to save time.

Kay Caskey
Manogue High School
Reno, Nevada

Quick Garlic Flavoring

Cut up fresh cloves of garlic; place in jar with salad oil. Cover. During summer months keep tightly covered jar in refrigerator. Great to add to meat marinades and salad dressings.

Asahi T. Oshima
Boulder Valley School District Re-2
Boulder, Colorado

Trussing A Turkey

Use giant safety pins to truss a turkey if skewers aren't available.

Asahi T. Oshima
Boulder Valley School
Boulder, Colorado

Uses For Bacon Fat

Pop popcorn in bacon fat instead of oil. This gives a delightful flavor to the popcorn and uses bacon fat which tends to accumulate.

Use bacon fat as about 1/4 of the shortening called for when making peanut butter cookies.

Mrs. Margaret Onerheim
Evans Junior High School
Ottumwa, Iowa

Scrubbing Vegetables

A piece of nylon net at the kitchen sink is great for scrubbing vegetables.

Kay Caskey
Manogue High School
Reno, Nevada

Hints For Vegetables And Fruits

Sweet potatoes will not turn dark if put in salted water immediately after peeling, using 1 tablespoon salt to 1 quart water.

Add small amount of vinegar to water when washing vegetables to freshen them.

Fresh tomatoes will keep longer if placed with stems down.

Soak potatoes in salted water for 20 minutes before baking in order to bake more rapidly.

Chewing gum while peeling onions helps to prevent tears.

Limp celery may be crisped by placing in a pan of cold water, adding a slice of potato and refrigerating for several hours.

Bananas may be kept for several days in refrigerator if wrapped individually in a piece of waxed paper.

Slice bananas with silver knife to prevent turning dark.

Mrs. Loretta Fowler Bennett
Thomas Jefferson High School
Alexandria, Virginia

Shopping Hints

Make a detailed shopping list from planned weekly menu but be flexible enough to incorporate supermarket specials into menu.

Try not to shop when tense, hungry or in a hurry.

Compare brands. Make use of unit pricing to help find the best buy.

Make as few trips to the supermarket as possible to help cut down on impulsive buying.

Sort through food coupons in newspapers and magazines to find those that fit your family needs.

Mrs. Elizabeth B. Lengle
Warrior Run High School
Turbotville, Pennsylvania

How To Prevent Gummy Rice And Pasta

Add 2 teaspoons cooking oil to boiling water before adding rice, noodles, macaroni and spaghetti to make foods glisten and separate.

Nancy Graham
Big Piney High School
Big Piney, Wyoming

Handling Pasta Dough Easily

Dust board with cornstarch instead of flour when rolling out pasta dough. Flour is absorbed and will cause sticking. Sprinkle cookie sheet liberally with cornstarch; spread out noodles or other pasta dough. Freeze until stiff. Store in freezer in plastic bag.

Eileen Silva
Escalon High School
Escalon, California

How To Make Powdered Sugar

Place granulated sugar in blender container; process until sugar is powdered. One-half cup granulated sugar makes almost 1 cup powdered sugar.

Phyllis T. Krumrine
Susquehannock High School
Glen Rock, Pennsylvania

Different Topping

Add 1/4 cup jam or jelly in prepared Dream Whip or Cool Whip for delicious topping.

Mrs. Loretta Fowler Bennett
Thomas Jefferson High School
Alexandria, Virginia

Greasing Tins Easily

Place hand in sandwich bag; dip bag in shortening to grease tins. Store bag in shortening can to use again.

Ruth M. Allard
Lyndon Institute
Lyndon Center, Vermont

How To Keep Fruit Pies From Running Over

Cut strips 2 inches wide and long enough to go around pie pan and overlap from old sheeting or similar fabric. Dampen strip and place around edge of pie before placing pie in oven. Remove strip as soon as pie is finished. Pie will not run over.

Mrs. Gladys Olson
Monmouth High School
Monmouth, Illinois

Substitutions and Cooking Guides

Substitute 1 teaspoon dried herbs for ·1 tablespoon fresh herbs.

Add 1/4 teaspoon baking soda and 1/2 cup buttermilk to equal 1 teaspoon baking powder. The buttermilk will replace 1/2 cup of the liquid indicated in the recipe.

Use 3 tablespoons dry cocoa plus 1 tablespoon butter or margarine instead of 1 square (1 ounce) unsweetened chocolate.

Make custard with 1 whole egg rather than 2 egg yolks.

Mix 1/2 cup evaporated milk with 1/2 cup water (or 1 cup reconstituted nonfat dry milk with 1 tablespoon butter) to replace 1 cup whole milk.

Make 1 cup of sour milk by letting stand for 5 minutes 1 tablespoon lemon juice or vinegar plus sweet milk to make 1 cup.

Substitute 1 package (2 teaspoons) active dry yeast for 1 cake compressed yeast.

Add 1 tablespoon instant minced onion, rehydrated, to replace 1 small fresh onion.

Substitute 1 tablespoon prepared mustard for 1 teaspoon dry mustard.

Use 1/8 teaspoon garlic powder instead of 1 small pressed clove of garlic.

Substitute 2 tablespoons of flour for 1 tablespoon of cornstarch to use as a thickening agent.

Mix 1/2 cup tomato sauce with 1/2 cup of water to make 1 cup tomato juice.

Make catsup or chili with 1 cup tomato sauce plus 1/2 cup sugar and 2 tablespoons vinegar.

CAN SIZE CHART

8 oz. can or jar	1 c.	1 lb. 4 oz. or 1 pt. 2 fl. oz. or No. 2 can or jar	2 1/2 c.
10 1/2 oz. can (picnic can)	1 1/4 c.	1 lb. 13 oz. can or jar or No. 2 1/2 can or jar	3 1/2 c.
12 oz. can (vacuum)	1 1/2 c.	1 qt. 14 fl. oz. or 3 lb. 3 oz. or 46 oz. can	5 3/4 c.
14-16 oz. or No. 300 can	1 1/4 c.		
16-17 oz. can or jar or No. 303 can or jar	2 c.	6 1/2 to 7 1/2 lb. or No. 10 can	12-13 c.

SUBSTITUTIONS

1 square *chocolate* (1 ounce) = 3 or 4 tablespoons cocoa plus 1/2 tablespoon fat.
1 tablespoon *cornstarch* (for thickening) = 2 tablespoons flour (approximately).
1 cup sifted *all-purpose flour* = 1 cup plus 2 tablespoons sifted cake flour.
1 cup sifted *cake flour* = 1 cup minus 2 tablespoons sifted all-purpose flour.
1 teaspoon *baking powder* = 1/4 teaspoon baking soda plus 1/2 teaspoon cream of tartar.
1 cup *bottled milk* = 1/2 cup evaporated milk plus 1/2 cup water.
1 cup *sour milk* = 1 cup sweet milk into which 1 tablespoon vinegar or lemon juice has been stirred; or 1 cup buttermilk.
1 cup *sweet milk* = 1 cup sour milk or buttermilk plus 1/2 teaspoon baking soda.
1 cup *canned tomatoes* = about 1 1/3 cups cut-up fresh tomatoes, simmered 10 minutes.
3/4 cup *cracker crumbs* = 1 cup bread crumbs.
1 cup *cream, sour, heavy* = 1/3 cup butter and 2/3 cup milk in any sour milk recipe.
1 cup *cream, sour, thin* = 3 tablespoons butter and 3/4 cup milk in sour milk recipe.
1 cup *molasses* = 1 cup honey.

Metric Conversion Chart

VOLUME

1 tsp.	=	4.9 cc
1 tbsp.	=	14.7 cc
1/3 c.	=	28.9 cc
1/8 c.	=	29.5 cc
1/4 c.	=	59.1 cc
1/2 c.	=	118.3 cc
3/4 c.	=	177.5 cc
1 c.	=	236.7 cc
2 c.	=	473.4 cc
1 fl. oz.	=	29.5 cc
4 oz.	=	118.3 cc
8 oz.	=	236.7 cc

1 pt.	=	473.4 cc
1 qt.	=	.946 liters
1 gal.	=	3.7 liters

CONVERSION FACTORS:

Liters	X	1.056	=	Liquid quarts
Quarts	X	0.946	=	Liters
Liters	X	0.264	=	Gallons
Gallons	X	3.785	=	Liters
Fluid ounces	X	29.563	=	Cubic centimeters
Cubic centimeters	X	0.034	=	Fluid ounces
Cups	X	236.575	=	Cubic centimeters
Tablespoons	X	14.797	=	Cubic centimeters
Teaspoons	X	4.932	=	Cubic centimeters
Bushels	X	0.352	=	Hectoliters
Hectoliters	X	2.837	=	Bushels

WEIGHT

1 dry oz.	=	28.3 Grams
1 lb.	=	.454 Kilograms

CONVERSION FACTORS:

Ounces (Avoir.)	X	28.349	=	Grams
Grams	X	0.035	=	Ounces
Pounds	X	0.454	=	Kilograms
Kilograms	X	2.205	=	Pounds

Equivalent Chart

3 tsp. = 1 tbsp.	16 oz. = 1 lb.	4 c. sifted flour = 1 lb.
2 tbsp. = 1/8 c.	1 oz. = 2 tbsp. fat or liquid	1 lb. butter = 2 c. or 4 sticks
4 tbsp. = 1/4 c.	2 c. fat = 1 lb.	2 pt. = 1 qt.
8 tbsp. = 1/2 c.	2 c. = 1 pt.	1 qt. = 4 c.
16 tbsp. = 1 c.	2 c. sugar = 1 lb.	A Few Grains = Less than 1/8 tsp.
5 tbsp. + 1 tsp. = 1/3 c.	5/8 c. = 1/2 c. + 2 tbsp.	Pinch is as much as can be taken
12 tbsp. = 3/4 c.	7/8 c. = 3/4 c. + 2 tbsp.	between tip of finger and thumb.
4 oz. = 1/2 c.	2 2/3 c. powdered sugar = 1 lb.	Speck = Less than 1/8 tsp.
8 oz. = 1 c.	2 2/3 c. brown sugar = 1 lb.	

WHEN YOU NEED APPROXIMATE MEASUREMENTS . . .

1 lemon makes 3 tablespoons juice
1 lemon makes 1 teaspoon grated peel
1 orange makes 1/3 cup juice
1 orange makes about 2 teaspoons grated peel
1 chopped medium onion makes 1/2 cup pieces
1 pound unshelled walnuts makes 1 1/2 to 1 3/4 cups shelled
1 pound unshelled almonds makes 3/4 to 1 cup shelled
8 to 10 egg whites make 1 cup

12 to 14 egg yolks make 1 cup
1 pound shredded American cheese makes 4 cups
1/4 pound crumbled blue cheese makes 1 cup
1 cup unwhipped cream makes 2 cups whipped
4 ounces (1 to 1 1/4 cups) uncooked macaroni makes 2 1/4 cups cooked
7 ounces spaghetti make 4 cups cooked
4 ounces (1 1/2 to 2 cups) uncooked noodles make 2 cups cooked.

MAKE 1 CUP OF FINE CRUMBS WITH . . .

28 saltine crackers
4 slices bread
14 square graham crackers
22 vanilla wafers

Index

"Life-Saver" Crafts

Index

"Life–Saver" Recipes

PHOTOGRAPH RECIPES

PHOTOGRAPHY CREDITS: Western Research Kitchens; National Macaroni Institute; Spanish Green Olive Commission; National Kraut Packers Association; United Dairy Industry Association; Florida Department of Citrus; American Concordgrape Association; Pickle Packers International, Inc.; National Canners Association; DIAMOND Walnut Growers, Inc.; California Strawberry Advisory Board; California Beef Council; Frozen Southern Vegetable Council; Libby, McNeill and Libby; American Dairy Association; Litton Microwave Cooking Products.

FAVORITE RECIPES of HOME ECONOMICS TEACHERS

NEW Holiday Cookbook

Delightful Holiday Foods For Every Special Occasion Of The Year

This is your very special Cookbook of delicious holiday foods. When the holiday magic takes over from the day-to-day world, you will find just the right dishes to serve from this Cookbook.

There are hundreds of recipes from Home Economics Teachers throughout the country . . . these special recipes will surely make your holidays unforgettable occasions. When you need a little inspiration for your own special way of entertaining, you will always find it in the NEW HOLIDAY COOKBOOK. Included are recipes for soups, meats, vegetables, salads, breads, relishes, desserts and beverages. All recipes are from Home Economics Teachers who have tested them in their own kitchens. Homemakers appreciate working with recipes that have the ingredients in order!

The NEW HOLIDAY COOKBOOK also offers more than just recipes for your holidays . . . there are Menus for every major holiday in each category; often decorations and entertainment ideas are included. Then, there is a very special section of *"Gourmet Gifts"* with lovely foods for that perfect gift. Be sure to include a NEW HOLIDAY COOKBOOK when ordering Favorite Recipes of Home Economics Teachers. Order Blanks are on page 200.

Favorite Recipes of Home Economics Teachers Cookbooks

Use these handy order forms to order individual books for yourself and for friends.

ORDER FORM 60890

PLEASE SEND ME THE FOLLOWING BOOKS:
(Note: Schools should request special discount order forms)

Name

Address

City   State   Zip

☐ Please Bill Me — Plus Postage and Handling.

☐ Enclosed is payment for full amount. No charge for postage and handling.

← *Pictured, Horse Apple Flowers from "Life-Saver" Cookbook*

Quan.	Cookbook Title	Item No.	Price Each	Total
	"LIFE-SAVER"	101032	$4.75	
	Bicentennial Cookbook	101030	5.50	
	Canning, Preserving and Freezing	101029	4.75	
	New Holiday	101028	4.75	
	Americana Cookery	101022	4.75	
	Quick and Easy	101014	4.75	
	Poultry	101026	4.75	
	Money-Saving	101021	4.75	
	Desserts	101013	4.75	
	Meats	101010	4.75	
	Total Order			

MAIL TO: FAVORITE RECIPES PRESS, ORDER PROCESSING, P.O. BOX 2020, LATHAM, NEW YORK 12111

ORDER FORM 60890

PLEASE SEND ME THE FOLLOWING BOOKS:
(Note: Schools should request special discount order forms)

Name

Address

City   State   Zip

☐ Please Bill Me — Plus Postage and Handling.

☐ Enclosed is payment for full amount. No charge for postage and handling.

← *Pictured, Horse Apple Flowers from "Life-Saver" Cookbook*

Quan.	Cookbook Title	Item No.	Price Each	Total
	"LIFE-SAVER"	101032	$4.75	
	Bicentennial Cookbook	101030	5.50	
	Canning, Preserving and Freezing	101029	4.75	
	New Holiday	101028	4.75	
	Americana Cookery	101022	4.75	
	Quick and Easy	101014	4.75	
	Poultry	101026	4.75	
	Money Saving	101021	4.75	
	Desserts	101013	4.75	
	Meats	101010	4.75	
	Total Order			

MAIL TO: FAVORITE RECIPES PRESS, ORDER PROCESSING, P.O. BOX 2020, LATHAM, NEW YORK 12111

ORDER FORM 60890

PLEASE SEND ME THE FOLLOWING BOOKS:
(Note: Schools should request special discount order forms)

Name

Address

City   State   Zip

☐ Please Bill Me — Plus Postage and Handling.

☐ Enclosed is payment for full amount. No charge for postage and handling.

← *Pictured, Horse Apple Flowers from "Life-Saver" Cookbook*

Quan.	Cookbook Title	Item No.	Price Each	Total
	"LIFE-SAVER"	101032	$4.75	
	Bicentennial Cookbook	101030	5.50	
	Canning, Preserving and Freezing	101029	4.75	
	New Holiday	101028	4.75	
	Americana Cookery	101022	4.75	
	Quick and Easy	101014	4.75	
	Poultry	101026	4.75	
	Money-Saving	101021	4.75	
	Desserts	101013	4.75	
	Meats	101010	4.75	
	Total Order			

MAIL TO: FAVORITE RECIPES PRESS, ORDER PROCESSING, P.O. BOX 2020, LATHAM, NEW YORK 12111